ONE GOD, ONE LAW

ANCIENT MEDITERRANEAN AND MEDIEVAL TEXTS AND CONTEXTS

GENERAL EDITORS
Jacob Neusner
Robert Berchman

STUDIES IN PHILO OF ALEXANDRIA AND MEDITERRANEAN ANTIQUITY

EDITED BY
Robert Berchman, Dowling College, Oakdale, NY
Francesca Calabi, Università di Pavia, Pavia, Italy

VOLUME II

EDITORIAL BOARD

K. Corrigan, Emory University, Atlanta, USA
L. H. Feldman, Yeshiva University, New York, NY, USA
M. Hadas-Lebel, La Sorbonne, Paris, France
C. Lévy, La Sorbonne, Paris, France
T. Rajak, University of Reading, United Kingdom
E. Starobinski-Safran, Université de Genève, Switzerland
L. Troiani, Universita' di Pavia, Pavia, Italy

ONE GOD, ONE LAW

Philo of Alexandria on the Mosaic and Greco-Roman Law

BY

JOHN W. MARTENS

BRILL ACADEMIC PUBLISHERS, INC.
BOSTON • LEIDEN
2003

Library of Congress Cataloging-in-Publication Data

Martens, John W., 1960–
   One God, one Law : Philo of Alexandria on the Mosaic and Greco-Roman law / by John W. Martens.
     p. cm. — (Studies in Philo of Alexandria and Mediterranean antiquity, ISSN 1543-995X ; v. 2)
   Includes bibliographical references and index.
   ISBN 0-391-04190-8 (hc)
   1. Philo, of Alexandria—Views on Jewish law. 2. Jewish law—History. 3. Philo, of Alexandria—Contributions in philosophy of law. 4. Law, Greek—Philosophy—History. 5. Roman law—Philosophy—History. I. Title. II. Series: Studies in Philo of Alexandria and Mediterranean antiquity (Brill Academic Publishers) ; v. 2.

B689. Z7M27 2003
296.1'8'092—dc21

2003042239

ISSN 1543-995X
ISBN 0-391-04190-8

© Copyright 2003 by Brill Academic Publishers, Inc., Boston

All rights reserved. No part of this publication may be reproduced, translated, stored in a retrieval system, or transmitted in any form or by any means, electronic, mechanical, photocopying, recording or otherwise, without prior written permission from the publisher.

Authorization to photocopy items for internal or personal use is granted by Brill provided that the appropriate fees are paid directly to The Copyright Clearance Center, 222 Rosewood Drive, Suite 910 Danvers, MA 01923, USA.
Fees are subject to change.

PRINTED IN THE UNITED STATES OF AMERICA

CONTENTS

Acknowledgements	ix
Abbreviations	xi
Preface	xiii
Introduction	xv

Chapter One: "Higher" Law and the Superfluity of the Law in Greek Thought: Unwritten Law	1
ἄγραφος νόμος: Unwritten Law	3
Laws Which Were Not Written	3
Custom	4
Unwritten, but Eternal	7
Conclusions	11

Chapter Two: "Higher" Law: The Law of Nature	13
Origins	13
Nature	16
The "Common" Law	18
The Law of Nature	19
Where Does One Find the Law of Nature?	21
Who Follows the Law?	22
Conclusions	28

Chapter Three: "Higher" Law: The Living Law	31
Early Greek Forerunners of the Living Law Ideal	32
The Pythagorean Fragments of the Hellenistic Period	38
The Followers	42
The King as Law: Roman Evidence	46
Inscriptional Evidence	48
The Historians	48
Philo	48
Pliny	49
Suetonius	49
Dio Cassius	50

Philosophers and Poets	51
Pomponius Porphyry	51
Seneca	51
The Lawyers	52
Gaius	52
Ulpian	52
Comments: The Historical Evidence	52
The νόμος ἔψυχος Ideal	53
The King is the Law	54
The King's Closeness to God	55
The King's Relationship to his Subjects	56
Harmony	57
Imitation	59
"Communion"	60
Other Hellenistic Kingship Traits	61
The "Just" King	63
Conclusions	65
The Task	66
Chapter Four: Philo and φύσις	**67**
φύσις: The Power of Growth and Life	68
φύσις: The Inherent Character of Things	69
φύσις: The Order of the Cosmos	74
φύσις: The Nature of God	77
Philo's Scheme of Nature	80
Nature and Law	80
Chapter Five: Philo and the Law	**83**
νόμος φύσεως: The Law of Nature	83
ἄγραφος νόμος: The Unwritten Law	86
Νόμος ἔμψυχος: The Living Law	90
The Law of Moses	95
Other Codes of Law	99
Conclusions	100
Chapter Six: The Unity of the Law	**103**
Who Follows the Law?	104
Higher Law and the Law of Moses	105

The Law of Nature and the Patriarchs 105
The Living Law and Present-Day Rulers 111
The Law of Nature in Philo's Day 113
The Law of Nature and the Law of Moses 118
Philo's Contribution: The Unity of Law 121
The Living Law 121
The Unwritten Law 123
The Law of Nature and the Law of Moses 124
Conclusions 126

Chapter Seven: Thesmos in Philo of Alexandria 131
Thesmos and Nomos 131
Θεσμός in Greek Literature 135
Νόμος in Philo 139
Thesmos in Philo 141
Thesmos in Physeos 143
Thesmos Agraphos: Θεσμός ἄγραφος 144
Understanding Thesmos in Philo 145

Excursus: Thesmos Philo and the Stoics on the καθήκοντα
and the κατορθώματα 151

Chapter Eight: Conclusions 159

Appendix 1: The Date of the Pythagorean Kingship
  Tractates 165
Appendix 2: Philo and the Oral Law 175

Bibliography 187

Index of Modern Authors 201
Index of Ancient Sources 203
Index of Subjects 213

ACKNOWLEDGEMENTS

In the course of completing such a study, many debts are accrued. I wish to repay my debtors in some manner by acknowledging all their help in bringing this study to fruition. First, I would like to thank my doctoral dissertation committee who many years ago supported the research which formed the basis of this study at McMaster University. These men, Alan Mendelson, Stephen Westerholm, and the late Ben F. Meyer, are responsible for directing me always in the right direction. My thanks also to Brad Inwood, of the University of Toronto, who graciously took me into his graduate seminar on Stoicism and came aboard my supervisory committee to steer me through the shoals of Greco-Roman law, particularly the law of nature in Stoicism.

My thanks are also due to Robert Berchman and Francesca Calabi for editing my manuscript and for their numerous suggestions and insights, all of which were valuable for me. I need also thank two of my teaching assistants, Karin Shrofel, now of Harvard University, for her research on θεσμός in Chapter 7, which was superb, and to Bjorn Einarson, of the University of Winnipeg, for his excellent work on the Indices. The staff of the University of Winnipeg was ever helpful and forgiving, particularly the members of Interlibrary loans. I would also like to thank the Department of Religious Studies at the University of Winnipeg, particularly Professor Peggy Day, for her support of all kinds over the years. Thanks are also due to my colleagues and the management of Klinic Community Health Centre in Winnipeg who for many years cleared my schedule and gave me leave so that I could continue to teach and research.

Professor Mark Golden of the Classics Department at the University of Winnipeg read my manuscript and caught numerous errors in the Greek and made many helpful corrections. I thank him for his careful, exact, and penetrating reading of this study. He saved me from my own self.

I would also like to thank my sons, Jake and Sam, for their patience while I struggled to bring this manuscript to the light of day. Thanks to all my family for their continued support of my studies. Finally, though, I must thank my wife Tabitha for her practical help, with typing, editing, and proof-reading, but most significantly with her moral and spiritual support and guidance, which encouraged me not only in my academic pursuits, but in the search of the knowledge and love of God. It is to her that this book is dedicated.

ABBREVIATIONS

References to scholarly literature are given in full on their first appearance and thereafter abbreviated in some form. The names of ancient texts are most often, though not always, abbreviated and accompanied by the author's name, where known. I have referred to a number of ancient Pseudo-Pythagorean authors, Ecphantus, Archytas, Sthenidas, and Diotogenes, whose works are extant only in anthology form, by name in the text, and have referred to their location in the anthology of Stobaeus either in the body of the text, in brackets, or in a footnote. Stobaeus is abbreviated as *Stob*.

Philo's treatises are referred to by the following abbreviations:

Opif.	De Opificio Mundi
Leg.	Legum allegoriae
Cher.	De Cherubim
Sacr.	De sacrificiis Abelis et Caini
Det.	Quod deterius potiori insidiari soleat
Post.	De posteritate Caini
Gig.	De gigantibus
Deus	Quod Deus sit immutabilis
Agr.	De agricultura
Plant.	De plantatione
Ebr.	De ebrietate
Sobr.	De sobrietate
Conf.	De confusione linguarum
Migr.	De migratione Abrahami
Her.	Quis rerum divinarum heres sit
Congr.	De congressu eruditionis gratia
Fug.	De fuga et inventione
Mut.	De mutatione nominum
Somn.	De somniis
Abr.	De Abrahamo
Ios.	De Iosepho
Mos.	De vita Moysis
Decal.	De Decalogo
Spec.	De specialibus legibus

Virt.	De virtutibus
Praem.	De praemis et poenis, de exsecrationibus
Prob.	Quod omnis prober liber sit
Contempl.	De vita contemplativa
Aet.	De aeternitate mundi
Flacc.	In Flaccum
Legat.	Legatio ad Gaium
Hypoth.	Hypothetica
Prov.	De Providentia
Anim.	De animalibus
QG	Quaestiones et solutiones in Genesim
QE	Quaestiones et solutiones in Exodum

PREFACE

This study grew out of a doctoral dissertation at McMaster University on law in Philo of Alexandria and the Apostle Paul. Stephen Westerholm, who had then just completed a study on Paul and the law, suggested to me that the possible influences of Greco-Roman law on Paul's reflections on νόμος had been left in many ways unexplored. As I began to explore Paul's view of the law in this context, I was fortunate enough to begin taking seminars with Alan Mendelson on Philo of Alexandria and the contrast between Paul's views of the Mosaic law and Philo's views began to intrigue me. The study incorporated background on Greco-Roman views of law and studies of the influence of this law upon Philo and Paul. The study of Paul and Greco-Roman law, it seems to me, still demands our attention, but the work on Philo needed immediate tending. If scholarship on Paul and the law is a vast array of acres and acres of cultivated fields, Philo and the law is a small garden with only a row or two.

Philo's writing continues to intrigue me not only for its vastness, but due to its intricacy. The more one reads Philo, on any topic, the more complex his thought becomes, true, but also the more clearly and directly it begins to assert itself. I have written here in broad strokes, aware that there is much more to be done, not only on Philo and the law, but on many particular passages concerning Philo and the law. I have foregone exegesis in some cases in order to paint a broad picture. I hope the broadness of this study allows for others to pick up particular passages, themes, or topics and to expand, explicate, and finish what has here been started. Philo's thought is fascinating in its own right, as a model of the tension between reason and revelation at any given historical moment, but his influence upon later Christian, Jewish, and pagan thinkers also demands our attention. It should also be said that Philo's thought demands our attention, as Philo demands, as all great ancient thinkers do, that we ask whether it is true what he says about the law and about nature. Modern scholars are apt to not even consider such a question, and Philo's grand project often draws smiles for its seemingly forced or archaic or supposedly unbelievable qualities. Reading Philo on his own terms has its rewards, not least of which is gaining the company of a man for whom the final and only goal is the true knowledge of God. I hope that the following study helps to make clear one aspect of his vast corpus and one aspect of his search for the Truth.

INTRODUCTION

The Problem

Philo of Alexandria challenges history-of-religion scholars through his distinct views of the law of Moses. One cannot claim that the views of Philo of Alexandria were representative of the Judaism of the time, but he did have a common interest with other branches of Judaism, and for all of his differences he accepted the Mosaic Law as divine in origin and charged with historic meaning. And yet, in its material form, Philo considered the Mosaic law apparently superfluous to moral behaviour in certain cases.

Philo affirmed that the law in its material form is unnecessary for people who themselves become an "unwritten law" (ἄγραφος νόμος), for those who have become an "embodiment of the law" (νόμος ἔμψυχος), or for those who follow the law of nature (νόμος φύσεως). For these people the law of Moses is dispensable for by their nature they obey its precepts.

The idea that the law in its material form is superfluous is not standard fare in Judaism. The normal assumption is that the law was given by God so that his people would study and obey it. How does Philo therefore come to see the law as fulfilled in other ways by some people? The purpose of this study to examine how Greek conceptions of law impinged on the reasoning of Philo.

For the problem of the written law in Philo is the problem of written law in Greek thought. The problem is one of arbitrariness. How do we know which law is good? Is the written law not simply an expression of a given society and so, finally, culturally relative? Most major Greek thinkers wrestled with the problem of how to root justice and law in reality, or some transcendent order, and so escape the arbitrary nature of law. By so doing, however, they laid a foundation upon which the written law was truly secondary. The written law was generally considered good, but the "higher" laws, the law of nature, the unwritten law, and the living law, were the true representations of justice.

This study looks at Philo's attempt to deal with Greek forms of higher law, and his attempt to deal with the relation of the written law to these forms of higher law. Some have suggested that in his attempt to relate the higher law to the written law, Philo, like the Greeks, pulled the foundations out from under the written law, in his case the law of Moses.[1]

"Higher" Law in Greek Thought

There is no one Greek conception of the law; one strong strain running through some Greek discussions of law, particularly Stoic, is the idea that there is a law of nature, a law which transcends written codes of law. The law of nature is an immutable law which human beings can perceive through study and reason, and which guides them by nature, not by codification, to do all that is right and to avoid all that is wrong. This law is unchangeable and can be realized and known without a written form. This leads to a second strain of thought found in Greek conceptions of law: some people *are* capable of the knowledge of this law and possess thereby such virtue as to render material forms of law superfluous to them. They keep the law through their very nature, or by comprehending nature itself.

Two other forms of what might be called "higher" law are related to the Stoic view of the law of nature, at least in their implications for how people should live: the idea of unwritten law; and the concept of the king as the living law. The idea of an unwritten law, or laws, is a vague, but prevalent conception in Greek sources. In its most important manifestation the idea of unwritten law speaks of immutable, eternal, or divine laws beyond the codified, or positive law which must be obeyed.

---

[1] There is a long history of this interpretation in modern Philonic scholarship: Charles Bigg, *The Christian Platonists of Alexandria* (Oxford: Clarendon Press, 1913), 49; E. R. Goodenough, *By Light, Light: The Mystic Gospel of Hellenistic Judaism* (New Haven: Yale University Press, 1935), 73–96, esp. 87f.; Sidney Sowers, *The Hermeneutics of Philo and Hebrews* (Richmond, Virginia: John Knox Press, 1965), 44–48, esp. 48; Samuel Sandmel, *Philo's Place in Judaism* (New York: Ktav Publishing House, 1971), 109; André Myre, "La Loi de la Nature et la loi mosaïque selon Philon d'Alexandrie" in *Science et Esprit* 28/2 (1976), 176f.; H. Kleinknecht and W. Gutbrod, "νόμος" in *TDNT* IV, (ed.) Gerhard Kittel, Geoffrey William Bromiley, and Gerhard Friedrich, Grand Rapids, Mich.: Eerdmans, 1964–1976), 1052–1054.

The living law is a concept which took form in the Hellenistic period, specifically in a number of fragments attributed to students of Pythagoras. These fragments, unique as they are, draw upon Greek traditions about the king as the most just man and the wise man who transcends the law. In the νόμος ἔμψυχος ideal the just and wise king himself becomes the law and replaces the codified law for his subjects. To obey the law, the king's subjects must follow the king; the written law is unnecessary.

This study is an attempt to understand the role of these three Hellenistic conceptions of "higher," or uncodified, law in shaping the beliefs of one Jewish thinker of the first century. The aim of the study is to determine how Philo was influenced by Hellenistic conceptions of "higher" law and the "ideal man" in his rethinking of the law, and so to determine how Hellenistic notions shaped Philo's thought on the law of Moses, and, as importantly, how Philo's view of the law of Moses shaped his reception of Hellenistic legal theory.

This study will also allow a better-based comparison of Philo with his Greek contemporaries, as well as a fresh appraisal of the originality in his thought on the law; it will also facilitate the effort to place him in the history of Greek and Jewish thought on law.[2] Much of the current debate regarding Jewish law has ignored Greek law and what it can add to our understanding of early Christianity and Judaism in the Greco-Roman period.

Philo and The "Higher" Law

Many have noted Philo's reliance on Greek philosophical conceptions in general. This general reliance on Greek philosophy finds its formulation in specific concepts and terms.

---

[2] Little appears to have been written on Philo and his view of natural law, unwritten law, and the ideal man. The topic does deserve a thorough restatement in and of itself regardless of its use in a comparison. One notable exception is the work of André Myre of the Université de Montréal whose work on Philo and the law appeared in the journal *Science et Esprit* from 1972 to 1976. Especially pertinent is his article "La Loi de la Nature et la Loi mosaïque selon Philon d'Alexandrie" in *Science et Esprit* 28/2 (1976). At the same time, Philo has too often not been considered as a "Jewish" interpreter of law; his use of Greek language has obscured his loyalty to the Mosaic law.

One of these concepts is Philo's idea of a law of nature (νόμος φύσεως) and the related concepts of the unwritten law and the living law.

The law of nature was a Stoic idea which found new meaning in the hands of Philo. Helmut Koester has gone so far as to strip the Greeks of the credit for the creation of the concept and hand it to Philo.[3] We will not follow Koester, but there is much left to be said about Philo's use of the concept and his alteration of it. Particularly distinctive are Philo's description of the relationship between the Mosaic law and the law of nature, and the close ties he creates between the law of nature, unwritten law, and the living law.

Certain connections, however, have been overlooked by studies of Philo and the law, connections Philo draws between the law of nature and the general idea of the superfluity of material law for certain people and the specific idea of who fulfills the law. The Stoics always maintained the ultimate transcendence of the law of nature over written codes of law. The reality of the law of nature in Philo's work means that certain people have fulfilled the law of nature and, theoretically, others are capable of fulfilling the law of nature. The fulfillment of the law of nature, without recourse to the Mosaic law, would seem to be a higher way. The law of nature would be the true law, and lend credence to Helmut Koester's claim that Philo's theory "produces the extremely momentous insight that a true law of nature is in fact an ultimately superior criterion for the life of the truly wise man."[4] What then of the Mosaic law? Is it not only a copy of the true law? Is the law of Moses in some fundamental way second best in Philo's scheme? Philo also connects the law of nature to the concepts of the living law and the unwritten law, both of which are altered in his work. Both of these ideals seem to subvert the high standing of the written law too. What becomes of the law of Moses?

---

[3] Helmut Koester, "νόμος φύσεως: The Concept of Natural Law in Greek Thought" in *Religions in Antiquity: Essays in Memory of E. R. Goodenough* (Leiden: Brill, 1968) 522, 532, 540. Koester's proposal is fatally flawed by overlooking the work of Cicero on the *lex naturae*, or law of nature, in Latin. By only considering the Greek term, he overlooks the fact that Cicero has clearly adopted the term from Middle Platonist forerunners. I will deal with the appropriate texts in chapters 2, 5, and 6. The error has been further carried into Philonic studies by the work of Naomi G. Cohen in *Philo Judaeus: His Universe of Discourse* (Frankfurt: Peter Lang, 1995) 274–76 who adopts Koester's results without question.

[4] Koester, "νόμος φύσεως" 535.

I will examine this tension between the higher forms of law and the law of Moses in depth. To this end, I will attempt to clarify Philo's views regarding law and nature, the relationship between the Mosaic law and the law of nature, his view of the "living laws" and "unwritten laws" and their relationship to the ordinary person, and his view of the possible superfluity of the Mosaic law. Finally, I will evaluate his status once again on these important questions as a Jewish and Greek thinker.

Philo had to come to terms with the law of Moses in the context of the cultural mosaic of Alexandria. To do so he looked to Hellenism. This has been acknowledged in Philo's case, but not allotted its due force. Yet, shared by Hellenism and Philo is the understanding that the material law may be in some cases superfluous. For Philo, the Mosaic law, a copy of the law of nature, seems to be second best, but meant to be kept because only rarely did anyone achieve the true law of nature. What has been lost in the study of Philo's law of nature, however, are his changes to the Greek law of nature: God is above nature; natural law has its particular manifestation in Judaism; and the various manifestations of higher law are united in his work. What has been lost is his Judaizing of a Greek concept. For all of his Greek language, Philo seems to remain true to Judaism. But did he, in borrowing these Greek concepts of law, subvert the law of Moses? This is the question which will guide us as we explore the connections between Philo and the Greek legal discussions in the Greco-Roman era.

The treatment of Philo's work must, of course, await a study of the concepts of higher law in the Greek literature. The following discussions of νόμος φύσεως, ἄγραφος νόμος, and νόμος ἔμψυχος are intended to see in what way these forms of law were considered "higher," how their proponents claimed they were based in eternal concepts of truth and justice, and in what way they could potentially undermine the material or written law. They are not intended to be exhaustive discussions on the history and meaning of these important concepts. The following chapter is meant to provide enough background information and sense of development to render the discussion on the law and its superfluity in Philo intelligible.

CHAPTER ONE

"HIGHER" LAW AND THE SUPERFLUITY OF THE LAW IN GREEK THOUGHT: UNWRITTEN LAW

Most scholars seem to agree that in spirit, at least, concepts such as ἄγραφος νόμος, νόμος φύσως, and νόμος ἔμψυχος go back beyond their first explicit formulations in the extant literature to something deeply ingrained in the Greek spirit: a belief in the divine ordering of the world.[1] The divine ordering of the world was apparent in early Greek thought;[2] more than that, authors such as Heraclitus show us that the divine order of the world extended to human law.[3] The foundation of Greek society, its legal systems, was supported by the gods. How this was so was not always clear, however, and as long as the Greeks had faith in the law it was not necessary that it be clear. The knowledge that the divine order supported the law somehow was enough. The fifth century brought a change into this relationship, among others, that led people to ask why their law was worth following and in what way it reflected truth and justice and not simply arbitrariness and convention. The relativism of the Sophists struck a responsive, if dissonant, chord.

The law, said the Sophists, was not that which made the Greeks moral and just; instead, law was to be seen in a negative light, as "convention," something imposed upon humankind arbitrarily by those who had power and with no true basis in morality or justice.[4]

---

[1] Victor Ehrenberg, *Sophocles and Pericles* (Oxford: Basil Blakwell 1954) 35–36, 48; James Luther Adams, "The Law of Nature in Greco-Roman Thought" in *JR* 25 (1945) 97; M. T. McLure, "The Greek Conception of Nature" in *Phil Rev* Peter Smith Publisher 23/63 (1934) 115; W. C. Greene, *Moira: Fate, Good, and Evil in Greek Thought* (Gloucester, Mass. 1944) 226–227; Werner Jaeger, *Paideia*. Vol. III (New York Oxford University Press 1944) 241; Rudolf Hirzel, *Agraphos Nomos* (Leipzig: B. G. Teubner 1900) 27.

[2] Greene, *Moira* 17, 36; W. K. C. Guthrie, *History of Greek Philosophy*. Vol. III (Cambridge: The University Press 1962–1981) 55.

[3] See G. S. Kirk, *Heraclitus: The Cosmic Fragments* (Cambridge 1954) 48 for fragment B114 which speaks explicitly, if not clearly, of this connection; see also F. Heinimann, *Nomos und Physis* (Darmstadt: Wissenschaftliche Buchgesellschaft 1965) 66.

[4] See Guthrie's "The Nomos-Physis Antithesis" in *History* Vol. III 55–134 for an

Some Sophists, indeed, spoke of a "law of nature," by which they meant, "might is right": this was true law, which no amount of talk about the goodness of law could disguise. Other Sophists spoke of law as true and good, but since there was no chance of this true law being practised by the majority of men, why should one pretend to follow the law? Still others found the law a useful device for social control, necessary for the maintenance of a civilized society; they nevertheless agreed that if the opportunity to break the law presented itself, without the fear of punishment, one should break the law, for the law had no status in questions of truth and justice.

These challenges rocked the foundations of Greek society and philosophic thought. If the law was not based on truth and eternal standards of justice, but was only the expression of societal convention, arbitrariness, or power, why should one obey the law?[5] It was the struggle to answer these challenges to the material law, the codified law of a people or city, that led to the creation of Greek concepts of what one might call "higher" law: law whose support came not from the shifting sentiments of human convention and the selfish dictates of power, but from divine standards of truth and an eternal sense of justice.

An odd effect of Greek thought on "higher" law was, ironically, that the material law which these concepts were to support was rendered, in various and limited senses, superfluous. The basis for human law was sought in the eternal and unchangeable, and while "higher" law theorists agreed that there was an ideal law, or laws, they were forced to admit that the material law fell short of the ideal in many cases. And if the material law fell short of the ideal, of the truth, it could, in fact it should, be replaced by the true law.[6]

---

outline of the rise of the Sophists and their thought. Guthrie also provides references to the other secondary literature. This material was later reprinted as *The Sophists* (Oxford: Oxford University Press 1971).

[5] Guthrie, *History* Vol. III, 55–134 discusses the variety of Sophistic arguments used to undermine the written law.

[6] The discussions of "higher" law are careful not to preach antinomianism. Such care is probably a result of reflection on the real dangers to which "higher" law could lead and in fact antinomianism was an unwanted byproduct of such legal thought. Ludwig Edelstein, *The Meaning of Stoicism*, Martin Classical Lectures XXI (London: Oxford University Press 1966) 83 says that the antinomian characteristics of the law of nature were never denied by the Stoics.

ἄγραφος νόμος: *Unwritten Law*

The term unwritten law generally refers only to a group of specific laws, not to a concept which defines a general system of "higher" law. Unwritten law could mean many things, sometimes even in the work of the same author. Victor Ehrenberg gets to the heart of the matter when he says,

> it would really be a mistake to connect the idea of unwritten laws with any definite rules beyond the fact that they were not put down in writing.[7]

There is, he continues, no real "definition or limitation" and, as a result, "the *agraphoi* nomoi could even express almost contradictory philosophies of life."[8]

We are able, however, to distinguish the main strands of Greek thought on unwritten law and, thereby, to come to some general conclusions about the contours of the discussion in the primary literature. There are three major meanings of unwritten law in the Greek literature: unwritten law could mean laws which were literally not written in a code of law;[9] it could refer to custom, customs, or social mores—"laws" which had no official status, but the breaking of which led to social sanction or some other type of community punishment; or it could refer to divine, or eternal law which was incumbent upon everyone, even though not written.

Laws Which Were Not Written

This, in at least two senses, meant "unwritten" law in a rather concrete way. It could mean that a law or laws in the course of a revision of a city's law were omitted and, hence, "unwritten"; or it could mean that certain laws were "unwritten" for certain people, that is, they were not intended for or not binding upon these people.

The first meaning is found in Andocides, *De Mysteriis*, 85f. In this case, he refers to the revised laws of Athens. Some of the old laws

---

[7] Ehrenberg, *Sophocles* 47.
[8] Ibid., 48.
[9] Generally these laws were at one time a part of the written law of a city, but a revision of the law codes omitted them; they are, therefore, "unwritten." See Douglas Maurice MacDowell, *Andocides* (Oxford: Clarendon Press 1962) 125–126.

were not written in the revised laws; nevertheless, some people had been charged on the basis of these old laws. These old laws, however, were no longer valid because they were ἄγραφοι, "unwritten."[10]

The second meaning is found in the work of an African author from the third century C.E., Pomponius Porphyry. In his commentary on Horace, *Satires*, 2.3.188, he records a Greek proverb.[11] Horace tells the tale of a commoner who is told by the King not to bury a comrade. When the commoner asks why, the king answers, "Because I say so." The commoner answers, "That is enough for me." Porphyry adds a proverb, embedded in Greek in his Latin text, which he believes is pertinent to this passage: μωρῷ καὶ βασιλεῖ ἄγραφος νόμος, "for the fool and the king the law is not written." The sense of this passage is clear: for differing reasons the law is not binding upon or not intended for the king and the fool. Somehow, they elude the law.

This proverb was preserved in a third century text, but we may suspect that it is quite a bit older; how old, however, is impossible to determine. That it had a wide and popular audience in the ancient world is shown by the fact that the proverb, transliterated, but not translated, is found in the Palestinian Talmud. The proverb, found in Palestinian Talmud *Rosh Hashanah* I,3,57a, is altered only in minor respects.[12]

Custom

Most, if not all, communities preserve customs, unspoken and unwritten, which are quietly obeyed by members of society, not for fear of punishment from a legal authority, but because of the fear of outcast status which sometimes accompanies the breaking of an "unwritten law." This sense of unwritten law continues to shape societies around the world today. This was one of the major meanings of unwritten law in Greek thought.

---

[10] Ibid., 125–126; E. C. Marchant, *Andocides: De Mysteriis and De Reditu* (London: Longmans 1906) 152; Hirzel, *Agraphos Nomos* 37.

[11] See Alfred Holder's (ed.) edition *Pomponi Porfyrionis: Commentum in Horatium Flaccum* (Innsbruck 1894) 302 for the passage in question.

[12] The Talmud citation adds παρά, "for," and the definite article before νόμος. See Saul Lieberman, "How Much Greek in Jewish Palestine?" in *Texts and Studies* (New York: KTAV, 1974) 221–222; *Greek in Jewish Palestine* (New York: P. Feldheim, 1965) 37–38; 38,#51; 144,#2. See also Heinrich Lewy, "Philologische Streifzüge in den Talmud.4. Ein griechisches Sprichwort" in *Philologus* 52 (1893) 567–568 for a discussion of the Talmudic passages.

Why it was called "unwritten" law is obvious: these "laws" were not codified, sometimes they were only apparent if broken. They carried with them, if broken, only the odium of the society in question. That they existed in a middle ground, between law and opinion, is clear from the many formulations of the term. Sometimes it was ἄγραφα νόμιμα, other times ἄγραφον ἔθος, but the term adopted by most writers was ἄγραφος νόμος.

Plato discusses unwritten laws as custom in *Leges* 793a–793d. Various suggestions have been made by Plato regarding the raising of infants; he believes that these suggestions should not be placed in the written law, but neither should they be passed over unmentioned. They inhabit a middle ground, and Plato calls them ἄγραφα νόμιμα or πατρίους νόμους; they are customs which should be done habitually and so buttress the order brought by the written laws.[13]

These "laws" are not considered eternal, but are seen to grow from concrete historical situations and communities.[14] They are something less than written law, but not arbitrary additions to a community's law. This is borne out by Plato's further discussion in *Leg.* 822d, 835e, 838b, and 839a. He implies, at least, that unwritten law, which is made manifest in custom, is based on a higher standard than arbitrary community standards, namely, nature.

Nevertheless, unwritten law is valid for certain communities, not humankind in general. When Plato speaks of these unwritten laws, such as the proper choice of a marriage partner (*Leg.* 773e), the control of sexual practices and the passions (*Leg.* 835e, 839a), and the silence of children among parents or the cut of one's hair (*Resp.* 425a-e), he maintains that they need not be inscribed in a written code. Their relative lack of importance does not justify their inclusion in a code of law (*Leg.* 822d; *Resp.* 425a–e). They are ancestral customs (*Leg.* 793a–d; *Pol.* 295a–296c, 298d), but it is not necessary that they acquire legislative force.

Demosthenes, in *In Aristocratem* 70, speaks of the ἄγραφα νόμιμα as a branch of city law, in this case of Athens. The dictates of these unwritten laws had been contravened by a certain Athenian jurist.

---

[13] The difference between νόμιμα and νόμος with the modifier ἄγραφος becomes slight, but it is clear that νόμιμα does not occupy the same status as νόμος. It appears that Plato wanted to use νόμιμα to distinguish between written law (νόμος) and unwritten custom. This distinction ultimately fell by the wayside.

[14] Cf. also *Leg.* 773e; 841b; *Rep.* 425b; *Pol.* 295a–e, 298d; Hirzel, *Agraphos* 19–20.

Demosthenes tells us that unwritten law is not simply a matter of theory, but a part of the law of a city, under which people, whether officially or not, are judged.[15]

Thucydides, 2.37,2 gives us perhaps the best definition of unwritten law as custom and the effect of its transgression. He names fear as a restraint on lawlessness. This "reverent fear" is found both in laws "ordained for the succour of the oppressed and those which, though unwritten, bring upon the transgressor a disgrace which all men recognize." The laws ordained for the "succour of the oppressed" are certainly the written laws. As to the unwritten laws, this is the classic formulation of the power which unwritten law contains, though officially having none.

Aristotle, whose combined writings on the unwritten law are the most extensive, also has a section in the *Rhetorica* on unwritten law as custom. In *Rhet*. 1.1374a,18f. he groups ἄγραφος νόμος under ἴδιος νόμος; the unwritten law is a particular component of the city law.[16] Here it is taken to mean the customs of a people.[17] Unwritten laws are "the notions, habits and practices prevailing in any given society," according to Cope.[18] It is, in this sense, in "excess" of the written law and is defined by community standards. Unwritten law as custom may also be based on "equity" (ἐπιείκεια); so defined, it modifies "deficiencies of the special and written law."[19] This definition of unwritten law does not describe unwritten law as universal law, even though based on "equity"; rather, it still is law based on application to a particular code of law by a given community.[20]

Later authors, too, are well aware of this sense of unwritten law as custom. Dio Chrysostom defines custom (ἔθος) as unwritten law:[21]

---

[15] Hirzel, *Agraphos* 26; W. W. Goodwin, *Demosthenes: On the Crown* (New York: Hildescheim, 1973) 169 believes that ἄγραφα νόμιμα here refers to unwritten law's "eternal" meaning, but this does not seem to be the case, as Aristotle's division in the *Rhetorica* 1368b ff. makes clear.

[16] Ἰδιος νόμος is opposed to κοινὸς νόμος, which is law valid for everyone, in *Rhet*. 1.1373b,4. Elsewhere, however, ἄγραφος νόμος is opposed to ἴδιος νόμος as a part of the κοινὸς νόμος. This will be taken up in the following section.

[17] Hirzel, *Agraphos* 3–11, especially his summary statement on page 11; E. M. Cope, *An Introduction to Aristotle's Rhetoric* (London: Macmillan 1867) 242–243.

[18] Cope *Aristotle's Rhetoric*, 243.

[19] Ibid., 243; cf. also Hirzel, *Agraphos* 11.

[20] Aristotle speaks further of unwritten law in *Pol*. 3.11,6; 3.6,5; *Eth. Nic.* 10.9,4. See Hirzel, *Agraphos* 13.

[21] Hirzel, *Agraphos* 18.

custom is a judgement common to those who use it, an unwritten law of tribe or city, a voluntary principle of justice, acceptable to all alike with reference to the same matters, an invention made, not by any human being, but rather by life and time (76.1).

Dio is not, however, the only writer to have read and digested the writings of his predecessors. Plutarch reports that dolphins are protected by an "unwritten law" that nobody hunt or injure them purposely (*Sept. Sap. Conviv.* 163a).[22] Plutarch also relates that laws in regard to bravery were unwritten (*Apoph. Lacon.* 221b).

The idea of unwritten law as custom is a major component of the concept of unwritten law, but the most important component, and probably the oldest, is the idea of the unwritten law as eternal or divine law. Though these two senses of unwritten law, custom and eternal law, often became confused, the distinction is clear.[23]

Unwritten, but Eternal

The earliest existing reference to ἄγραφος νόμος is found in Sophocles' *Antigone* 450f.[24] In this passage the unwritten laws refer to what may be called religious law. According to Ehrenberg, "they were the rules of the divine order of the world."[25] They are valid for everyone everywhere: they transcend human boundaries.[26] This sense of unwritten law begins to approach what was later called the law of nature, specifically in the universality of the laws, but there are some differences: there was no attempt to systematize unwritten law and to draw from it a way of life;[27] and it is not clear from what or whom these laws draw their authority—sometimes the gods, sometimes Nature. The unwritten laws are generally only a group of laws; they are rarely, if ever, considered a code of law. As in Sophocles, they often are concerned with religious law. They are not specifically opposed to the written law, but if a written law undermined the unwritten law, the unwritten law should take precedence.

---

[22] Ibid., 18–19.
[23] Ibid., 29–31; MacDowell, 125–126.
[24] Ehrenberg *Sophocles*, 28–29.
[25] Ibid., 30; cf. also with Cope, 240 and Hirzel, *Agraphos* 24.
[26] Ibid., 37.
[27] Ibid., 48.

In Xenophon, *Memorabilia* 4.4,19f., Socrates speaks of ἄγραφος νόμος as law which comes from God. He raises the issue of unwritten law to counteract the relativism of the Sophist Hippias. The laws of which Socrates speaks are certainly considered eternal and binding upon all people.[28] These laws transcend racial borders and human borders; they are meant to be obeyed by all people. Socrates actually names some unwritten laws; hence some scholars have argued that there was a code of unwritten law. Ehrenberg has successfully shown that there is no certain content which is intended whenever the term appears, though some laws, it is true, appear more frequently under the heading of unwritten law.[29]

Demosthenes, too, knows of the unwritten law which is binding upon all. In *De Corona* 274–275, Demosthenes tries to make a distinction between someone who sins wilfully and someone who sins unintentionally. The person who fails in an action, while attempting to act in the common interest, should not suffer vilification. This course of judgement is found "not only in the laws" (here read as "written"), "but even nature herself prescribes it in the unwritten laws (ἀγράφοις νόμους) and in human practices."[30] Here is the idea at its height: the idea of unwritten law is that of a law which is borderless, inherent, and natural.[31] It is, in fact, taught by the morality inherent in man. Whether the written law is in agreement with it, it is the law.

There are a number of other passages where Demosthenes seems to play with the idea of unwritten law; here one must tread more carefully. In *In Stephanum* 1.53 he claims that one who bears false witness "violates not the written laws alone, but also the ties of natural relationships." Unwritten law is not mentioned here, but it may be implied. In *In Aristocratem* 61, Demosthenes advocates his right to defend himself against violence. To be denied this right is

> manifestly contrary to law,—I do not mean merely to the statute law (τὸν γεγραμμένον νόμον), but to the unwritten law of our common humanity (ἀλλὰ καὶ παρὰ τὸν κοινὸν ἁπάντων ἀνθρώπων).[32]

---

[28] Hirzel, *Agraphos* 23–24; Cope *Aristotle's Rhetoric*, 240.

[29] Ehrenberg *Sophocles*, 167–172.

[30] My translation. cf. K. J. Dover, *Greek Popular Morality in the Time of Plato and Aristotle* (Oxford: Basil Blackwell 1974) 82. He understands this passage to demonstrate "those forces which make for mutual love and social cohesion." He seems, however, to accept the universal scope of these unwritten laws (83).

[31] W. W. Goodwin, *Demosthenes* 169.

[32] This translation is taken from Demosthenes, Vol. III in the Loeb Classical

Again, unwritten law does not appear in the text, but the opposition to written law implies it. Whatever the situation in these two cases, Demosthenes is familiar with the idea of an eternal, unwritten law (*De Cor.* 274–275).

Thucydides, who like Demosthenes speaks of unwritten law as custom, also discusses the unwritten law as eternal law. Thucydides, in 5.105,1–2, states that men are like gods in one respect, namely, if they have power, they rule. This is a type of law for Thucydides, though

> we neither enacted this law nor when it was enacted were the first to use it, but found it in existence and expect to leave it in existence for all time.

Though Thucydides does not use the term "unwritten law" here it underlies his discussion of an always existing law.[33]

Parts of Archytas of Tarentum's treatise on the law and righteousness, Περὶ νόμου καὶ δικαιοσύνης, are preserved by Stobaeus (4.1,132,135).[34] In it he speaks of the unwritten law in a most comprehensive and clear fashion.

> The unwritten laws of the gods, which are opposed by the laws of wicked custom, inflict an evil lot and punishment on those who do not obey them, and are the fathers and guides of the written laws and teachings which men enact (*Stob.* 4.1,132).[35]

Library, trans. J. H. Vince. It points to a problem with the translation of the concepts of higher law, and it is not Vince's problem alone. The terms are often only implied, or not fully stated in the primary text; translators often "flesh" out the terms. For instance, φύσις is often rendered as the law of nature. Sometimes, the additions can be correct, but it is probably wise not to let years of accumulated interpretation haze our understanding of these terms.

[33] Hirzel, *Agraphos* 21–22.

[34] The genuineness of most of the Pythagorean texts from the Hellenistic period is generally doubted. See Holger Thesleff, *An Introduction to the Pythagorean Writings of the Hellenistic Period* (Åbo Akademie, 1961). This text, however, is considered early, not only by Thesleff (114), but also by J. S Morrison, "Pythagoras of Samos" in *CQ* 6 (1956) 155 and Armand Delatte, *Essai sur la politique pythagoricienne* (Liége: Bibliothèque de la Faculté de Philosophie et Lettres de l'Université de Liége, 1922) 121–124. Lucien Delatte, Armand's son, is silent regarding Archytas in *Les Traités de la Royauté d'Ecphanté, Diotogène et Sthenidas* (Liége: Bibliothèque de la Faculté de Philosophie et Lettres de l'Université de Liége, 1942) which is a surprise. Lucien rejects his father's dating for Ecphantus, Sthenidas, and Diotogenes in no uncertain terms, so his silence with respect to Archytas is interesting and, perhaps, revealing. The question of date will be discussed in depth later in the chapter.

[35] E. R. Goodenough, "The Political Philosophy of Hellenistic Kingship" in *Yale Classical Studies* 1 (1928) 59.

He attributes the unwritten laws to the gods, and calls them the fathers and guides of the written laws. Though the relationship between the written and unwritten law is not spelled out in full, two important elements of the relationship are apparent. The unwritten laws are divine and higher than the written law. There is also a relationship between the two forms of law. Archytas is the first witness to state that the unwritten law guides the written law, implying that the unwritten law is either a code of some kind or divine legal guidance.[36] The unwritten laws are not simply laws which exist beyond the written law, they exert an influence on the written law. Whether Archytas exercised influence with his view of the unwritten law, he shows that in at least one instance the unwritten law was considered to be the pattern by which people should guide their lives. The written law was a copy, so to speak, of a higher law.

This takes us to the most important discussion, namely, that of Aristotle. Aristotle, as we have seen already to some degree, wrote about ἄγραφος νόμος in a nuanced, and complex, manner. He distinguished between two forms of law in the branch of unwritten law concerned with custom alone. He also spoke of unwritten law as a branch of κοινός νόμος, or "common" law, by which he meant common to all humankind.[37]

This sense of unwritten law is particularly clear in *Rhetorica* 1368bf. The κοινὸς νόμος is described here as unwritten (ἄγραφα) laws which are recognized universally. These unwritten laws are

> the great fundamental conceptions of morality, derived and having their sanction from heaven, antecedent and superior to all the conventional enactments of human societies, and common alike to all mankind.[38]

These common or unwritten laws are laws that are superior to the written laws of any given society; they are the laws whose claims ought to be first in the minds and hearts of people. While Aristotle more often speaks of the unwritten law as custom, in this case the

---

[36] There are great differences with Heraclitus' conception of divine guidance of the law. See A. Delatte, *Politique pythagoricienne* 81.

[37] There is, indeed, a fourth category of higher law, that of "common law" (κοινὸς νόμος). It not only appears in Aristotle, but is also attributed to many of the early Stoics. The common law in the context of the early Stoics will be taken up in the section on natural law.

[38] Cope, *Aristotle's Rhetoric*, 240.

unwritten law is considered according to nature (κατὰ φύσιν) and recognized universally. Here, as in Archytas, the unwritten law seems more a code than a few commands or prohibitions.[39]

The author of the pseudo-Aristotelian *Rhetorica ad Alexandrum* 1421b,35f also writes of universal, unwritten laws.[40] What is just, says the author, is "unwritten custom" (ἄγραφον ἔθος). He names a number of such customs, such as honouring one's parents, and repaying favours to benefactors. These are not based upon written laws, but on unwritten custom and common law. Here, too, the unwritten law is tied to the common law, probably under the influence of Aristotle. Because the unwritten custom is separated from the law of the city (1422a), it seems that the author indeed envisions these laws to be held universally.[41]

Dionysius of Halicarnassus speaks too of a universal law as an unwritten law. Ἄγραφος νόμος can mean custom in Dionysus' work, but it also means universal or common law.[42] In *Antiquitates Romanae*, 7.41 he mentions an unwritten natural right that all may receive equal treatment before the law. In 7.52 he states again that there is an unwritten natural right (although in this case ἄγραφος does not appear). Cicero, too, in at least one passage (*Pro Milone* 10) refers to unwritten law, not as custom but as a product of nature.

Conclusions

This short survey should point to the problems of the concept of unwritten law. It can mean various things, even in the same author's work. The terminology is not always common, and it is unclear how different terminology alters the meaning of the concept in general.[43]

---

[39] See Hirzel, *Agraphos*, 3–14, for the full discussion of the tension between the two views of unwritten law in Aristotle and the various attempts to ease the tension. With Hirzel, I agree that both views are Aristotle's (11–13).
[40] See my comments on pages 42–43 for a discussion of the date and authorship of the pseudonymous *Rhetorica ad Alexandrum*.
[41] Hirzel, *Agraphos* 23–24.
[42] Ibid., 18.
[43] The term ἄγραφα νόμιμα appears, as does ἄγραφον ἔθος and ἄγραφος νόμος. Does νόμιμα always imply something less than νόμος? Does ἄγραφος νόμος imply a code of law and ἄγραφος νόμοι a group of laws? When ἄγραφον ἔθος appears it oddly does not refer to custom but to eternal law.

Even this quick overview warns us against making hasty conclusions.

Nevertheless there are places in which the unwritten law is clearly a law, or code of law, which is seen to be eternal or divine and higher in status than the written law. It is law which transcends the written law, or guides the written law. The superfluity of the written law is not overtly broached but it is an unavoidable implication of the concept. If the law comes from God, it is eternal and true; if it is universal, it is valid whenever it contradicts other, written law codes. It is a form of law which has the first claim on the lawful actions of people.

Of course, the unwritten law never did become the moving force that the law of nature did. What could be said about it? It was not clear whence its authority came. Its content was difficult to outline, though this can be said of the law of nature too. Without a developed theory of unwritten law, it was difficult to guide one's life by it. It generally involved statements of morality so vague that it could not be codified.

It was an attempt, however, to ground morality in a divine order. As such, it had a measure of success, as it fought to maintain law as a guide which did not bend to arbitrariness and political power. Yet, its vagueness could not guarantee it support. Such support was given to another form of higher law: the law of nature.[44]

---

[44] One must be careful not to join injudiciously the concepts of the law of nature and unwritten law. Though the similarities are sometimes strong, they are different concepts. Hirzel often considers the two concepts synonymous in *Agraphos Nomos*. This is really putting words in the ancients' mouths. Only one ancient author, Philo, joins these concepts together in a programmatic way.

CHAPTER TWO

"HIGHER" LAW: THE LAW OF NATURE

The law of nature, a concept whose origin lies with the Stoics, has had a long and turbulent history. The concept was early on adopted by Christian theorists and had a large role to play in European religious, philosophical, and political history. It has been used to support the whims and perversions of dictators.[1] But it has also been used to protect the rights of all human beings. It continues to be discussed in learned law journals even today.[2]

Given the long history of the concept, one must tread carefully in an historical study, making sure that the path that is followed is the path blazed by the ancient Greek authors, not by later trailblazers.

Origins

There is not as much information on the law of nature in ancient Stoic sources as one might believe. English translators of Greek texts, for example, often translate κατὰ φύσιν, "according to nature," as "according to the law of nature." However valid this may be in some cases, it is often an addition dependent on later developments and does not always reflect the intent of the author in question. It

---

[1] For the history of the concept in Europe and modern times in general see Otto Friedrich von Gierke's *Natural Law and the Theory of Society* (Introduction by Ernest Barker; Cambridge: The University Press, 1934); see also J. P. Mayer, *Political Thought: The European Tradition* (London: J. M. Dent and Sons, 1939); Leo Strauss, *Natural Right and History* (Chicago: The University of Chicago Press, 1953); Ernst Bloch, *Natural Law and Human Dignity* (trans. Dennis J. Schmidt; Cambridge, Mass. MIT Press, 1986); Michael Bertram Crowe, *The Changing Profile of the Natural Law* (The Hague Martinus Nijhoff, 1977); John Finnis, *Natural Law and Natural Rights* (Oxford: Clarendon Press, 1980); Lloyd L. Weinreb, *Natural Law and Justice* (Cambridge, Mass. Harvard University Press, 1987).

[2] See for example Anton-Hermann Chroust, "On the Nature of Natural Law" in *Interpretations of Modern Legal Philosophies* (New York: Oxford University Press, 1947) 70–84 and Max L. Laserson, "Positive and 'Natural' Law and their Correlation" in *Interpretations of Modern Legal Philosophies*, 443–449 among many examples.

blinds the modern reader to the fact that until Cicero (writing in Latin, but dependent upon Greek sources) and later Philo, the term only appears six times.[3] This has led to the question who the originator of the law of nature concept was, a question which has generally been answered with the Stoics. Today new answers abound.

Almost everyone or every school who could be has been claimed as the originator of the law of nature concept at one time or another. Some have claimed the pre-Socratics, specifically Heraclitus.[4] A great number have supported Plato as the founder of the concept.[5] Some have opted for Aristotle.[6] Others, naturally, have stayed with the Stoics.[7] The choices, however, do not end here. Cicero, long considered only as a bearer, not as a creator of tradition, has won support.[8] Helmut Koester has chosen Philo as his unlikely hero.[9]

---

[3] Helmut Koester, "νόμος φύσεως" in *Religions in Antiquity* (ed. Jacob Neusner; Leiden: E. J. Brill 1968) 523.

[4] Anton-Hermann Chroust, "On the Nature of Natural Law," 80–81,#5; Raghuveer Singh, "Heraklitos and the Law of Nature" in *JHI* 24 (1963) 458. This conclusion is especially based on frag. B114 of Heraclitus. Singh says that the "traditional conception of Natural Law as embodied in the writings of Roman jurists and Christian thinkers appears to be an elaborate footnote to Heraklitos" (461). Elaborate indeed!

[5] R. F. Stalley, *An Introduction to Plato's Laws* (Indianapolis: Hackett, 1983) 33; W. C. Greene, *Moira* 277; Joseph P. Maguire, "Plato's Theory of Natural Law" in *Yale Classical Studies* 10 (1947) 152f.; Jerome Hall, "Plato's Legal Philosophy" in Indiana Law Journal (31 (1956) 183,202f.; Friedrich Solmsen, *Plato's Theology* (Ithaca, N. Y. Cornell University Press, 1942) 167–168, 184; Rudolph Hirzel, *Themis, Dike, und Verwandtes: Ein Beitrag zur Geschichte der Rechtsidee bei den Griechen* (Hildesheim: Olms, 1966), 390f.; Glenn Morrow, *Plato's Cretan City* (Princeton: Princeton University Press, N. J. 1960) 565; and the star of the firmament, the thorough study by John Wild, *Plato's Modern Enemies and the Theory of Natural Law* (Chicago: University of Chicago Press 1953). How can so many claim for Plato the origination of this concept? It probably depends on a slight difference of terminology. Plato did indeed see law as based in the eternal forms of justice and right, but is this the same as law of nature? I think it is quite different, as will be argued shortly.

[6] E. Barker in the *Introduction* to Gierke's *Natural Law and the Theory of Society*, xxxv; Sir Frederick Pollock, "History of the Law of Nature" in *Essays in the Law* (London: Macmillan 1922).

[7] The list is too long to itemize, but most recently, and very persuasively, Gisela Striker, "Origins of the Concept of Natural Law" in *Proceedings of the Boston Area Colloquium in Ancient Philosophy* Vol. II (Boston, University Press of America 1987); Paul Vander Waerdt, *The Stoic Theory of Natural Law* (Diss. Princeton, 1989). An important article, also arguing for the Stoics, and breaking down the components of the law of nature, is Gérard Verbeke, "Aux Origines de la Notion de 'loi naturelle'" in *La Filosofia della natura nel medievo*. Atti del 3 Congresso internazionale di filosofia medioevale. Posso della Mendola (Trento), 31 agosto—5 settembre 1964 (Milan: Società Editrice Vita e Pensiero 1966) 164–173.

[8] Gerard Watson, "The Natural Law and Stoicism" in *Problems in Stoicism* (London: The Athlone 1971).

[9] Helmut Koester, in "νόμος φύσεως," says that the Stoics never managed to

It is, indeed, not apparent initially that the Stoics were the originators of the law of nature. The term appears infrequently, and not in many early Stoic writers. Yet, the concept and its origins are not as muddled as might first appear. The problems point not only to a paucity of sources, but to questions of definition. It was only with Philo and Cicero that the term νόμος φύσεως (*lex naturae*) found currency, but it is rare that someone argues for one of these two as the originator of the concept. What one must argue for the Stoics is that the idea of the law of nature was present, but in the early sources that remain, specifically for pre-Roman Stoic sources, the term itself is missing. But if only the idea of a nature which guides is present in the early Stoics, why can one not argue for Heraclitus or Plato as the originators of the concept? Do they too not share these ideas? Not exactly, and this is the problem of definition.

As Gisela Striker puts it,

> the reason for the dispute seems to me to lie in the lack of distinction between the thesis that there is such a thing as natural justice on the one hand, and the thesis that there is a natural law on the other.[10]

The concepts, while closely related, do not imply each other.[11] The reality is that, with the exception of the Sophists, all Greek thinkers saw some kind of divine or eternal support for law and justice.[12] It is wrong to move quickly from "natural justice" (or divine justice, or eternal justice) to "natural law."[13]

If we speak of immutable nature as the guide for law, as law itself, only one group of philosophers can truly be considered: the Stoics.

---

solve the antithesis between law and nature, but that Philo did (523). See Richard Horsley's refutation in "The Law of Nature in Philo and Cicero" in *HThR* 71 (1978). He believes the idea might have come to both of them through Antiochus of Ascalon, but he supports Stoic provenance of the idea in general (39–40). Cf. Vander Waerdt, *Natural Law*, for the claim that Cicero's view of the law of nature is, indeed, from Antiochus, esp. 231–263, but the claim is made throughout the dissertation. Naomi Cohen, *Philo Judaeus: His Universe of Discourse* (Frankfurt: Peter Lang, 1995) 274–277 also argues for Philo as the originator of the law of nature, but she is completely dependent upon Koester's arguments and simply recites his conclusions.

[10] Striker, "Origins" 80.
[11] See Vander Waerdt, *Natural Law* 123–143.
[12] Werner Jaeger, "Praise of Law: The Origin of Legal Philosophy and the Greeks" in *Interpretation of Modern Legal Philosophies* (New York 1947) 372.
[13] Victor Ehrenberg, "Anfänge des griechischen Naturrechts" in *Archiv für Geschichte der Philosophie* xxxv Band, Neue Folge xxviii (1923) 112–143, considers ἄγραφος νόμος as the equivalent of νόμος φύσεως, which mars his otherwise excellent article.

Only Stoicism claimed that nature supported justice and law in a systematic way, even before the widespread use of the term νόμος φύσεως.[14] Philosophically, one can see the connections between Plato and the Stoics, but the demands of history and philology are more narrowly defined. The Stoics alone depend on immutable nature as their guide; and if the term "law of nature" is missing among the early Stoics, Cicero, among others, allows us to fill in the missing pieces.

Nature

Long before nature had been called a "law" it had been opposed to law as "reality" or "truth" to convention.[15] The history of nature (φύσις) in Greek thought, like the history of most such powerful concepts, is not clear-cut or one-dimensional. Scholars of early Greek philosophy have discussed, and argued, at length whether φύσις meant first, and most importantly, genesis, "becoming" or "growth," or whether it first signified the "true character" of a thing.[16] Wherever the truth may lie, the direction in which the word developed was that of "true character" and φύσις became the norm against which the Sophists judged what was real and what was conventional or artificial.[17] But the φύσις which some Sophists—Hippias, Antiphon, and Callicles—[18] took as their guide, brutal, cold, and opposed to the law, became the guide which the Stoics saw as orderly, purposeful, and the creator of law.

---

[14] Maryanne Cline Horowitz, "The Stoic Synthesis of the Idea of Natural Law in Man: Four Themes" in *JHI* 35 (1974) 3–5; Striker, "Origins," 90–92; Brad Inwood, "Commentary on Striker" in *Proceedings of the Boston Area Colloquium in Ancient Philosophy* Vol. II. (Boston: University Press of America, 1987), 96.

[15] See the still classic work of Heinimann, *Nomos und Physis*, for the complete history of the antithesis.

[16] For "true character" see John Burnet, "Law and Nature in Greek Ethics" in *Essays and Addresses* (London: Chatto and Windus, 1930); and A. D. Lovejoy, "Meaning of Physis" in *Phil. Rev.* 18 (1909) 369–383; for "becoming" see F. J. E. Woodbridge in *Phil. Rev.* 10 (1901) 359–374 ; for both see Heinimann, *Nomos und Physis* 92f.; W. C. Greene, *Moira* 410, App.27. Even at the earliest point in the word's development, there were secondary meanings. Hans Leisegang, "φύσις" in *Pauly-Wissowa Real Encyclopädie* 20.1, 1130–1164 gives a good overview of the historical development of the term and its variety.

[17] Heinimann, *Nomos und Physis* 125.

[18] Guthrie, *History* Vol. III 136–143; Greene, *Moira* 232–244.

If the Sophists struck a blow against conventional morality and law—claiming them as arbitrary and ultimately meaningless—the Stoics sought to base morality on something unchanging and eternal. That the Stoics chose nature as their guide implies not a universe of disorder, but one with order as its very character and essence. It may be, in fact, that the Stoics took the Sophists' criticisms of conventional morality to heart, including the limited character of the written law; but then they turned the tables: indeed, nature is the true law, but instead of being chaotic and meaningless, it embodies meaning and truly grounds law in the purposeful and eternal.

According to Diogenes Laertius 7.87, Zeno, the founder of Stoicism, was the first to call the goal (τέλος) of life a life according to nature. A life according to nature is a virtuous life; and it is nature which leads to virtue. Diogenes goes on to state that the Stoic leaders who followed Zeno claimed the same "goal." Men such as Chrysippus, Cleanthes, Posidonius, and Hecato all claimed nature as the guide to a virtuous life. Early on, according to Diogenes, this life according to nature became linked to an eternal or divine law. It was a life in which we refrain

> from every action forbidden by the law common to all things, that is to say, the right reason which pervades all things, and is identical with Zeus, lord and ruler of all that is. (7.88)

Important in this passage are the links between nature, God, right reason (ὄρθος λόγος), and law (here called the κοινὸς νόμος). As we will see, these are synonymous in Stoic thought.

Cicero, too, clearly dependent on Middle Stoic sources,[19] says that the only true end, or goal, for humanity is following nature (*De Fin.* 20–26). The "root of justice" he says is found in nature (*De Leg.* 20). Cicero on numerous occasions makes the link between nature and

---

[19] Vander Waerdt, *Natural Law* 245–263, has argued that Antiochus of Ascalon is responsible for Cicero's theory in specific and fundamental revisions to the early Stoic theory of natural law. This, I will argue later—while suggesting certain modifications of Vander Waerdt's thesis—must be the case, but he too admits that "all we can say is that Antiochus' reinterpretation of the theory of natural law was prepared, perhaps in crucial respects, by certain developments in Stoic ethics already taking place under the influence of Panaetius and Posidonius" (234). Vander Waerdt is also right to stress that Cicero is not simply acting as a scribe: "there is no reason to assume that Cicero is simply copying out of one of his [Antiochus'] books" (236–237).

law. In *De Legibus* 18–19 he calls the law the highest reason implanted in nature.²⁰

It is nature as reason, God, even law, which the Stoics took as their guide to the virtuous life. That the guide for the virtuous life of the Stoic came to be called the law of nature is not odd in light of their connections between the two concepts; it was odd, however, in light of the long antipathy in Greek thought between the concepts of law and nature.²¹ The Stoics resolved this antithesis by tinkering both with the meaning of law and with the meaning of nature. Law was not truly the written law, but law based in unchanging nature: its commands and prohibitions therefore were not mere convention.²² Nature was reasonable, purposeful, even Zeus; far from being chaotic, it was the storehouse of order.²³

The "Common" Law

The early Stoics, as already mentioned, spoke of the link between nature and law. Before this was developed into the evocative phrase νόμος φύσεως, the Stoics talked of a κοινὸς νόμος, as did Aristotle. That the "common law" was an important concept for the early Stoics has not been duly noted, but the phrase appears in connection with every major Stoic thinker.²⁴ It seems that the common law existed as a concept beside nature, closely related, but not yet fully integrated with it.

Zeno, for instance, in Plutarch's *De Alexandri magni Fortuna aut Virtute* 329a–b (*SVF* 1.262), contends that there should be one way of life

---

²⁰ For other examples in Cicero, only a sampling, see *De Leg.* 1.34; 2.13; 3.2–3; *De Rep.* 3.33; *Parad. Stoic.* 14; *Nat. Deor.* 34, 82, 86; *De Off.* 1.98–100.

²¹ Gerard Watson, "The Natural Law and Stoicism" 218, says "we find it difficult at first to realize just how paradoxical such a close juxtaposition of φύσις and νόμος must have sounded even at the time of the first Stoics."

²² Rudolf Bultmann, "The Stoic Idea of the Wise Man" in *Primitive Christianity* (Cleveland and New York: Meridian Books, 1956) 137, says "the law of nature does not depend on human whims and fancies, but is the norm of society, on which all positive law must be based. Positive law is never actually identical with natural law."

²³ Against Koester, "νόμος φύσεως" 523, who believes that the Stoics never resolved the tension between law and nature.

²⁴ Vander Waerdt, *Natural Law* 82 notes the presence of the κοινὸς νόμος but does not, it seems to me, grant it the importance it deserves.

and order for people. The human family should be like that of a herd, being nurtured by a common law (νόμῳ κοινῷ). Chrysippus makes the connection between nature and one law even clearer. In Diogenes Laertius 7.87–89, already examined, it was Chrysippus who added that the life according to nature meant that one should not transgress the κοινὸς νόμος, which is the ὀρθὸς λόγος and identical to Zeus. When Chrysippus (*SVF* 3.314) speaks of law as king of all things, following Pindar *Frag.* 69, it should be obvious that he is speaking of a common and divine law. Chrysippus argued further (in Diogenes Laertius 7.128) that law exists by nature. Cleanthes, in his famous *Hymn to Zeus* (*SVF* 1.537), writes of the law of Zeus (line 2) and later of the θεοῦ κοινὸν νόμον, the common law of god (line 24).

In all of these cases, the law is seen to be something more than simply the written law of the city. It is connected with nature or God. Clearly, the way to the law of nature was being prepared, even if the term itself was not present. The law of nature was close at hand.

The Law of Nature

The law of nature would have been considered a "jarring" phrase, even contradictory.[25] It was the bringing together of opposites, and not only in the eyes of the Sophists.[26] The attempt to loosen the antithesis was made before the Stoics,[27] but it is only with the Stoics that the opposition was dissolved in unity.[28] Law, as the two previous sections have stressed, became that order and justice which was inherent in nature. Far from being arbitrary, the law was eternal.

---

[25] For further discussion of the antithesis cf. also Max Pohlenz, "Nomos und Physis" in *Hermes* 1953 (81); Guthrie, *History* Vol. III 55–134. Vander Waerdt, *Natural Law* 83, admits the "jarring" nature of the phrase, but believes that the reason the law was not referred to as the "law of nature" was because it was "a singularly inappropriate term to describe their theory" (83). Why? Because it referred to the right reason of the sage, not a code of *praecepta*. This does not explain, however, why the early Stoics spoke of a "common law," as they all did. They had no specific content in mind, save the sage's right reason, but this did not dissuade them from using the term. For this reason, I am inclined to believe the standard explanation that the "law of nature" was not initially used because of its "jarring" character.

[26] Heinimann, *Nomos*, 85–89, 115–125.

[27] Ibid., 153–154.

[28] Ibid., 169; Hirzel, *Agraphos* 98.

The fact that there existed many laws of many peoples did not alter the reality of true law; rather it meant that the true law was not being followed.

The law inherent in nature, sometimes considered the nature of humankind, but generally the nature of all or the universe itself,[29] is due to the reason in nature.

> In following reason, man acts in accord with the right reason of the universe, which, for Stoics after Chrysippus, is identical with νόμος κοινός, universal law.[30]

That right reason, ὀρθὸς λόγος, is considered the bedrock of the law is seen in the early Stoic sources. It is especially clear in Cicero. Cicero states what others continue to hint at: right reason is law which is in agreement with nature (*De Rep.* 3.33). The connection is made as well by Epictetus,[31] Seneca,[32] and Marcus Aurelius.[33]

The missing link, of course, is the link between the early Stoics and Cicero, who used the phrase *lex naturae* without explanation. The earliest use of the term *lex naturae* (νόμος φύσεως) on a regular basis in a Stoic sense of the concept, implying right reason and a connection between eternal law and purposeful nature, is by Cicero. Cicero is certainly dependent on the Middle Stoics, Panaetius and Posidonius, and Antiochus of Ascalon, in many respects—though source work on Cicero is a knotty problem[34]—and the idea of a νόμος φύσεως as formulated in Cicero almost certainly came from these thinkers.[35] The Roman student Cicero is, however, the preserver of the idea of the law of nature, and happily, he was an excellent student.

Much of what Cicero reports is not much different from what the early Stoics reportedly said. "Law is the highest reason, implanted

---

[29] The nature of humankind and the nature of all is ultimately the same thing. Humanity, as a product, and a reasonable product, of nature, shares in eternal nature and does not disagree with its dictates.

[30] Horowitz, "Four Themes" 4; cf. also Inwood, "Commentary" 99.

[31] 1.29,19; 4.3,11–12.

[32] *Epist.* 30, 45, 48, 66.

[33] 1.17,6; 4.4,1–4; 7.9.

[34] See, for example, on the question of source work in general, Olaf Gigon, "Cicero und die griechische Philosophie" in *ANRW* I.4 226–261.

[35] Elizabeth Rawson, "The Interpretation of Cicero's 'De Legibus'" in *ANRW* I.4 340–342 believes that by the time of Cicero it was common Stoic thought.

in nature, which commands what ought to be done and forbids the opposite. This reason, when firmly fixed and fully developed in the human mind, is Law" (*De Leg.* 1.18–19).[36] The difference between Cicero, or the Middle Stoics, and the early Stoics, is that Cicero gives us a systematic view of law, comprehensively developed, and with the title firmly entrenched: the law of nature.[37] Cicero also gives it to us often. The law of nature, however, is simply that true law, equal to God, the right reason of nature, which is incumbent on everyone, and of which the early Stoics also spoke.

That such a law existed is one thing, but what was the content of this law? What was its relationship to the written law? And who actually practised this law?

Where Does One Find the Law of Nature?

The law of nature was not to be located in any existing written code of law, at least not in its ideal or complete form. Cicero himself said that the law of nature placed Roman civil law in a "small and narrow corner" (*De Leg.* 1.17). It was a foolish notion, he said, to consider that everything which every nation considers law is just (*De Leg.* 1.42). There are, in fact, evil statutes which should not be called laws (*De Leg.* 2.13). A code of written law was to the law of nature "a mere outline sketch" (*De Off.* 3.69). Philo says that some written laws are not law in the true sense of the word at all. Epictetus, likewise, writes of the laws which come from God as worthy of following, not those from human legislators (4.3,11–12).

The law of nature transcended human laws, rendered them superfluous in some cases. The law of nature was reasonable, just, and according to nature. As a result, it was possible for one to do the higher law while transgressing the written law.[38] Diogenes Laertius

---

[36] See Vander Waerdt, *Natural Law* 81–142 for the definitive statement of the early Stoic provenance of what Cicero comes to call *lex naturae*. There can be no doubt, in light of his study, that Cicero follows, through his sources, the early Stoics.

[37] Cf. p. 125 n. 39 for the possible influence of Cicero himself on the formulation of the law of nature.

[38] Edelstein, *Meaning* 83, says "here the daring of Stoic ethics is conspicuous. No member of the school denied that a positive law is morally right or good only if it agrees with the law of nature and that otherwise it must be regarded as an aberration." Cf. Vander Waerdt, *Natural Law* 85, 95–98.

claims that the Stoic sage had all authority (ἐξουσία) over the law (7.125). Brad Inwood believes that the authority to transgress the written law is representative of early Stoic views. He says,

> morality for the Stoics is emphatically not a matter of obeying fixed specific rules,[39]

and,

> in breaking rough and ready but rigid rules of morality, the sage is obeying the law of nature in a higher, but more flexible, sense.[40]

The true law is not a matter of written codes, for written codes often do not reflect true law.

The true law, the law of nature, is available through reason, though most people are unable to harness reason and follow nature. As Dio Chrysostom says, if all men were good, there would be no need of laws (76.4). And Cicero contends that Socrates and Chrysippus could break certain laws because of their virtue (*De Off.* 1.148). Was the wise man to obey all the laws? Even when they were not really law? This, according to Cicero, is nonsense (*De Rep.* 3.18). For the wise man only the law of nature was truly law.[41]

Who Follows the Law?

The law of nature was that law which the wise man followed by the reason inherent in him; it came naturally to him.[42] Because reason is common to all people, though, everyone has the ability to follow the law of nature. This is a pleasant thought, but reality is much grimmer. The seeds of success lie within each person, but if the law of nature is in each of us potentially, and in the wise man certainly,

---

[39] Inwood, "Commentary" 97–98.

[40] Inwood, "Commentary" 101; For the unfixed nature of Stoic morality see I. G. Kidd, "Moral Actions and Rules in Stoic Ethics" in *The Stoics* (Berkeley and Los Angeles: University of California Press, 1978) 247–258.

[41] There is tension between my claim and Socrates' unwillingness under any circumstances to abandon the written law in the *Crito* (cf. 46b, 50b). The laws, however, do give Socrates a choice: he can either obey them or persuade them to follow universal justice (51b, 52a). The Stoic sage, it seems, who knew the universal law of nature, was obligated to follow it.

[42] Horowitz, "Four Themes" 16.

our chances of success are dimmed by the fact that very few people if any are truly wise. It was hard to find one who lived according to nature.

Sextus Empiricus never tired of mocking the Stoics on this score. He repeatedly states that it is impossible to find a wise man.[43] This might be tossed aside as mere sniping on the part of a critic, but in fact it formed a real problem for the Stoics. Cicero was not certain if there had been a wise man. He vacillates between saying there was none (*De Off.* 3.16; *De Rep.* 3.7) and saying that there were a handful (*Nat. Deo.* 1.23).[44] At any rate, there were not many, and had never been many, wise men. Nevertheless, the Stoics did not think of the wise man in theoretical terms: they believed he could exist.[45]

What would the wise man be like? In this they were not unlike other Greek thinkers who also imagined a wise man; they were part of a long Greek tradition. Plato stated that those adequate in their own nature would not need laws (*Leg.* 875a–d). In this they would be like the first men (*Leg.* 679e–680a). For Plato, though, this was a dream, or at most, a hope. Aristotle called the wise man a god among men (*Pol.* 3.8,1–2), perfect (*Eth. Eud.* 4.2,34), and above the law (*Pol.* 1.1,9; *Eth. Nic.* 4.8,10). Aristotle, too, though, held out little hope of finding such a man. So while the views of Plato and Aristotle blend easily with those of the Stoics, the Stoics spent much more time developing the concept and, more importantly, their philosophical system to a large degree was built around the Sage.

The Sage was all things. According to Diogenes Laertius the wise man is free from passions; he only feels proper emotions (7.116). He never feels, for instance, vanity or grief (7.117–118). The wise man also never has an opinion, that is, he always knows the truth and

---

[43] Sextus Empiricus, *Pyrrhoniae Hypotyposes* 2.38–42; *Adv. Dogm.* 1.432; 3.133; 5.181. Or Horace, *Epist.* 1,106–108: the Sage is "second only to Zeus: rich, free, honoured, beautiful, king of kings, especially while he is healthy and not troubled by a cold."

[44] This is discussed by G. B. Kerferd, "What Does the Wise Man Know?" in *The Stoics* (ed. John Rist; Berkeley and Los Angeles: University of California Press, 1978) 126–127; Eduard Zeller, *The Stoics, Epicureans, and Sceptics* (London: Longmans, Green: 1870) 294; J. M. Rist, "The Stoic Concept of Detachment" in *The Stoics*, 267.

[45] Edelstein, *Meaning* 11–12.

does not agree to the false (7.121). The wise man does all things well (7.125) and is in fact infallible (7.122). A Stoic paradox claimed that the wise man alone is free (7.121) and that only the wise are kings (7.122). For between virtue and vice, there exists no intermediate position: only the wise are wise; all others are foolish (7.127). It is no surprise then that Diogenes tells us that wise men were godlike (θείους) (7.119).

Cicero shares much the same understanding. The wise man is the true king (*De Fin.* 3.75). He never is wrong and he never hurts anyone (*De Fin.* 3.71). True goodness or "right" is only attainable by the wise man (*De Off.* 3.15). Given all this, one ought not be surprised that the wise man is always happy (*De Fin.* 2.104).

Plutarch gives us interesting information on how the Sage becomes wise. It happens in an instant (*Virt. Sent. Prof.* 75d); overnight the wise man becomes virtuous (*Stoic. Repug.* 1057e). One does not necessarily know, however, that the wise man has become wise: it simply happens (1061e). It is possible that even the Sage does not know it himself. Plutarch also draws a distinction between the reason of the wise man and the law, by which he means the written law (1038). The reason of the Sage, the law of nature, is different from the written law.

Seneca has preserved perhaps the most information on the wise man. The wise man does not "feel" his troubles, he simply overcomes them (*Epist.* 9.45). He also does not feel pain, or if he does, it does not bother him at all (*Epist.* 66.18). He is always joyful (*Epist.* 59.513). The completely wise man is not in ethical "motion" at all, for he is perfect (*Epist.* 35.245). The wise man also benefits others, according to Seneca. He enjoys giving more than a recipient enjoys receiving (*Epist.* 81.2). The wise man can tame vice in himself, too, and presumably that of others (*Epist.* 85.41).

The wise man lives, of course, according to nature (*Epist.* 17.115). He comes to know truth and nature and the law of life *(Epist.* 99.36). He is like a god because he becomes wise through perfect reason and obedience to nature (*Epist.* 87.19). He is as happy as a god (*Epist.* 73.14). And though Seneca argues that the wise man remains only a man (*Epist.* 71.27), Marion Altman argues that in some ways the wise man in Seneca is an equal of the gods.[46]

---

[46] Marian Altman, "Ruler Cult in Seneca" in *CP* 33 (1938) 202.

There are, of course, a number of attributes which stem from the wise man's perfection, but, for our limited discussion, of paramount concern is the perfect morality of the wise man. More to the point: our concern is the ability of the wise man to free himself from the restraints of material law through his ability to fulfil the higher law, the law of nature. The sources are not as clear and forthcoming as one would hope. There are, however, a number of clues and hints.

First, it is clear there was law which transcended the laws of cities and states.[47] While this law was first known by the Stoics as "following" nature or called the common law, it finally became the law of nature. This law was accessible through reason and, more specifically, right reason.[48] It was a problem of Stoicism, however, that the true law was only known to the wise man and that the material law, any civil code, contained only the outlines of the law of nature. Cicero, no antinomian, claims that "the most foolish notion of all is that everything is just which is found in the customs and laws of nations."[49] Cicero reflects the struggles the Stoics had with the civil law:

> But I ask, if it is the duty of a just and good man to obey the laws, what laws is he to obey? All the different laws that exist?[50]

This was not the answer, of course, for the law sufficient to all was the law of nature.

This was to be the law which the wise man obeyed and if it contradicted the laws of a given state, so be it. In theory this stance of the superiority of the law of nature over the written law was always upheld,[51] though the sources are careful not to preach anarchy or lawlessness. In any case, the rightful breaking of the law was not a common occurrence, simply because the wise man was not common.[52]

---

[47] Epictetus calls upon his readers to obey the laws sent by God: "to these you ought to subject yourselves, not the laws of Masurius and Cassius" (4.3,11–12). Elsewhere, 1.29,19, the laws of God are called the laws of nature.

[48] Alexander, *De Fato* 207, 5–21 (*SVF* 2:1003).

[49] Cicero, *De Leg.* 1.42.

[50] Cicero, *De Rep.* 3.18. Cf. also *De Leg.* 2.13; and *De Off.* 3.69 for further statements on the limited usefulness of the material law.

[51] Ludwig Edelstein, *Meaning* 83, calls this stand "the daring of Stoic ethics."

[52] Those who are not wise need the positive law and must follow it (Epictetus, 3.24,107). Marcus Aurelius calls the transgressor of ὁ νόμος κύριος (cf. Pindar, frag. 169; and Cleanthes, *Hymn to Zeus*, *SVF* 1.537) a fugitive slave. While ὁ νόμος κύριος may seem to refer to a "higher" law, in this case it is simply the written law; the sage at any rate did not break the law of nature.

There is no unanimity in the sources regarding the existence of the wise man.⁵³ The fact that there was a question about this put the Stoics on the receiving end of much ancient humour. Sextus Empiricus and Plutarch never tired of mentioning it.⁵⁴ Yet the Stoics never wavered in maintaining that there could be a wise man.⁵⁵

The once and future wise man was free from error. He had all the virtues and no vices.⁵⁶ His perfect moral character allowed the sage to see what was truly just and virtuous, what was, in fact, truly law. In perceiving the law of nature, and in following it, they were able to perceive the truth which the framers of positive law could not.

Cicero stresses that just because Socrates and Chrysippus broke the laws of a given city, others do not have the right to ignore the laws of their city.⁵⁷ The crux is found in Cicero's claim about Chrysippus and Socrates: they earned the right to ignore aspects of the material law. For Plato, the ideal state would need no law.⁵⁸ For the Stoics, all members of the ideal state, at least following Zeno's model, would possess the law themselves.⁵⁹ Due to the unlikelihood of a Stoic ideal state—only wise men and women comprise the state—the positive law, flawed as it is, remains. Since it is not as perfect as the sage, the sage may at times disobey it.⁶⁰

Only the Stoic sage knows this "perfectly correct law."⁶¹ If he was to break a written law in the course of following the law of nature, he would be directed by reason: "it is obedience to the rationality imbedded in him" which guides his behaviour.⁶² He has all authority over the written law.⁶³ He must be subject to the law of nature.⁶⁴

---

[53] Cicero, *De Rep.* 3.7; *Nat. Deo.* 1.23. Johnny Christenson, *An Essay on the Unity of Stoic Philosophy* (Copenhagen: Munksgaard 1962) 69.
[54] Sextus Empiricus, *Pyrr. Hyp.* 2, 38–42; *Adv. Dogm.* 1. 432; *Adv. Dogm.* 3. 133.
[55] A. A. Long and D. N. Sedley, *The Hellenistic Philosophers*, Vol. I (Cambridge: University Press, 1987) 383. Kurt Deissner, "Das Idealbild des Stoichen Weisen" in Greifswalder Universitäts Reden (Greifswald: Ratsbuchhandlung L. Bamberg, 1930) 3.
[56] Diogenes Laertius, 7.123.
[57] Cicero, *De Off.* 1.148; cf. Seneca, *Epist.* 14.
[58] Hall, "Plato's Legal Philosophy," 192.
[59] H. C. Baldry, "Zeno's Ideal State" in *JHS* 79 (1959) 3–15.
[60] Inwood, "Commentary" 101.
[61] Rist, "Detachment" 267.
[62] A. A. Long, "The Early Stoic Concept of Moral Choice" in *Images of Man in Ancient and Medieval Thought*, (Leuven: Leuven University Press, 1976) 92.
[63] Diogenes Laertius, 7.125; Dio Chrysostom, 76.4; Cicero, *De Fin.* 3.75.
[64] Epictetus, 3.3,11–12.

The sage could not possibly oppose a law of nature; it would contradict reason and this the sage cannot do.

The idea of the godlike, perfect wise man makes it clear why they were so rare. Unfortunately, a consequence of this idea of the wise man was the notion that the rest of humanity was foolish.[65] It meant, in practice, that everyone was foolish. This, too, was cause for laughter on the part of critics. Taken to its absurd extreme, or logical end, Plato was no better than a common criminal (Plutarch, *Stoic. Repug.* 1048e; *Virt. Sent. Prof.* 76a). Later Stoics, particularly Seneca (e.g., *Epist.* 35), devised a system of progress to give hope to the great mass of fools, but it was not very successful in bridging the gap between the wise and the fools. Those who were progressing were still on the side of the fools. Seneca argues that those who are progressing are a long way from the fools (*Epist.* 75), but they are still on the wrong side of happiness. As Plutarch put it in *Adversus Stoicos* (1062a), the Stoics considered that one was drowning, whether five hundred fathoms under the sea or one arm's length from the surface.

The situation was clear, if not pleasant. The law of nature would be done by the sage, if he could be found. Only he, however, would know the law of nature. This leads to the problem of content. What was in the law of nature? No one knew for sure, although people made attempts at defining individual laws. But apart from a smattering of individual laws here and there in the works of various writers, the law of nature was contentless. As Lapidge put it:

> one looks in vain for how man was to live in harmony with universal nature.[66]

There was no answer. Wisdom was what the wise man thought.[67] Only he could know the natural law.[68] Marcus Aurelius said that it was possible to be extremely godlike and not be recognized (7.67); so if the wise man existed, he did not tell how he did the law of nature or what was in this law.[69]

---

[65] Rist, "Detachment" 260; Long and Sedley, *The Hellenistic Philosophers* 384–385.
[66] Michael Lapidge, "Stoic Cosmology" in *The Stoics* 162.
[67] Kerferd, "The Image of the Wise Man in Greece before Plato" in *Images of Man in Ancient and Medieval Thought: Studia Gerardo Verbeke* (Leuven: Leuven University Press 1976) 27.
[68] Rist, "Detachment" 267.
[69] Vander Waerdt, *Natural Law* 235–263 claims in an important discussion that

Conclusions

The law of nature was the universal, divine law that was also known as the right reason of nature. It was known to the wise man through his reason and his understanding of nature. Because of the higher status of the law of nature, it transcended the written laws of cities and peoples.[70] Civil law, even at its best, did not reflect the entirety of the law of nature, as Cicero (*De Leg.* 1.17,42,44; 2.13; *De Off.* 3.69; *De Rep.* 3.18), Seneca (*Epist.* 30), and Epictetus (1.26,1–2; 4.7,34) attest. The law of nature, located in its entirety only in the reason of the sage, gave the sage "complete authority to violate the duties or laws when appropriate."[71] The sage who knew the law of nature was able then to "break" various written laws if in so doing he was actually fulfilling the law of nature.[72]

> Obviously none of the precepts which guide the conduct of ordinary human beings govern the wise man's conduct, since he has the rational disposition for which these precepts are supposed to provide a practical substitute.[73]

Antiochus, followed by Cicero, knows of a code of laws, or *officia*, which contain the content of the law of nature (253). Antiochus replaces, therefore, the κατορθώματα of the sage for the καθήκοντα, which even the ordinary person could follow. This is an important distinction, and the result of fine scholarship. But while I think it is true that Antiochus made this move, I do not think that he had a code of *officia*. I also do not think that the wise man's ability to follow the law of nature completely falls by the wayside. In a passage significant for his claim that there was a code of *officia* (*De Leg.* 2.8–11) it is still admitted that "divine mind is the supreme Law, so, when [reason] is perfected in man, [that also is law; and this perfected reason exists] in the mind of the wise man" (*De Leg.* 2.11). Cicero also says in *De Off.* 3.69 that we have no true representation of the law of nature. How do we determine which laws are just? By referring them to the standard of nature, says Cicero (*De Leg.* 1.44). This implies that one can "determine" how to act according to nature in individual circumstances, but it does not imply to me that it had been accomplished and set down in a code of *officia*, nor does it imply that anyone but the sage could do this perfectly and so truly follow nature. If all this seems to undercut Vander Waerdt, I still agree in general that the move had been made by Antiochus to try and find in general rules to guide the ordinary person; I do not believe that such rules had been codified or that the role of the sage had been cast aside.

[70] Seneca, *Epist.* 95.40; 66.40; Kidd, "Stoic Intermediaries" 164–167; "Moral Actions and Rules" 247–257; Inwood, "Commentary" 97–101.

[71] Vander Waerdt, *Natural Law* 34. His claim is based upon Diogenes Laertius 7.125.

[72] Inwood, "Commentary" 101.

[73] Vander Waerdt, *Natural Law* 95.

The only true law was the law of nature (cf. *Epictetus* 4.7,34).

Cicero, according to Watson,[74] and Antiochus, according to Vander Waerdt,[75] attempted to ground the law of nature on a code of precepts, perhaps even on a model much like Roman civil law, rather than on the reason of the sage. Cicero continued to maintain, however, the elusiveness of the law of nature; its fixity in a code of written law was not a *fait accompli* but a continuing project (*De Leg.* 1.42,44; 2.13; *De Rep.* 3.18,33). The law of nature exists in full, according to Cicero, in the perfected reason of the wise man alone (*De Leg.* 2.11).

What was the wise man to do when confronted with "bad" laws? Or when reason led him against the dictates of the civil code? The sage is told to obey the laws and customs of civil society (Cicero, *De Off.* 3.63; Seneca, *Epist.* 14; Epictetus 3.24,107), but there is a clear sense in which these strictures are provisional.

The law of nature is the superior law for Cicero (*De Leg.* 1.18–19) and for Epictetus (4.3,11–12). According to Cicero, the law of nature is the only true law (*De Off.* 1.100). Epictetus states that the laws which matter are not those of Masurius and Cassius—jurists of the first century C.E.—but those of God (4.3,11–12). The civil law desires to follow the law of nature (Cicero, *De Off.* 3.69; Seneca, *Epist.* 30), but it has not achieved this goal (Cicero, *De Leg.* 1.44; Epictetus 1.11,15).[76]

The wise man, as a result, can "break" laws which do not agree with nature or which oppose reason. Though the ordinary person is bound by a civil code, the sage is not (Cicero, *De Off.* 1.148; Plutarch, *Stoic. Repug.* 1038a; Diogenes Laertius 7.125).

> In some cases ... he [the sage] has no choice but to violate the precepts or rules by which his fellows live in order to remain consistent with the higher law of Zeus.[77]

The Stoics are saved from antinomianism or, worse, anarchy on two counts. Not every written law is opposed to the law of nature. The sage is often warned to keep the customs of the people with whom

---

[74] Watson, "Natural Law" 231–236.
[75] Vander Waerdt, *Natural Law* 231–263.
[76] Cf. I. G. Kidd, *Posidonius. Commentary* Vol. II. Part II (Cambridge: Cambridge University Press, 1972) 654–656.
[77] Vander Waerdt, *Natural Law* 96.

he lives, and some laws, perhaps most, agreed with the law of nature. Also, the wise man was extremely rare, perhaps he never even existed, and only the wise man has the authority over law which allows him to disobey written law. Nevertheless, the Stoics never backed off from their position that the true law, the law which had priority, was the law of nature; and the reason of the sage would not allow him to ignore this higher law.

CHAPTER THREE

"HIGHER" LAW: THE LIVING LAW[1]

In the famous fragment of Pindar (69), the law is called king of all, living and dead.[2] This was the pride of most Greeks: they were ruled equally by the law, not by the whims of a tyrant. In this section, we want to discover how it is that this commonplace, which underpinned the democratic πόλις, came to be formulated in the Hellenistic period in a way that would have sent, perhaps would still send, shivers down the spines of democrats: the switch of subjects, from "the law is king" to "the king is law," leads us from a concept which underpins democracy to one which underpins an absolutist monarchy.

The Greeks, perhaps more than most ancient peoples, feared tyranny, even monarchy itself.[3] Yet, even the Greeks from early in their history, written at any rate, accepted the authority of the kingship of Zeus and recognized his influence upon earthly kings. Werner Jaeger says of Homer's kingship conception:

> the kings received their sceptre and with it the *themistes* from their pattern in heaven, Zeus, the king of the gods, whom Homer conceived as the divine source of all earthly justice.[4]

---

[1] I have yet to run across a discussion on how ἔμψυχος ought to be translated in this phrase. Some scholars have chosen "animate" and others "embodiment," as in "embodiment of the law;" both of these have their virtues. Most scholars, however, have opted for "living" and this seems to capture the nuances of both the word and the idea. Archytas contrasts the king as ἔμψυχος with the written law which is ἄψυχος (*Stob.* 4.1,135). Of the three possibilities, "living" seems to me to get to the heart of the contrast. As we shall see, the king *is* the law. He is not simply the law's embodiment. Animate is possible, but living seems more appropriate for a person. In *E. N.* 8.10–11, and elsewhere, Aristotle refers to a slave as an ἔμψυχον ὄργανον, a "living tool;" the same translation seems appropriate for the νόμος ἔμψυχος, namely, the "living law."

[2] This piece of Pindar's work influenced a great number of writers: Herodotus, 7.104; Lysias, *Epitaph.*, 18–19; Plato, *Gorgias*, 484b; Cleanthes, *Hymn to Zeus* (SVF 1.537), Dio Chrysostom 75.1; Marcian 1 (*SVF* 3.314).

[3] E. Barker, *Greek Political Theory* (London: Methuen 1951) 205 says monarchy was "most unpopular in the Greek world."

[4] Jaeger, "Praise of Law" 353.

Before democracy, then, there was kingship, and ideally this kingship was just because the kings followed the pattern of perfect justice in heaven, Zeus. Be this as it may, in the centuries which intervened between Homer and Hellenism, law came to be king of the Greeks. Law did not choose favourites: it did not tyrannize the poor and favour the rich. By the time of Hellenism, the concept of law as king was well established.

Yet, from the time of the Sophists, at any rate, the law itself was not always a straightforward matter. Questions of the relativity of law, the origin of law, true law, and higher law were all debated. And alongside the dominant stream of thought, "the law is king," lay this other trickle, which never really ran dry and which came to the fore during the Hellenistic period, "the king is law."

The trickle, which seemed to gain force from the time of Alexander the Great's ascendancy, was the idea of a just or perfect king who ruled virtuously and wisely. At its height, it opposed the king to the written law and called the king the "living law." That is, it gave a philosophic basis to a powerful reality: the king whose law was his word. The demands, of course, were not light; not any king with horrible power was the living law. The king must be perfect, truly just, and like a father to his subjects if he was to be the living law.

Early Greek Forerunners of the Living Law Ideal

The νόμος ἔμψυχος ideal at its full flower, whether with the title or not, is not found in early sources. The centre of the ideal, however, the opposition between the king on one side and the written law on the other, is found, even if undeveloped, in a number of Greek authors whose influence on the living law ideal is probable. Even here, though, one must be careful not to claim too much: a king can be the law in deed without needing to defend his claim philosophically. With this is mind, these are the early Greek forerunners of the νόμος ἔμψυχος ideal.

Xenophon presents us with the first clear opposition between the written law and the king in a Greek source. We are presented with the Persian king Cyrus. Cyrus attempted to set before his subjects "a perfect model of virtue in his own person" (*Cyropaedia* 8.1,21). What was the purpose of this? Xenophon tells us that Cyrus seemed to understand that even through the written laws man became better, but he believed that the good ruler was a law keeping watch on behalf of men (*Cyropaedia* 8.1,22).[5]

Cyrus in fact believed that the king was superior to the written law, perhaps because he was able to respond to the individual subjects in his kingdom. Whatever the case, the contrast is clear. The μέν-δέ formulation sets up the contrast, and the choice of verbs fulfils it. Cyrus "understood" that written law made one better, but he "believed" that the good ruler was a better law. The written law and the king are two options for a people. This is why Cyrus needed to be a "perfect model of virtue": he was the law.[6]

The text goes on to sing the praises of Cyrus, describing his lasting legacy and his virtues. It adds that from the first the Persians imitated him (*Cyr.* 8.1,24), a concept which becomes significant in the developed living law ideal.

Plato, too, at times, considered the idea of an absolute rulership which implied that the king, or ruler, was the law. In the *Respublica* (473c–e), the rule of the philosopher-kings is "absolute—absolute in the sense that they are untrammelled by any written law."[7] The same is true of the *Politicus* (293b–d,301d,302e), in which Plato has built a system wherein the written law is unnecessary for the true philosopher-king.[8] The antithesis, as in Xenophon, is between the "personal rule of a wise sovereign and the impersonal rule of law."[9]

In the *Leges*, it is true, Plato moves somewhat away from the absolutism of the *Respublica* and the *Politicus*, but he does not abandon his earlier views entirely. He still speaks of "those who have no need

---

[5] My translation. The translation of Walter Miller, *Cyropaedia II* in the *LCL* does not fully bring out Xenophon's contrast between the law and the king. G. J. D. Aalders, "Νόμος ἔμψυχος" in *Politeia und Res Publica* (Wiesbaden: Steiner 1969) 319, believes that Xenophon does identify the king with the law in this passage and others, but also points back to Isocrates as a starting point in this process, though he does not think that the identification is complete in the work of Isocrates (317–318).

[6] Sextus Empiricus, *Adv. Rhet.* 2.33 records the story that when the king of the Persians died the people practised five days of ἀνομία so that they would perceive the worth of the king, who was also the law.

[7] Barker, *Greek Political Theory* 205. They are not, however, free from basic principles of justice (421e; 423c–d; 424b–c).

[8] L. Delatte, *Les Traites* 131–132; Barker, *Greek Political Theory* 271–287.

[9] Barker, *Greek Political Theory* 280.

of laws" (644b) because they are capable of ruling themselves (875c–d), but he does seem to rule out an absolutist monarchy, in which the king was sovereign over the laws. Plato seems finally to opt for the laws being sovereign over the king.[10]

Aristotle, however, presents a powerful case for the authority of the king as the law. In a discussion of humour—not necessary for a king, but definitely necessary for his subjects—Aristotle says that the cultivated man "will therefore regulate his wit, and will be as it were a law to himself" (*Eth. Nic.* 4.8,10). This is not directly to the point, but it does give us a taste of Aristotle's view on the ability of man to govern himself. More to the point is *Eth. Nic.* 5.4,7 in which Aristotle describes the ideal magistrate as "living justice" (δίκαιον ἔμψυχον). The magistrate not only practices the law, he becomes justice itself.

It is in the *Politica*, though, that we find the expression of these ideas in their political dress. Aristotle has said that a man can be a law to himself and the magistrate "living justice," but what of the king? In *Pol.* 1.1,9 Aristotle gives his famous description of man as a "political animal" by nature. If one is, therefore, beyond the bounds of the πόλις, he is either below common humanity or he has transcended it. It is the man who transcends the city who is of concern to us, and whom Aristotle describes in Book 3 of the *Politica*.

One cannot number among the members of a state people who are outstanding in virtue. They are gods among men. As a result, legislation is not directed towards these people: they are themselves law (3.8,1–2). Aristotle in this passage is content to state only their transcendence over and freedom from the state. Later, though, he discusses absolute monarchy and the case against it (3.11,1–9). Aristotle acknowledges that it is not just to have a king who himself takes the place of the law (αὐτὸν ὡς ὄντα νόμον), but he adds that one king is unjust only among people who are equal. If one man, or a whole family, transcends the other citizens in virtue to a great degree, this man, or family, should not be ostracized or banished, nor should he, or they, be subjected to the rule of others. The community should obey such a man "not in turn but absolutely" (3.11,11–13). The community should treat him as the law.[11]

---

[10] Ibid., 310–311 sees this backstep on Plato's part as influenced by contemporary Persia, which had fallen into disarray.

[11] Aristotle's discussion on kingship in *Eth. Nic.* 8.10–11, while not discussing the

The idea of the king as the law is also present, albeit negatively, in a section of Euripides' *Suppliants*. Theseus, speaking in favour of the κοινὸς νόμος, which in this case means the laws belonging to all the members of the state, declares that with a tyrant the law is kept in private hands and is no longer public property. This is, probably, only a reflection of the sad truth of tyranny, and not a statement, even negatively, of a nascent νόμος ἔμψυχος ideal. Nevertheless, it presents to us once again the idea of the king as the law.[12]

The best example of the living law ideal, indeed, its first statement is found in the tractate Περί Νόμου καὶ Δικαιοσύνης of Archytas. Archytas as a forerunner of the Hellenistic Pythagorean fragments may strike some as odd. He is gathered with the other pseudonymous Pythagorean texts in Stobaeus' anthology and E. R. Goodenough considered Archytas' writings Hellenistic forgeries with the name of an ancient attached, as with Diotogenes and Sthenidas.[13] Could his texts be genuine? It is not an easy decision. Holger Thesleff, however, has argued convincingly for the early character of the writing, and he will be followed in one respect. Whether the text is a genuine writing of Archytas, it seems to be a forerunner of the living

---

king as law, displays many of the same attributes as the living law texts. The king is a father to his subjects (8.10,4). The king benefits his subjects (8.11,1-2). These are, though, general kingship attributes, not found only in the living law ideal. See Aalders, "Νόμος ἔμψυχος," 321-323, though, for a more confident assessment of the ideal in the work of Aristotle.

[12] See also Isocrates, *Ad Demonicum*, 36; cf. Goodenough, "Hellenistic Kingship" 62-63.

[13] E. R. Goodenough, "Hellenistic Kingship" 60-61. Goodenough, too, admits to having some doubts about whether Archytas' tractate is a Hellenistic production (101). It was dated as pre-Platonic by A. Delatte in *Essai sur la politique pythagoricienne*. This was disputed by Willy Theiler (*Gnomon* 2[1926] 147-156), who opted for a Hellenistic date (150-151). Holger Thesleff (*An Introduction to the Pythagorean Writings of the Hellenistic Period*) dates most of the kingship fragments to the early Hellenistic period, but considers this work of Archytas' earlier (109,114).

Interestingly, L. Delatte's late dating of the kingship fragments in *Les Traites de la Royauté*, disputed by Thesleff in *An Introduction* 65-71, does not include Archytas. Walter Burkert, in the discussion which followed papers given by Thesleff ("On the Problem of the Doric Pseudo-Pythagorica: An Alternative Theory of Date and Purpose") and Burkert ("Zur geistesgeschichtlichen Einordnung einiger Pseudopythagorica") on the dating of the Pythagorean fragments, *Fondation Hardt: Pour L'Etude de L'Antiquité Classique Entretiens: Tome XVIII—Pseudepigrapha I* (Geneve: Fondation Hardt 1972) 100 agreed that much of the pseudepigraphal material is based upon genuine material from Archytas.

Given the general scholarly consensus, it seems right to consider the tractate of Archytas genuine, or if not genuine, of an earlier date than the other Hellenistic discussions.

law fragments because of its less developed ideas of absolute kingship.

Archytas is not a thorough-going monarchist, or at least not a supporter of an absolute monarchy. He sees the written law, which is nourished by unwritten law, as in some way god-given (*Stob.* 4.1.132).[14] It is only in relation to these god-given laws that the king is just (*Stob.* 4.1.135). The king is just (νόμιμοις) with reference to this law of God. This law is the law which, as we saw earlier, is unwritten and nourishes the written laws. It can, however, also nourish the king. For the king, not only the written laws, can serve as the law:

> but the law is the living king (ἔμψυχος βασιλεύς) or the inanimate written law (ἄψυχος γράμμα) (*Stob.* 4.1.135,20–21).[15]

The king is an alternative to the written law. The written law is not bad, and the king is not better, but they both fulfil the same function for Archytas and only one is necessary.

The phrase Archytas uses is evocative, ἔμψυχος βασιλεύς, the living king, as opposed to the inanimate (ἄψυχος) written law. This is the first statement of the living law ideal, or at least the earliest literary record. It is from this statement, which recognizes two types of "just" law, and carries the seeds of the living law ideal and phrase itself, that we move to the classic formulation of νόμος ἔμψυχος, which is concerned with really only one type of law, the king. Archytas seems to be the link between the earliest Greek formulations and the development of the full-blown ideal.

Archytas' tractate contains other reminders of the living law ideal as found in the pseudepigrapha, as we shall see. The comparison of the law with ἁρμονία (*Stob.* 4.1.135,15) and the description of the well-ruled state as harmonious (*Stob.* 4.1.135,7–13) remind us of the living law fragments. So, too, does the description of the king who acts only out of concern for his subjects (*Stob.* 4.5.61). The king must love his subjects to be a true king. Archytas gives this expression:

> And the true ruler must not only be understanding and powerful in ruling well, but he must also be a lover of men, for it would be strange for a shepherd to be a hater of sheep and ill disposed toward his own

---

[14] Where page and line references are given to material cited from Stobaeus the edition of C. Wachsmuth and Otto Hense is followed (Berlin: Weidmann 1884).

[15] My translation.

flock... He would do nothing in his own interest, but only for the sake of his subjects, just as the law exists not for its own sake but only for those subject to it.[16]

The goal of the king is to serve his subjects. More specifically, one can point to terms which later came to be commonplaces in the general concept of Hellenistic kingship, terms such as φιλανθρωπία (*Stob.* 4.5.61,13) and εὐεργέτης (*Stob.* 4.5.61,19) which are found in this passage.

Goodenough has actually stressed the differences between the other Greek sources, such as Xenophon and Aristotle, and Archytas.[17] Clearly Archytas presents a new concept in many ways, but there are a number of similarities and some continuity between their formulations. The decision seems to hinge on the degree to which one attributes Eastern influences and the degree to which one believes the ideas are indigenous to the Greeks. While there are impulses from the East, Egypt and Persia, which have influenced this conception, especially in its earliest stages, it seems to me highly likely that in fact it finally took root in Greek soil because it was a development of Greek needs and desires at the time.[18] The Greeks were no strangers to despots and tyrants, and, like all people, they hated them. In light of their great hatred of tyranny, and their love of freedom, it seems inexplicable that they could have adopted the idea of absolutist monarchy without having an indigenous need for it. A tyrant may be imposed and there is little a people can do about him, until they gain the force to remove the tyrant. That a people who despised tyranny were able to consider absolutist monarchy, aware of the dangers to which such rule could lead, suggests that the desire for the perfect ruler who brought justice and peace sometimes overwhelmed the fear of tyranny and spoke to needs found in the people themselves. What is finally astounding about the idea is that so many thinkers considered it in the Greek world. Their consideration led to something far more serious: the idea of the king as the true law.

---

[16] Translation of Goodenough, "Hellenistic Kingship" 59. Unless otherwise noted, all translations of the Hellenistic Pythagorean authors are from "The Political Philosophy of Hellenistic Kingship" by Goodenough.

[17] Goodenough, "Hellenistic Kingship" 61–64.

[18] Aalders, "Νόμος ἔμψυχος," 316, for a similar assessment of the origin of the concept.

The Pythagorean Fragments of the Hellenistic Period

The texts which contain the νόμος ἔμψυχος ideal are also contained in the anthology of Stobaeus and attributed to Sthenidas of Lokri, Diotogenes, and Ecphantus, three followers of Pythagoras. It is agreed by all scholars consulted, with the exception of Armand Delatte, that these texts are not written by their attributed authors. There is less agreement as to the date of these texts. As a result these texts cannot be discussed without an overview of the knotty and bedevilled topic of their date. To ensure that the important question of the date of these texts does not distract from the ideas, the issue of dating these texts will be carried out in an Appendix. These are the authors and their ideas.

Ecphantus, of the three Hellenistic Pythagorean sources, produced the most thorough statement of the living law ideal.[19] Both Diotogenes and Sthenidas, though, contain important material, some of which is not duplicated in Ecphantus.[20] At any rate, all three comprise the most important material for the development of the living law ideal.

Ecphantus calls the king a copy of god (272,14f.). Since the king is most like god (274,1f.), the ordinary person should make himself like him in order to purify himself when he sins. Ecphantus says that the subject should do so, whether the ruler is the king or the law (274,4–9). The contrast between the king and the law is known already from Archytas; here the contrast is complete: one's ruler is either the law or the king. They are equal, but discrete choices: one does not need both. The other important information is the closeness, the nearness of the king to god. He is, in fact, a special being.

Ecphantus stresses as well the virtue of the king, who imitates the virtue of the heavenly king. The king's virtue is so great, that one might think it came from God (274,20–275,5). The close relationship between the king and God is seen in the king's virtue and in his relationship with his subjects.

---

[19] These texts are found in *Stob.* 4.7,64,65,66; lines 271,13–274,20.
[20] The work of all three authors, however, will only be treated here to the extent that it contributes to our understanding of the idea of the superfluity of the law; where important in the study of Philo's view of the law, these texts will be taken up again.

> He who rules in accordance with virtue is called, and is, the king, for he has the same love and communion with his subjects as God has with the universe and the things in it (276,2–9).[21]

The idea of the king as law appears here again. Perhaps surprising is the warm feeling these subjects are said to have for their "law;" but, then, their law is perfect and just.

Their "law," the king, loves them and enters into "communion" with them, an important concept in the kingship fragments. He loves them as God loves his creation, because he imitates God in his role as their king. The imitation of God is an important concept, and appears more than once in Ecphantus.

The king is like the rest of humankind bodily, "but he is fashioned by the supreme Artificer, who in making the king used himself as an Archetype."[22] The uniqueness of the king is of paramount importance:

> Accordingly the king, as a copy of the higher king, is a single and unique creation, for he is on the one hand always intimate with the one who made him, while to his subjects he appears as though he were in a light, the light of royalty.[23]

The king functions as a mid-point between God and humanity, inferior to the one, but towering over the other.

The king possesses a secondary position between humanity and God through his imitation of God. As a result, he is not only an example for his subjects, but he is able to drive evil out of them and replace it with good. In two passages Ecphantus describes how the king brings virtue to his subjects and allows them to participate in this virtue:

> And there must exist complete good will, first on the part of the king toward his subjects, and second on their part toward the king, such as is felt by a father toward his son, a shepherd toward his sheep, and by a law toward those who use it (276,4–9).[24]

The king's subjects need only accept him to receive virtue:

---

[21] Goodenough, "Hellenistic Kingship" 84.
[22] Ibid., 76.
[23] Ibid., 76–77.
[24] Ibid., 84.

> The king alone is capable of putting this good into human nature so that by imitation of him, their Better, they will follow in the way they should go. But his λόγος, if it is accepted, strengthens those who have been corrupted by evil nurture as if by drink, and who have fallen into forgetfulness; it heals the sick, drives out the forgetfulness which has settled upon them as a result of their sin, and makes memory live in its place, from which so-called obedience springs.[25]

The virtuous king, a law for his subjects, allows his subjects to lead virtuous lives through participation in his virtue; this participation is a direct result of imitation of and obedience to the king.

To Sthenidas of Lokri is attributed a short kingship fragment.[26] The king is an imitator of God and zealous for him (270,13–14).[27] The king, for all of his greatness, is only a copy of the true king, God, says Sthenidas. According to L. Delatte, who has made a number of textual changes, the contrast between the king and God is even clearer:[28]

> For he [God] is the first king by nature (φύσει) and being (ὠσίᾳ), but the other by birth and imitation (270,14–16).

The king, therefore, takes his example from God and is called to imitate God in all things, especially in acting like a father to his subjects (270,20–21). For God is recognized as God by acting like a father; so, too, the true king is recognized as the king by his behaviour toward his subjects (271,1–2). God is also called the lawgiver (271,6–7), and it follows that as a perfect imitator of God the king too has the role of lawgiver for his subjects.

Diotogenes, however, gives us our most straightforward account of the living law and the first usage of the term νόμος ἔμψυχος.[29] He calls the king most righteous and most lawful (263,15–16). Without justice there is no law, and without law there is no justice, says Diotogenes. The king, however, is the living law (νόμος ἔμψυχος) or most lawful leader (νόμιμος ἄρχων), so he is indeed most just and lawful (263,16–20).[30] The king is the law for his subjects because he meets the standards of justice.

---

[25] Ibid., 89.
[26] Sthenidas' fragment on kingship is found in *Stob.* 4.7,63; lines 270,12–271,12.
[27] Delatte, *Les Traites* 275–276.
[28] Ibid., 276–277 adds ὠσίᾳ and φύσει, which he believes to have been lost in the transmission of the texts. My translation accepts these additions.
[29] Diotogenes' fragments are found in *Stob.* 4.7,61; 263,14–270,11.
[30] Delatte, *Les Traites* 248 takes these two descriptions of the king, as either the

The king is also the saviour of his people (264,9), a common designation of kings in the Hellenistic period. Through his role as their king, he brings them into harmony and acts as their benefactor (εὐεργέτεν) (264,12–265,1). Diotogenes expresses clearly how the king benefits and affects his subjects and leads them to lawful and virtuous lives:

> So he will succeed in putting into order those who look upon him, amazed at his majesty, at his self-control, and his fitness for distinction. For to look upon the good king ought to affect the souls of those who see him no less than a flute or harmony (265f.).[31]

The very presence of the king affects the souls of those subject to him. He is like a god to them. The function of creating harmony, already seen in Archytas, is a common Pythagorean theme. "Benefactor" is probably the most common of all the titles of Hellenistic kings.

Diotogenes, too, calls the king an imitator of God, who through his act of imitation creates a microcosm of the cosmos in his state (265,1–10). This act of imitation of God's role in the cosmos means that the king brings order and harmony to his kingdom (265,10–12). Diotogenes says that

> on the one hand, in public matters the king is to bring the whole kingdom into harmony with his single rule and leadership, while private matters of detail must be brought into accord with this same harmony and leadership.[32]

Diotogenes also calls the king an imitation of God, and the state an imitation of the cosmos. The king brings harmony to the state, just as God brings it to the universe. As in Diogenes, the role of the king on earth is that of God in the cosmos.

Through his virtuous acts he will come to be loved by the multitude; through his superiority he becomes close to the gods (267,1–268,12).

---

living law or the most lawful leader, as a mitigation of the absolute character of kingship as found, for instance, in Ecphantus. Diotogenes, it seems to me, is simply looking for the right phrase. The living law is lawful; he does not rule without guidance by external standards. By what law he is lawful is not explained, but the standard is probably the law of God. At any rate, in this passage, Diotogenes considers the king the law. He does not follow a written law. The king is said again to bring his life in order with the law in 266,19–23.

[31] Goodenough, "Hellenistic Kingship" 72.
[32] Ibid., 67.

This closeness to God, as in Ecphantus, allows him to affect the souls of his subjects when they only so much as look at him (268,12–14). Yet, he also takes an active role in the lives of his subjects. He is just, he helps the needy, and aids all those in distress (268,14–269,17). He is like the gods in his virtue, especially like Zeus, for royalty is an imitation of God (270,1–11).

In these fragments, the outline of a "living law" concept begins to emerge. For all the work which has been done on the concept no one has yet defined how the king embodies the law. The concept can be divided into four major sections: the king as the living law; the king's closeness to and imitation of God; the king's love for his subjects; and the justness and virtue of the king. Included in these sections are specific concepts such as "harmony" (ἁρμονία) between the king and his subjects, "communion" (κοινωνία) between the king and his subjects, the love of men which the king displays (φιλανθρωπία), and his role as benefactor (εὐεργέτης) of his subjects.

The ideal is not only found in these fragments. It continued to exercise influence on a number of authors. All the concerns found in the Pythagorean fragments are echoed in the work of the followers.

The Followers

The idea continued to have influence, although it is unlikely that the influence comes directly from these fragments. Perhaps the influence did come from Middle Platonism, although this is not certain. From wherever the influence came, the νόμος ἔμψυχος ideal influenced a wide range of work which comprises a remarkably unitary witness to the ideas expressed in the fragments.

The earliest witness following the Pythagorean tractates is the *Rhetorica ad Alexandrum*. The treatise, once attributed to Aristotle, has long been considered a forgery.[33] It is usually dated to around the beginning of the third century B.C.E. Paul Wendland, followed by

---

[33] Cope, *Introduction to Aristotle's Rhetoric* 410f.; W. S. Hett and H. Rackham, *Aristotle Vol. 16* in *LCL*, 258–262; E. S. Forster (trans.), *The Works of Aristotle Translated into English: Vol. 11* (ed. W. D. Ross; Oxford: Clarendon Press 1908–1952), preface; Goodenough, "Hellenistic Kingship" 91–92; Paul Wendland, "Die Schriftstellerei des Anaximanes" in *Hermes* 39 (1904) 419–443; 499–542.

Goodenough, believed that the letter was an original of Anaximenes, reworked to conform to Hellenistic kingship models.[34] Whether this is so, or whether the whole treatise goes back to the third century, it is apparent that the influence of the Pythagorean kingship models is prevalent.

The contrast between the written law and the king appears early in the treatise. For those whose political constitution is democracy, the subjects appeal for justice is to law. For those who are under a king, the subjects appeal for justice is to his reason (λόγος) (1420a, 20–23). The king's reason performs the function of law in a democracy (1420a,23–25). The author stresses the contrast again:

> you must realize that the model set before most men is either the law or else your life and the expression of your reason (1420b,12–14).[35]

This is the choice of the kingship fragments: the king or the law. Though the phrase νόμος ἔμψυχος is not used here, λόγος ἔμψυχος (1420a,22–25) is used, and the terms are synonymous. The king performs the functions of the law for those who are subject to him. The model of the king who brings virtue to his subjects is found here as well. The *Rhetorica ad Alexandrum* exhorts Alexander to

> exert yourself to the utmost, so that those who spend their lives in these pursuits, using the elements of virtue in them to produce a beauteous copy of the model set before them, may not direct themselves toward ignoble ends but make it their desire to partake in the same virtues (1420b,15–19).

The king, through the reason embodied in him, is to guide his subjects "along the path of their advantage" (1420a,22–25). The king is the guide to the good life.

The idea appears in the writings of Cicero, in a number of places. The concept was, therefore, widely known, even in the Roman world in the first century B.C.E. It appears in *De Legibus* 3.2–3, in a slightly altered form. Cicero calls the magistrate a "speaking law" (*legem loquentem*). The law governs the magistrate and he governs the people. The magistrate is the law, but he is not separate from the law. Elsewhere Cicero speaks of the virtuous ruler as the best form of

---

[34] Wendland, "Anaximanes" 500f.; Goodenough, "Hellenistic Kingship" 93–94.
[35] The translation of Forster in *The Works of Aristotle in English: Vol. 11* is used for the *Rhetorica ad Alexandrum*.

government. This ruler puts his "own life before his fellow citizens as their law" (*De Rep.* 52). In *De Off.* 41–42 Cicero states that the reason for making laws was the same for making kings; laws were invented only because of a lack of just kings. Though Cicero may not have held out any hope for such a king, he knows the concepts of the νόμος ἔμψυχος and of the contrast between law and kingship.

In regard to the relationship between god and the king, Cicero has Scipio Africanus speak of it in the context of a discussion of the king as law (*De Rep.* 52–56). One God rules in heaven and this Scipio takes as precedent for the rule of a king on earth. The imitation of God by the king is here discussed, and the relationship between the subjects and the king described as that between a father and his children.

Cicero calls the good king a father to his subjects (*De Rep.* 1.54). He is eager to protect them. Those who were ruled by such a king "thought that life, honour, and glory had been granted to them through the justice of their king" (*De Rep.* 1.62). Cicero is too much of a realist to leave unsaid that the king "often becomes a despot" (*De Rep.* 2.43), but he knows of the concept of the king who "shielded the weaker classes from wrong" (*De Off.* 2.41).

Then there is the case of Musonius Rufus. Musonius Rufus contains perhaps the oddest, and also one of the clearest, of the examples. Odd, because it is not at all clear who his source is; but clear, because the idea is expressed in its fullness. It is the king's duty to arbitrate justice among his subjects and so he himself must be just.[36] The good king must be faultless and perfect, a "living law" "effecting good government and harmony, suppressing lawlessness and dissension, a true imitator of Zeus and, like him, father of his people."[37] Musonius also claims that the king is the best man. Musonius supplies a ready example when he says that the king must be "faultless and perfect in word and action."[38]

There are a number of connections with the Hellenistic Pythagorean fragments, but Musonius, who adds this paragraph on the νόμος

---

[36] The text is found in *Stob.* 4.7,67. A Greek text and English translation are provided by Cora Lutz in "Musonius Rufus: The Roman Socrates" in *Yale Classical Studies* 10 (1947). The particular text is "VIII: That Kings Also Should Study Philosophy," 60–67. All English translations are from Lutz's translation.
[37] Lutz, 65.
[38] Ibid., 65.

ἔμψυχος without discussion, seems to have copied it from an existing text. The language is formal and the concept seems set. Musonius' claim that the king should be "zealous for Zeus" (ζηλητὴν δὲ τοῦ Διός) is directly comparable to the passage in Sthenidas, though the language is somewhat different. So when A. C. Geytenbeek says that "the content of Musonius' discourse is so general, it is difficult to prove influence by any special school of thought,"[39] one must disagree in respect to these passages: the influence of the Pythagorean living law ideal is clearly seen.

Finally, there is Plutarch's important treatise *Ad Principem Ineruditem* (779d–782f.). For Plutarch also, the king is the "living reason," or λόγος ἔμψυχος. The king is not ruled by law in books, or on tablets, but by the reason embodied in him (780c). The king becomes the law for his subjects, because law "is the work of the ruler" (780e). The ruler who must form himself in the image of God is also forming himself in the image of the true law, for Zeus is "himself justice and right and the oldest and most perfect of laws" (781b). The king, in molding himself in the image of God, copies the true law, embodies reason, and becomes law for his subjects.

Plutarch also considers the king's effect on his subjects as the core of his mission. He says,

> Just as a rule, if it is made rigid and inflexible, makes other things straight when they are fitted to it and laid alongside it, in like manner the sovereign must first gain command of himself, must regulate his own soul and establish his own character, then make his subjects fit his pattern (780b).

The king is the rule by which the subjects become lawful and virtuous.

None of these followers exhibits all four aspects of the living law ideal, but most of them contain two or three elements of it and show the influence of the ideal clearly.[40] Especially clear is the contrast between the law and the king, the living law, which forms the core of the contrast. The next section, however, is concerned not so

---

[39] A. C. Geytenbeek, *Musonius Rufus and Greek Diatribe* (Assen: van Gorcum 1963) 127.

[40] Philo, who presents the ideal *par excellence*, will be studied separately. Later authors, such as Clement of Alexandria (*Stromata*, 5.5,29.2–3) and Themistius (ed. Wilhelm Dindorf, *Themistius*. Leipzig, G. Knobloch 1832) (212d, p. 259; 228a, p. 277) who present the ideal as well cannot be discussed.

much with literary evidence of the theory, but with literary, and other, evidence, which may show that the idea was actually applied in the Roman world in the first century B.C.E. and the first century C.E. How far did the influence of the living law extend?

The King as Law: Roman Evidence

The influence of the νόμος ἔμψυχος ideal was widespread and appeared in a number of literary sources. That the influence of the literary sources extended to the first century C.E. is clear from the expressions of the idea in Philo and Musonius Rufus. But did this influence spread from theoretical and philosophical discussions to use in actual forms of government? Did it influence the cult of the Caesars? Many have claimed a wide range of influence for the concept.

Claims such as W. Richardson's regarding the influence of the νόμος ἔμψυχος ideal in Luke-Acts and E. R. Goodenough's regarding the O. T. cannot be sustained, but there are other, more serious propositions.[41]

Some have seen in the living law ideal the core of Hellenistic kingship. Lester Born says that in Cicero's use of the idea he

> is employing the terms of Hellenistic political theories, whose Greek equivalents are not only illustrated in the fragments to which frequent reference has been made, but are often found in the actual titles of the kings themselves.[42]

---

[41] W. Richardson, "Nomos Empsychos: Marcion, Clement of Alexandria and St. Luke's Gospel" in *Studia Patristica. Vol. VI (vol. 81)* (ed. F. L. Cross; Texte und Untersuchungen zur Geschichte der Altchristlichen Literatur; Berlin: Akademie, 1964); "A Motif of Greek Philosophy in Luke-Acts" in *Studia Evangelica. Vol. II (vol. 87)* (ed. F. L. Cross; Texte und Untersuchungen zur Geschichte der Altchristlichen Literatur; Berlin: Akademie 1964); E. R. Goodenough, "Kingship in Early Israel" in *JBL* 48 (1929) 169–205. What Goodenough sees as the νόμος ἔμψυχος ideal in the O. T. is related to Near Eastern and Persian kingship in general; what Richardson claims is evidence of the νόμος ἔμψυχος ideal in Luke-Acts is simply common Graeco-Roman language regarding the Sage.

[42] Lester Born, "Animated Law in the Republic and Laws of Cicero" in *TAPA* 64 (1933) 136; cf. also, Francis Dvornik *Early Christian and Byzantine Political Philosophy: Origins and Background*, Vol. I. (Washington, D.C.: Dumbarton Oaks Center for Byzantine Studies 1966) 474–477, 494; and Glenn Chesnut, "The Ruler and the Logos in NeoPythagorean, Middle Platonic, and Late Stoic Political Philosophy" in *ANRW* II 16.2 (Berlin; New York: W. de Gruyter 1972–), 1310.

Kenneth Scott makes the same claims in his study of the living law in Plutarch.[43]

More important to us are claims that the living law ideal was current in Rome in the first century not only as a philosophical ideal, but as a support for Roman imperial declarations. Dvornik says that Musonius' use of the living law ideal

> proves that the concept of animate law as applied to kings must have been current in the first century of our era and had been in use for a long time during the Hellenistic period.[44]

Glenn Chesnut adds that the idea of the king as the embodiment of the law was further developed in Roman political theory.[45] The Pythagorean fragments, he says, are "an extreme version of the official political philosophy which formed the intellectual underpinning for the Romano-Hellenistic ruler cult."[46] He concludes:

> the notion of the emperor as the embodied Law or Logos of God, which appeared in a variety of contexts, both pagan and Jewish, was therefore a widespread and quite commonplace idea in the Roman world during the period of the Early Empire. It was simply a part of the general intellectual atmosphere.[47]

In what way was the living law the official political philosophy?

In fact the living law ideal, as distinct from Hellenistic kingship in general, does not appear that often in our sources. The term itself appears only three times before Philo, and then three times in Philo's work. This is the extent of the appearance of the term νόμος ἔμψυχος, though the concept appears in a number of other contexts. But the grand claims for the living law ideal seem to be made on the basis of a conflation between the specific concept and notions of Hellenistic kingship in general. Such a conflation is invalid. The general idea of Hellenistic kingship does not allow us to assume that the specific

---

[43] Kenneth Scott, "Plutarch and the Ruler Cult" in *TAPA* 60 (1929) 129; Cf. also Dvornik, *Early Christian* 272–273; and Chesnut, "The Ruler and the Logos" 1324.

[44] Dvornik, *Early Christian* 247–248.

[45] Chesnut, "The Ruler and the Logos" 1310.

[46] Ibid., 1315; Goodenough, "Hellenistic Kingship" 100 also classifies it as "the official philosophy of kingship in the period."

[47] Ibid., 1329.

idea of the king as the living law was present. What is the evidence that the living law ideal supported Roman monarchical policy?

We know that from the time of Alexander the idea of a deified king became more and more prevalent, taking root with the Diadochi, and coming to full flower with Augustus and the Roman emperors. There would seem to be a link between the Hellenistic kingship ideal in general and Roman imperialism.[48] The implicit assumption, however, is that this means there is also a connection between Roman imperialism and the living law ideal. This is the evidence that such a connection existed.

Inscriptional Evidence

Before or during the first century C.E. there is little evidence to suggest that the Roman emperor was considered the living law from the inscriptional evidence. The only pertinent inscription dates from 69 C.E. In this inscription the Emperor Vespasian is released from the laws and decrees of the Roman people (C. I. L. 6.930). This is obviously a special status granted to Vespasian, however, and, moreover, he neither replaces the law nor renders it superfluous; he simply does not have to follow it.

The Historians

Roman historians offer a number of passages which are worth comparing with the living law ideal.

Philo
Philo, whose general portrayal of Gaius does not differ often from the Roman historians, offers us the only outright claim that a Roman emperor considered himself the law. Gaius, according to *Legatio ad Gaium* 119, thought he himself was law. This evidence has been accepted as factual.[49]

---

[48] Lily Ross Taylor, *The Divinity of the Roman Emperor* (Chico, Ca.: Scholars Press 1981), *Divinity*, chaps. 7,8,9; Gertrud Herzog-Hauser, "Kaiserkult" in *Pauly-Wissowa Real Encyclopädie. Supplement IV* 806–853.

[49] Anton von Premerstein, *Vom Werden und Wesen des Principats* (Munich: Verlag der Bayerischen Akademie der Wissenschaften 1937) 177.

The only consideration speaking against its factuality is the negative portrait of the living law ideal given in this tractate. Both Wayne Meeks and Goodenough have pointed out that Gaius is presented in this tractate as the perversion of the νόμος ἔμψυχος ideal.⁵⁰ This antithetical portrait may then simply be a bit of propaganda. Given Philo's overall fair portrait, however, it is possible that he also reports the truth: Gaius considered himself the living law. Our final consideration is that, though dressed in Philo's philosophical clothing, the portrait of Gaius as the living law may be based upon Gaius' own claims.

Pliny (23 C.E.–79 C.E.)

Pliny's evidence is somewhat late, but it is sometimes considered as evidence for the Hellenistic kingship ideal and so ought to be briefly considered here. There are two passages of interest.

Pliny reports that the Emperor Tiberius controlled the Senate, allowing only some legislative responsibility to trickle down to the Senate (*Epist.* 3.20). He also seemed to be able to make any legal decision, as evidenced by his use of the *decreta* in response to a question of Pliny's (*Epist.* 10.56).⁵¹ Though the Emperor has the power to make law, he is not the law, and the apparatus of the justice system remains in place, even if not often considered.

Suetonius (c. 70 C.E.–c. 120 C.E.)

Suetonius records that Julius Caesar considered his own word law (1.77). This appears to be close to the living law ideal. Though Suetonius is not always a reliable source, the evidence is good that Caesar actually made the statement. Suetonius claims that it was a public statement and records Titus Ampius as the source for the statement.⁵² Suetonius regards the statement as arrogant, but if it is genuine, and there seems to be no reason to doubt it, it may conceivably show that Caesar was conversant with the living law ideal.

---

⁵⁰ Wayne Meeks, *The Prophet-King* (Leiden: E. J. Brill 1967) 49–51; E. R. Goodenough, *The Politics of Philo Judaeus* (New Haven: Yale University Press 1938) 101–108.

⁵¹ W. W. Buckland, *A Textbook of Roman Law from Augustus to Justinian* (Cambridge: The University Press 1963) 18, says, "where they {the decreta} did make new law, they had the force of law."

⁵² On Titus Ampius see E. Klebs, "Ampius" in *Pauly-Wissowa Real-Encyclopädie* I.2, 1978–1979. Titus Ampius is known through a number of sources, such as Josephus and Cicero, and would be a reliable source.

Suetonius also records a number of statements concerning or by Gaius which may have some connection with the νόμος ἔμψυχος ideal. Gaius had full and absolute power given him by the Senate (4.14). He reportedly said, "I have the right to do anything to anybody" (4.29). Again, though, the power given Gaius by the Senate did not render the laws of Rome null and void. Gaius did have the power to make law, but he was not the law himself. That he had the right to do anything need not imply a philosophical basis; it implies a lust for power. That he was *de facto* the law need not be argued—this is one of the perquisites of tyranny—but he seems to be driven by megalomania—he considered himself the equal of Plato (4.34) and Alexander (4.52)—and not by ideology.

Dio Cassius (c. 155–164 C.E.–c. 230 C.E.)

According to Dio Cassius, Julius Caesar founded a monarchy (52.1,3), and became a king, whether he admitted it or not (52.40,1–2). Caesar was advised to take control of the law and make law in collaboration with the best men in Rome (52.15,2). In reality, whatever pleased Caesar would be law (52.15,3). This power would not be a license to act with impunity (52.34,1), but a chance to do good, in order that the Romans might consider Caesar a father and a saviour (52.39,3).

There are connections to Hellenistic kingship in terms of the justness which Caesar should possess, and in how his subjects would regard him, but it is the claim that his word would be law which reminds us of of the living law ideal. It also reminds us of Suetonius' claim about Caesar. Caesar is in some ways to be the law; the force of this is muted somewhat by the fact that Caesar would still make law in conjunction with others, and that the legal system would still be in operation (52.34,6–8), but it hints at the ideal and the genuineness of Suetonius' report.

Dio also reports that Augustus, as Emperor, was in possession of the laws of Rome. When Augustus considers giving up his rule, he refers to his adopted father Julius and the power his deified father held:

> As for immortality, we could not possibly achieve it; but by living nobly and by dying nobly we do in a sense gain this boon. Therefore, I, who already possess the first requisite and hope to possess the second, return to you the armies and the provinces, the revenues and the laws (53.9,5).

Augustus does this under the pretence of returning Rome to democratic rule, but the important information is that the emperor possessed the laws. This does not truly impinge upon the living law ideal, though, for the possession of the laws differs from the king actually being the law.

Augustus, too, though he made a show of a return to democracy, attained autocratic power and the stature of a king (53.11,4–12,1). He was as such freed from the laws and written ordinances of Rome (53.18,1–2). Again, however great his power was, the laws are not abolished and Augustus is not the law; he simply has power over them and need not obey them.

Gaius, who had the same power as Augustus, used it, apparently, only to break the law (59.10,2;14,3;15,1) not to become the law.

Philosophers and Poets

This mixed group provides a mixture of historical truth and proverbial wisdom, which can, of course, also contain truth.

Pomponius Porphyry
This African of the third century C.E. preserves a kingship proverb in his commentary on Horace. In Horace *Sat.*, 2.3,188 a king forbids the burial of a certain Ajax. When asked why, the king replies: "I am the king." To which the questioner, a commoner, replies that this answer satisfies him. In his commentary, written in Latin, Porphyry adds to this a proverb in Greek: "for the fool and the king the law is not written."

This proverb, also preserved in Hebrew, may indeed be ancient, and certainly precedes Porphyry, but its usefulness for the living law ideal is minimal. It does not seem to reflect any official kingship philosophy, but, as the reference to the fool makes clear, a measure of, perhaps bitter, reality.

Seneca
Seneca speaks in two places of the power of the Caesars and reflects the reality, not the philosophy, of the Roman monarchy. In *Ad Poly.* 7.2 he speaks of Caesar who is able to do all things (*cui omnia licent*). In *De Clem.*, 1.8,5 he refers to Nero as omnipotent. In both of these cases Seneca seems to be relating statements of fact and not

philosophy, apart from which the ideal of the living law is not really under consideration.

The Lawyers

This evidence is often cited, but it is quite late and its usefulness for our purposes is doubtful; it is also not as clear as it initially seems.

Gaius
In his *Institutes*, Gaius, a lawyer, speaks of the emperor as taking the place of the law (*legis vicem obtinet*) (1.4–5).

Ulpian
Ulpian, preserved in *Justinian's Digest*, speaks once of the Princeps not being bound by the laws (1.3,31) and of the emperor as the law (1.4,1).

The first case in Ulpian does not really enter into the picture; it is a common expression of the idea that the Roman emperor is released from certain laws. Both the other passages do recall the νόμος ἔμψυχος ideal. They are from the third century C.E., though, and most authorities agree that they are taken out of context and refer to an individual case and not the idea of law in general. Nevertheless, the language of the living law is here, and was of course finally adopted by the Romans; the problem we face is not being certain that the idea was being put into practice in the first century C.E.[53] These statements do reflect the development of the role of the Emperor in Rome, but they are, for our purposes, too late.

Comments: The Historical Evidence

Our conclusions are mixed. Only in two or three cases can we see the influence of the living law ideal on the development of Roman monarchical claims in the first century B.C.E.–first century C.E. This

---

[53] The concept was a commonplace in the sixth century C.E. if Justinian's usage in his *Novellae* is any indication. In *Novella* 105, 4 (lines 7–15) he refers to the emperor as the "living law" (νόμος ἔμψυχος) in the context of a discussion of the office of the ὑπατεία, or "consular governor." The king is given to his subjects as a special honour, says Justinian, and God counsels him regarding the laws. He becomes, therefore, a "living law."

is something. It is far from the official theory of Roman political policy. It is important to bring some perspective to the reality of the situation; the influences of Hellenistic kingship do not necessarily imply the influence of the νόμος ἔμψυχος ideal.

The concerns of kingship are not unique to the living law ideal, especially the claim that the king is just and the best man, but the elements which follow, it seems to me, must be present for the living law ideal to be present. The following section is an attempt to categorize the essential elements of the νόμος ἔμψυχος literature in order to define the parameters of the discussion.

The νόμος ἔμψυχος Ideal

The term νόμος ἔμψυχος is not found until the Hellenistic period, but the idea of the good and just king is found throughout much Greek literature. Connected with this is the idea of the lawgiver, which the king was sometimes considered.[54] The leap to the idea of the king as "living law" may not seem a great leap, it may even be implied in earlier sources, but it is in fact a momentous step.[55] In claiming the king as somewhat divine, or perfect, or just, our sources do not move much beyond other, earlier Greek claims, but in claiming the king as the living law, they oppose the king to the written law, and open the door to a powerful, new, and dangerous concept.

Throughout Greek history the idea of the king as a philosopher or wise man is present, but the king usually brings himself into agreement or conformity with the law, or more to the point, follows the written law. While the idea that the king is "lawful" by reference to some other measure is sometimes present in the Hellenistic living law sources, and the king does not necessarily contradict the law of his city, the new dimension is clear: the written law is superfluous for the king and his subjects, for the king is the law.

There are a number of aspects of the king as law which are unique to the νόμος ἔμψυχος ideal or particularly important to it. There are a number of ideas which it shares with all Greek monarchical thought,

---

[54] Plato, *Pol.*, 300c; *Rep.*, 425a–c; Aristotle, *Pol.*, 3.11,13. Cf. also Hall, "Plato's Legal Philosophy" 183, 192.

[55] See Delatte's discussion in *Les Traites* 123–163 for the development of the kingship ideal, with special attention to the living law ideal, in Greek thought.

and though these are important, our concern is with what makes the living law ideal unique.

The King is the Law

The material of Archytas of Tarentum, we have argued, is the foundation of the living law ideal and perhaps genuine. Archytas' view of law is based on a distinction between the νόμοι θεῶν ἄγραφοι, which are the πατέρεςκαὶ ἀγεμόνες of the written laws, and laws of "wicked customs" (*Stob.* 4.1,132). Archytas makes a further distinction in the "written" law. The law is either the king, a living law (ἔμψυχος), or the inanimate, written law (ἄψυχος γράμμα) (*Stob.* 4.1,135).[56] Diotogenes says that the king is the most just man and that justice is inherent in the law (*Stob.* 4.1,61). He then claims the king as the living law (νόμος ἔμψυχος) or the "lawful leader" (νόμιμος ἄρχων).[57] The term νόμος ἔμψυχος is not used by Ecphantus, but the king is considered a law: the goodwill of the king is like that of a father for his son, a shepherd for his sheep, and a law for those who use it.[58] Ecphantus contrasts law and the king elsewhere, saying that purification from sin comes from the subjects making themselves like their rulers (ἀρχόντεσσιν) "whether it be law or king who orders affairs where they are" (*Stob.* 4.7,64).

The references to the king as law are not confined to the Hellenistic fragments. They appear in the *Rhetorica ad Alexandrum*, in which the author opposes democracy, whose final appeal is to law, and kingly rule, whose final appeal is to the reason (λόγος) of the king (1420a, 21–23). The term "living law" does not appear, but the term "living reason" (λόγος ἔμψυχος) does (1420a,22–25).[59] Plutarch also calls the king the "living reason" (780c). This phrase becomes synony-

---

[56] *Stob.*, 4.1,132,135,136,137,138; 4.5,61; Goodenough, "Hellenistic Kingship" 59f; A. Delatte, *Politique Pythagoricienne* 83–85; Holger Thesleff, *Texts* 33–36.

[57] *Stob.* 4.7,61,62; Goodenough, "Hellenistic Kingship" 64–73; Thesleff, *Texts* 71–75; L. Delatte, *Les Traites* 37–45, 245–273.

[58] *Stob.* 4.6,22; 4.7,64–66; Goodenough, "Hellenistic Kingship" 75–89; Thesleff, *The Pythagorean Texts of the Hellenistic Period*. Acta Academiae Aboensis, Ser. A: Humaniora, V. 30, no. 1 (Åbo: Åbo Akademie, 1965) *Texts* 79–84; Delatte, *Les Traites* 25–37, 164–244. The oddity of this passage seems to be the affection that Ecphantus presumes people have for the law.

[59] The term λόγος ἔμψυχος may indeed be an indication of Stoic influence. The Logos was a far more important idea for the Stoics than for the Pythagoreans.

mous with the living law and has the same significance: one is either ruled by the written law or the king. The "living reason" did not entirely replace the "living law" though. Musonius Rufus, with little elaboration, calls the king a νόμος ἔμψυχος, one who suppresses "lawlessness and dissension."[60]

The idea appears in other sources, too, but the point is clear. The living law ideal replaces the written law with the king, known either as the living law or the living reason. This is no license for mayhem on the king's part; far from a license, the king is to be most just and, indeed, perfect. The written law is superfluous because the king functions in the role of law. It is true that not every discussion of the king as the living law opposes written law to the king; sometimes the king is said to be conformed to the law; but even then the written law is no longer necessary because the king fulfills its role. The king becomes law for his subjects and they need only follow him.

The King's Closeness to God

The ability to become the law for his subjects derives in part from the close relationship the king has to God. This close relationship, and the special status of the king, allows the king to function as a god to his subjects in some cases, and to recreate God's cosmic order in the political community. In Archytas' treatise, it is God's unwritten law which informs the king and enables him to become a living law. As the law, the king, through his closeness to God, brings harmony to the human soul and the political order, because the "law educates the soul and organizes the life."[61] Diotogenes claims that "it is right for the king to act as does God in his leadership and command of the universe."[62] By acting as God, the king brings the whole kingdom into harmony; this harmony mimics that of the cosmos. The king then becomes a "deity among men."[63]

> For majesty, a godlike thing can make him admired and honored by the multitude; . . . he must separate himself from the human passions,

---

[60] *Stob.* 4.7,67; Lutz, *Musonius* 64–65.
[61] *Stob.* 4.1,132; Goodenough, "Hellenistic Kingship" 59; Delatte, *Politique Pythagoricienne* 83.
[62] *Stob.* 4.7, 61:263f.; Goodenough, "Hellenistic Kingship", 67.
[63] Ibid.," 68.

and draw himself up close to the gods, not in arrogance, but in high-mindedness and in the exceeding greatness of his virtue.[64]

This closeness to the divine allows the king to affect the souls of his subjects. Ecphantus especially stresses the unique and high status of the king—the king is shaped, uniquely, in the image of God, and occupies a place between man and God.

> He is like the rest [of mankind] indeed in his earthly tabernacle [σκᾶνος], inasmuch as he is formed out of the same material; but he is fashioned by the supreme Artificer, who in making the king used himself as an Archetype.[65]

Sthenidas, too, states that the king is a wise man and because he is wise "he will be a copy and imitator [ζηλωτάς] of the first God."[66] By imitating God, the king adopts God's many attributes: he is merciful, a support to his subjects, a teacher of beauty, and the lawgiver. Most of all, he is a father to his subjects.

Plutarch, too, speaks of the ruler as forming himself in the image of God, so as to become the law for his subjects (781b). Musonius Rufus stresses the importance of the king as an imitator of Zeus, and, therefore, a father to his people.[67]

This close relationship to God defines the king in the Hellenistic Pythagorean fragments, and among many of the authors who are dependent upon the concept. The king is an imitator of God. By virtue of the imitation, however, he becomes a god to men, and is able to guide and, indeed, "save" his subjects. His own function as a divine being is related closely to his role as faithful subject.

The King's Relationship to his Subjects

This last point leads directly to our next theme: the love between the king and his subjects. Since they are often like gods to their subjects, the king has a profound influence upon them and they in turn desire to follow the king.[68] The king must love his subjects, and desire to help them, to be a true living law.

---

[64] Ibid., 72.
[65] *Stob.* 4.7,64; Goodenough, "Hellenistic Kingship" 76.
[66] *Stob.* 4.7,63; ibid., 73–74.
[67] Lutz, *Musonius* 65; Stob. 4.7,67. Compare to Sthenidas' use of ζηλωτάς in *Stob.* 4.7,63.
[68] Goodenough, "Hellenistic Kingship" 59.

Archytas says that the king must love his subjects and act only in their interest.[69] Diotogenes expresses more clearly how the king actually brings his subjects to good and virtuous lives: simply by looking at the king, their souls will be brought into harmony.[70] Sthenidas also claims that the king must be fatherly and merciful to his subjects,[71] but it is Ecphantus who supplies the most beautiful witness to the relationship between the king and his subjects. If the Logos of the king is accepted, says Ecphantus, it heals the corrupted, the sick, and the sinful; the king is able to cause his subjects to turn to the good.[72] Quite simply, he can make them better.

This is found in a number of other sources too. The author of the *Rhetorica ad Alexandrum* tells Alexander that he is a model for his subjects, a model which causes them to desire the virtues of the king (1420b,15–19). Plutarch considers this function of the king as the core of the king's purpose: the king is to make himself virtuous, and then lead his followers to virtuous lives (780b). Cicero, too, speaks of the king who protected the weak from wrong (*De Off.* 2.41) and acted like a father to his subjects (*De Rep.* 1.54).

The king's love for his subjects and his ability to make them virtuous are found in a number of sources which echo the Hellenistic Pythagorean fragments. This is a central point of the living law ideal. No less central to the ideal is the king as a virtuous and just man.

Harmony (ἁρμονία)

More significant is the distinctly Pythagorean ideal of the king who brings harmony to his subjects and to his state.[73] Archytas says that the law is to the soul and life as harmony is to hearing and speech.[74] Law brings harmony to the soul and life; so too does the king, who

---

[69] *Stob.* 4.1,135; Goodenough, "Hellenistic Kingship" 60.
[70] *Stob.* 4.7,62:265f.; ibid., 72.
[71] *Stob.* 4.7,63; ibid., 74.
[72] *Stob.* 4.7,65; ibid., 89.
[73] Delatte, *Les Traites* 164f.
[74] *Stob.* 4.1,135–82,15–17; Goodenough, "Hellenistic Kingship" 59; Delatte, *Politique Pythagoricienne*, 84 says, "il est remarkquable encore que la comparison de la loi avec l'harmonie soit exprimée sous la form d'un rapport:

$$\frac{\text{Loi}}{\text{âme et vie}} = \frac{\text{Harmonie}}{\text{ouïe et voix}}."$$

is the living law. Archytas further states that virtue arises from a harmony of reason (the king) and the irrational (the ruled) (*Stob.* 4.1,135).

Diotogenes states that the goal of the king is to bring the same harmony to his kingdom that God brings to the universe.[75] In this regard, the king imitates God and the state imitates the universe. Ecphantus relates the harmony of the state directly to the king's role. But not only the harmony of the state rests with the king: "private matters of accord must be brought into accord with his single rule and leadership."[76] The harmony which the king brings knows no boundaries.

Ecphantus states that the nature of every being is in harmony with the cosmos (*Stob.* 4.7,64). The function of the king is integral not only to his subjects, but to the order of the world itself. To follow the "law" is to take one's place in the cosmos.

Indeed, the state is "an imitation of the order and harmony of the world." Law is central to the king's rule and to the harmony of the state, because law is central, inherent, in the cosmos. This means that the king, in imitating God, becomes the living law, an "absolute" (ἀνυπεύθυνον) ruler, and a god among men (θεὸς ἐν ἀνθρώποις).[77] It also means that the harmony of the state and its subjects rests squarely with the king.

The king knows "that the harmony of the multitude whose leadership God has given him ought to be attuned to himself," and so "the king would begin by fixing in his own life the most just limitations and order of law."[78] There is no harmony, therefore, if the king is not lawful, that is, just. If, however, the king meets the requirements of his position, merely looking at him brings harmony to his subjects and to the political community (*Stob.* 4.7,62).[79]

It is not surprising to find this concentration on harmony in the Pythagorean fragments—it was a centre of Pythagorean thought[80]—

---

[75] *Stob.* 4.7,61–264,11; 264,15; 264,18; 265,10; 4.7,62–268,12; 269,2; 269,3; Delatte, *Les Traites* 37–45; Goodenough, "Hellenistic Kingship" 65–73.
[76] *Stob.* 4.7,61; Goodenough, "Hellenistic Kingship" 67.
[77] *Stob.* 4.7,61; ibid., 68.
[78] *Stob.* 4.7,62; ibid., 71.
[79] Delatte, *Les Traites* 271.
[80] See, for instance, Flora R. Levin, *The Harmonics of Nicomachus and the Pythagorean Tradition* (Amer. Class. Stud. 1; University Park, Pa.: American Philological Association 1975) 1. She says: "that there is an intrinsic symmetry in the natural universe, founded on a mathematical necessity and expressible in the commensurable terms of a musical *harmonia*, is a conception consistently connected with Pythagorean doctrine."

but statements regarding harmony are found in the secondary witnesses as well. Musonius speaks of the king as effecting "good government and harmony."[81] Plutarch echoes the idea of harmony when he speaks of the subjects molding themselves to fit the king's pattern (780b).

Imitation (μίμησις)

The idea of imitation, in the classical sense of the term—forming oneself in the image of the original—runs throughout the kingship texts. The first occurrence is in the writings of Archytas. Archytas claims that "the law will be conformed to nature, if it imitates the justice (δίκαιον) of nature."[82] This Stoic-tinged sentence illustrates the degree to which the law was simply a part of the cosmic order; the king, in the same way, is to imitate the order and take his place in it: he, too, is the law.

The idea of imitation, however, comes especially to the fore in the work of Ecphantus. The beauty of the cosmic order, says Ecphantus,

> is revealed straightway, if the one [the king] who imitates [God] in his virtue is beloved at once by him whom he is imitating and by his subjects.[83]

The greatness of the political, and cosmic, order is revealed through imitation, for when true imitation occurs, each element functions properly. The king is king not by virtue of his place, but by virtue of his actions; the same is true of the subjects of the king.

Even God, though, would like the subjects of the king to imitate God and those who do imitate God do "all things better than other people."[84] The king who occupies a position between man and God is the true imitator of God, however, and he is the true focus of his subjects. For "the king alone is capable of putting good into human nature so that by imitation of him, their Better, they will follow in the way they should go."[85] The imitation of the king drives evil from his subjects' souls.

---

[81] Lutz, *Musonius* 65.
[82] *Stob.* 4.1,136–83,19; My translation; cf. with Delatte, *Politique Pythagoricienne* 91–92.
[83] *Stob.* 4.7,64; Goodenough, "Hellenistic Kingship" 77.
[84] *Stob.* 4.7,65; ibid., 89.
[85] *Stob.* 4.7,65; ibid., 89.

Sthenidas, too, calls the king an imitator (ζηλωτάς) of God (*Stob.* 4.7,63). To be a king one must be an imitator of God, for the attributes of God must belong to the king if he is to be a true king. A true king is worthy of imitation.

Musonius, echoing Sthenidas, says the king must be ζηλητήν for God: a true imitator.[86] The author of the *Rhetorica ad Alexandrum* states simply that the king is to be the model upon which his subjects pattern themselves (1420b,13–19).

It is in the act of imitation, by the king of God, and by the people of their king, that harmony is maintained and justice and good order reign, not only in the cosmos and the political order, but in personal lives.

"Communion" (κοινωνία)

The most common concept in the kingship fragments, at least in terms of number of appearances, is the idea of "communion" or "fellowship" (κοινωνία). The idea of communion between a king and his subjects has a special resonance in these texts. It speaks of a special, almost mystical, relationship which arises as a result of ἁρμονία in the community. At times it seems to be a mystical or religious union between the king and his followers. It is confined to the Hellenistic texts.

The term can imply, of course, simply a community.[87] But even here the sense of community is that of a community harmonized by the proper function of each of the member parts. If the parts do not function, the community is in disarray.

More common, however, is the mystical nature of the term stressed by Ecphantus:

> for the first and most necessary of all things for the human race is that communion shared in by the king over men as well as by the master who rules all things in the universe. For apart from love and communion existence is impossible.[88]

---

[86] Lutz, *Musonius* 64. The expected translation of ζηλητήν, zealous, is not in view in this passage. See H. G. Liddell, R. Scott, H. S. Jones (eds.), *A Greek-English Lexicon* (Oxford: Clarendon Press 1978) 755; they offer this passage, and that of Sthenidas, as examples of the meaning "true imitator," or "emulator."

[87] As in Archytas, *Stob.* 4.1,135–82,19; the obvious choice for this meaning, however, is usually, τὸ κοινόν.

[88] *Stob.* 4.7,64; Goodenough, "Hellenistic Kingship" 83.

This κοινωνία is special because God and the king do not actually need ordinary communion. This κοινωνία is necessary because it is "love which shares in a common purpose in a city {which} is a copy of the unanimity of the universe."[89] This κοινωνία among God, the king, and the ruled produces harmony. For the subjects, it produces obedience and love for the king. The king, in turn, loves and has communion with his subjects, just as God has with his cosmos (*Stob.* 4.7,64).

One of the ways in which the king is just is through equal communion with all of his subjects (*Stob.* 4.7,66). Because he loves them equally he can not treat any of them unjustly.

Diotogenes, too, links κοινωνία to justice.

> For justice bears the same relation to communion as rhythm to motion and harmony to the voice; for justice is a good shared in common between the rulers and the ruled and is accordingly the harmonizing principle in the political community.[90]

It is from this special relationship, this mutual κοινωνία, between ruler and ruled that equity is established, and mercy and justice emerge.

Other Hellenistic Kingship Traits

This section is designed to stress the "Hellenistic" nature of the kingship treatises; though unique, these treatises were also part of a larger body of Hellenistic kingship speculation.[91] The terms discussed here are also central to one or more of the Pythagorean writers in their discussions of kingship. They also appear in later writings in the living law tradition.

Interestingly, most of the terms are specific to certain authors in the fragments we are examining. While Archytas, Ecphantus, and Diotogenes all use a form of σωτήρ to describe the king, only Ecphantus uses εὔνοια and only Diotogenes uses εὐεργέτης.[92] The terms we do have, however, are called by W. Schubart the "Hauptbegriffe, die . . .

---

[89] *Stob.* 4.7,64; ibid., 83.
[90] *Stob.* 4.7,62; ibid., 72.
[91] Aalders, "Νόμος ἔμψυχος," 316–317, 322.
[92] Sthenidas contains no "Hellenistic" kingship terms, but his tractate is by far the shortest; it is difficult to know what is missing.

das Wesen des hellenistischen Königtums am reinsten ausdrucken."[93]

Archytas (*Stob.* 4.1,138), Ecphantus (*Stob.* 4.7,64), and Diotogenes (*Stob.* 4.7,61) all refer to the king as the saviour. This is a pure expression of Hellenistic kingship speculation, and a pure expression of what people wanted from a king.[94] Yet, the term does not generally refer to a spiritual saviour; more often than not it refers to the physical salvation of a given city or people by a king. Goodenough is correct to see something more than simply the physical salvation of a body politic referred to in the Pythagorean fragments, particularly with Ecphantus, but a warning should nevertheless be sounded: the somewhat mystical personal/political ideal does not approach the religious heights of Philo's view of God, and the concepts should not be conflated.

An important concept is also that of the king as εὐεργέτης or "benefactor" of his people.[95] This appears only in Diotogenes, and it is fundamental to his work. The king is to "do good" to his people, to "benefit" them. Though this becomes a title of great significance for Hellenistic kings, it is again grounded in practicality: the king is to physically benefit, bring boons, to his people. It is not clear whether the king who administers these acts takes on a more intense, heightened mystical significance—it is possible—but the acts he administers never leave the realm of human actions.

The third major concept, εὔνοια, occurs only in Ecphantus. Ευνοια is the "good will" which is to exist between the king and his subjects. In light of Ecphantus' concentration on κοινωνία and μίμησις, εὔνοια conjures up images of a special, even religious, bond between ruler and ruled.[96]

All of these concepts speak of the functions of the good king, and sometimes the response of the subjects. They are all powerful con-

---

[93] W. Schubart, "Das hellenistische königsideal nach Inschriften und Papyri" in *Archiv für Papyrusforschung und verwandte Gebiete*, Band 12. (Leipzig and Berlin: B. G. Teubner 1937) 13.

[94] Goodenough, "Hellenistic Kingship" 85, 98; Delatte, *Les Traites* 225–226, 249; A. D. Nock, "Soter and Euergetes" in *Essays on Religion and the Ancient World* II (ed. Zeph Stewart; Cambridge, Mass.: Harvard University Press 1972) 720–735; Paul Wendland, "σωτήρ" in *ZNW* 5 (1904) 335–353; Julius Kaerst, *Geschichte des Hellenismus*. II (Leipzig and Berlin: B. G. Teubner 1926) 313, 318f.

[95] Schubart, "Das hellenistische Königsideal" 13–15; Delatte, *Les Traites* 138, 253; Goodenough, "Hellenistic Kingship" 98; Nock, "Soter and Euergetes" 720–735.

[96] Schubart, "Das hellenistische Königsideal", 5, 8–9, 13; Delatte, *Les Traites* 227, 231–232.

cepts in the Hellenistic world and beyond. Some important Hellenistic kingship terms are not present, such as κτίστης (creator), but most of the most significant terms are found in the Pythagorean texts. Even some secondary terms occur.

Diotogenes states the king must be a μισοπονηρία (hater of evil). This is an important designation, and almost achieves the status of a title in the Hellenistic era.[97] Ecphantus' reference to the king as one who appears or manifests himself (ἐπιφαίνεσθαι) is a central term of kingship. The idea of the "appearance" of the king takes on mystical proportions in the Hellenistic period, with ἐπιφανής becoming a most popular title for a king.[98] Other, less important, Hellenistic kingship terms appear intermittently throughout the texts, such as εὐνομία (good government) and εὐσέβεια (piety).

What all of these terms point to, of course, is the provenance of the texts, the early Hellenistic era, but also to the special nature of the νόμος ἔμψυχος writings. Though these terms show them as part of Hellenistic speculation, it is the other terms, previously examined, which make them unique.

Interestingly, Hellenistic kingship terms abound in the work of Musonius Rufus as well. Derivations of σωτήρ and σῴζω abound, as do εὐεργέτης, δίκαιος, and εὐνομία.[99] Similar terms occur in Plutarch, Philo, and in the *Rhetorica ad Alexandrum*.

The Just King (ὁ δίκαιος)

Though no less central, the idea of the just king is somewhat less important in the unique concept of the king as living law, because the ideal of the just king is found in almost all Greek sources on kingship.[100] Not many people desire an unjust king! Nevertheless the idea is integral to this concept, as well as to Hellenistic kingship.[101]

---

[97] Schubart, "Das hellenistische Königsideal" 8.
[98] Nock, "Notes on Ruler–Cult I–IV" in *Essays on Religion and the Ancient World* I 152–159; Goodenough, "Hellenistic Kingship" 98.
[99] Lutz, "Musonius" 60, 62, 64.
[100] See Born, "Animated Law in the Republic and Laws of Cicero" 131f., #26. Here he appends a list of attributes found among most Greek authors on kingship. Some of these are Justice, Virtue, and Wisdom. He lists these with references.
[101] Schubart, "Das hellenistische Königsideal" 7.

Archytas states that the most reasonable man should rule, for he is the best man.[102] Diotogenes agrees, claiming that "the most just man would be king, and the most lawful would be most just."[103] The king is the best in the earthly realm, as God is the best in the heavenly realm.[104] Sthenidas, too, designates the king a wise man, and links this with the king's imitation of God, but it is Ecphantus who tells us that the king is a unique creation, shaped in the image of God. And like God, the king is perfect in virtue (*Stob.* 4.7,64).

What is unique about this common Greek theme in these sources is that the king is just because he is the law. He is also "conformed" to the law. The idea of the just king who aligns himself with the law is found in Archytas,[105] Diotogenes,[106] Ecphantus,[107] and Sthenidas.[108]

Musonius says that for the king to arbitrate justice for his subjects, he must be just. The king, above all, must be trained in justice. Plutarch expresses the same ideal, in perhaps its most elegant statement:

> Now justice is the aim and end of the law (and) law is the work of the ruler, and the ruler is the image of God who orders all things ... by his virtue he forms himself in the image of God (780e).

Cicero says that kings existed so that people would enjoy justice (*De Off.* 2.42–42). It seems true that the expression of the king who conforms himself to the law and becomes the law is found preeminently in the Pythagorean fragments, but the idea of the just and lawful king is found in all the witnesses.

The last element of the just king, already touched upon, is his affection and love for his subjects. Archytas says that the king must be a lover of men. Diotogenes claims that the king is occupied with doing well for and benefiting his subjects. Sthenidas concentrates on the king's mercy and fatherly attitude toward his subjects. Ecphantus says that the king "has the same love and communion with his sub-

---

[102] *Stob.* 4.1,135; Goodenough, "Hellenistic Kingship" 59.
[103] *Stob.* 4.7,61; ibid., 65.
[104] *Stob.* 4.7,62; ibid., 68.
[105] *Stob.* 4.1, 135–138.
[106] *Stob.* 4.7, 61–62.
[107] *Stob.* 4.7, 64–66.
[108] *Stob.* 4.7, 63.

jects as God has with the universe and the things in it."[109] The king, according to Ecphantus, has complete good will for his subjects, and his subjects good will for him.

Goodenough, in fact, claims that in understanding the relationship between the king and his subjects, we have "grasped the meaning which lies behind the conception of the Animate Law."[110] What is this meaning?

> The king is personally the constitution of his realm, that all the laws of localities under him must be ultimately moulded by and express his will. But more, he is the saviour of his subjects from their sins, by giving them what the Hellenistic world increasingly wanted more than anything else, a dynamic and personal revelation of deity.[111]

The king as the law was the Hellenistic answer to a search for meaning and hope, and an escape from the arbitrariness of law and morality. The subjects under the living law

> will at last have achieved the dream ... of all Greek ethical thinking ... to live spontaneously by divine law and dispense with the seriatim compulsion and injustice of the written code.[112]

In many ways they were free from the written law.

Conclusions

The living law ideal is a powerful concept. More than in any other concept of "higher" law the entire written law is replaced. The king substitutes himself for the law. The written law is indeed superfluous. Of course, the king must be lawful and just and act only out of compassion for his subjects, but the dangers inherent in the concept are obvious. It was perhaps not a ubiquitous concept, but it was present, and, moreover, it was dynamic. It may well be that it was the danger of the concept which caused it to be mentioned so rarely; tyrants hardly need philosophical justification to legitimize their doings.

---

[109] Goodenough, "Hellenistic Kingship" 84.
[110] Ibid., 91.
[111] Ibid., 91; see also Chesnut, "The Ruler and the Logos," 1312.
[112] Ibid., 91.

As the living law, however, the king was to be "lawful," to bring himself in line with divine or eternal law, though this is stated clearly only once or twice, and bring about virtue in the lives of his subjects. The "higher" quality of the living law seems to rest on his imitation of God, his perfect justness, and, especially, his ability to be the law for his subjects in such a way that they desire to follow the law.

The Task

These complex and powerful ideas have come down to us not only as ancient history, as the survey here indicates, but as living concepts in modern life. The ideas have lasted because they speak to the need to root law in something other than convention and arbitrariness: surely there is truth?

These ideals seek to root the essence of law, a norm for moral behavior, and its function, the insurance of justice, in sources which transcend the mundane and the arbitrary. Law may be intrinsic, written in the nature of the world and of humankind, or extrinsic, living in the true king, or enshrined in the heavens as eternal norm, but these concepts affirm that law is not subject to whim.

Our purpose now is to apply them to the thinking of Philo. What are the connections between this Jewish thinker and philosophic thought on the superfluity of the written law in the Greco-Roman era?

CHAPTER FOUR

PHILO AND φύσις

In a study of "higher" law in the Greco-Roman world, Philo presents to us a picture unlike any other. He weaves a tapestry of complexity and beauty. This tapestry reveals to us not only the patterns of Philo's thought on Greek law, but, indeed, as much, or more, information on ἄγραφος νόμος, νόμος φύσεως, and νόμος ἔμψυχος as is found in most other ancient sources. Indeed, Philo is the only ancient author who explicitly discusses all three of these concepts. Philo is not simply an object of study in terms of how he uses these sources, he is a source himself.

The goal of this study is narrowly defined but wide in its scope. Did Philo in his use and adoption of these concepts somehow render the Mosaic law superfluous for some people? Does the presence of ideas of "higher" law reduce the Mosaic law in Philo's writing to something which is less than necessary for certain, gifted people? The concepts with which Philo works are susceptible to such interpretations, if only—as with the Greek authorities he follows—for a small group of people.

Because of the importance of φύσις in understanding the law of nature and the related forms of higher law in Philo, and for understanding the place and role of God and humanity in the cosmos, our study will begin with an overview of nature in Philo's work. This overview is significant because Philo's view of nature differs from the Stoic view, and because Philo's view of the world, a united whole, is important for understanding his view of law.

The major strands of Greek thought on φύσις are found in Philo. These include φύσις as the power of life and growth; φύσις as the particular characteristic of any thing or being; and φύσις as the inherent order and reason of the cosmos, seen *par excellence* in the νόμος φύσεως, but manifesting itself in every living thing.[1] Philo's thought

---

[1] See Hans Leisegang, "Physis" in *Pauly-Wissowa Real Encyclopädie* 20.1 1130–1164; Greene, *Moira* 223–228; 410,413; F. Heinimann, *Nomos und Physis*. Nature as the

also includes the idea of the φύσις of God, separate from and towering over the created nature.[2]

φύσις: *The Power of Growth and Life*

This is perhaps the earliest Greek view of nature.[3] Nature as the power of growth and life is clearly evident throughout Philo's work (*Deus* 37–38). Seeds and fruit are the works of nature, not culture (*Her.* 121). The ability of a plant or an animal to bear fruit is determined by nature (*Congr.* 4). A vine is a piece of nature's handiwork (*Mut.* 162). Nature's work is to be seen everywhere. Though transformed by τέχνη, food is also a gift of nature (*Spec.* 2.158–159). Nature also divides the seasons (*Legat.* 190) and establishes the equinoxes (*QE* 1). Nature bestows on humanity "all gifts" (*Sacr.* 98–102; *Agr.* 7–8; *Post.* 103–104).

Nature also gives life to human beings. Nature is the common mother of all humankind (*Decal.* 41–43; *Agr.* 30–31; *Somn.* 2.262; *Legat.* 126). The sense-perceptions are created by nature (*Somn.* 1.27). The tongue is a gift of nature (*Spec.* 2.6). Nature has also formed the marriage union (*Abr.* 248–249), presumably to foster life, for on numerous occasions Philo refers to the womb as the workshop of nature (e.g. *Legat.* 56–57). The course of nature is active until the

---

reason inherent in the cosmos includes under its rubric the two first categories. This points to the difficulties of these divisions. There is great unity in Philo's universe and it is manifested throughout the cosmos. The character of a plant, for instance, is specific, but insofar as it fulfils its specific nature, it shares in the nature of the universe.

[2] A number of commentators over the years have argued that φύσις and God are synonymous in Philo; I hope to demonstrate that this is not so. See Hans Leisegang, "Physis" 1160–1161. He is most emphatic: Physis = God; E. R. Goodenough, *By Light, Light: The Mystic Gospel of Hellenistic Judaism* (New Haven: Yale University Press 1935) 31–54; James Drummond, *Philo Judaeus or the Jewish-Alexandrian Philosophy* (Amsterdam: Philo Press 1969; repr. of London 1888 ed.) 62,167; Gerhard Delling, "Wunder-Allegorie-Mythus bei Philon von Alexandrie" in *Studien zum Neuen Testament und zum hellenistischen Judentum* (Göttingen: Vandenhoeck & Ruprecht, 1970) 72–129. See also Adele Reinhartz, "The Meaning of νόμος in Philo's *Exposition of the Law*" in *SR* 15/3 (1986) 341–342.

[3] There are a great many articles dealing with this, and many have been discussed in Chapter Two. An argument for this view is provided by F. J. E. Woodbridge, "The Dominant Conception" 359–374; an argument against by A. O. Lovejoy, "The Meaning of *Physis*" 369–383.

birth of the child, after which nature no longer participates in its development (*Abr.* 193–195). The course of nature also contains death, which is simply a part of the process of life (*Mos.* 2.281).

The creative force of nature, the force of growth and life, comes to us too in the shape of needs and longings, to which our bodies must respond. There is a course of nature for each thing (*Leg.* 1.107), for nature has created all things in a unique and particular way (*Leg.* 3.64). The need to eat, as well as other bodily needs and functions, was appointed by nature (*Leg.* 3.145–147).

The opposite of the existence of natural drives is the limits which nature sets upon all things (*Mos.* 1.26–28; *Decal.* 41–43). These limits must be obeyed. Nature "intends" for all things "something" specific (*Spec.* 2.48). Each living thing, given the power of growth and life by nature, strives to become, and to maintain, what it truly is (*Aet.* 35–37).

This view of nature is probably the most common view of nature even today: nature is the inherent growth and life found in each living thing. What is different is the idea that each living thing has a role proper to itself which it ought to fulfil to be truly itself. This touches already upon the view of nature as the inherent character of things.

φύσις: *The Inherent Character of Things*

The unique, characteristic nature of each living thing is a powerful component of the Greek view of nature. It is found throughout Philo's writings. The specific nature which all living things contain is a part of the greater nature of the whole. It is the "stuff" of any thing or being, that which characterizes and defines it. Philo can therefore speak of the "nature" of the Good, and on the other hand speak of people who are "by nature" combatants: in both cases Philo is speaking of the inherent character of the thing in question.[4] Both a human being (*Opif.* 82–85) and a number (*Opif.* 95–97) have characteristic natures. Important for us, however, are Philo's discussions

---

[4] It can also mean they share in "nature" writ large, that is, they are what they are by virtue *of* nature, as well as *by* their own nature. This ultimately amounts to the same thing in Philo's thought, as is true in Stoic thought.

of human nature. The nature of a number, for instance, is not in doubt; but when it comes to human nature, the true nature of humankind is open to question.

Not every human "nature" is positive. Philo can speak of people whose personal nature is contrary to light (*Leg.* 1.18). Other human natures though reject pleasure, and so are wholesome (*Leg.* 2.105). It is no surprise then that Philo can speak of natures which are mutually hostile (*Leg.* 3.7). It is God who has made some natures evil and some good (*Leg.* 3.75).[5] Though the true nature of humanity is to partake in the good, there are contending natures of good and evil which may be present in each person (*Sacr.* 4).

Noah had an excellent nature from birth (*Leg.* 3.77–78; cf. *Somn.* 1.171–172 for Isaac). Others are said to have generously gifted natures (*Deus* 61–63). Elsewhere, Philo points out rational (*Migr.* 68; *Somn.* 1.106) and logical (*Migr.* 78) natures. There are also imperishable (*Mut.* 14) and happy (*Mut.* 84–86) natures. The wise man, who is born good, like Isaac, has a nature which acts as a light to all who have rational natures (*Somn.* 1.176). There are great "natures" (*Ios.* 118; *Mos.* 1.21–22, 59–60). The greatest nature of all belonged to Moses, who perfected his "nature" (*Mos.* 2.58).

Philo can also speak about "fleshly" natures, which are opposed to spiritual, or good, natures (*Det.* 83–84; *Gig.* 30). Some, says Philo, are altogether dull in their natures (*Somn.* 1.236). Philo says that even Joseph could not direct irrational natures (*Agr.* 56; *Somn.* 1.109–111), and that "Egypt"—which almost always connotes the baser elements of humankind[6]—cannot rise above its own nature (*Mut.* 117).

While Philo affirms what most anyone can observe, namely, some people are good and other people are bad, he roots these tendencies in human nature. On the other hand, Philo affirms that all human beings have the same nature (*Post.* 160). Philo speaks as well

---

[5] Here the problem of the creation of evil and the question of free-will and predestination are met. Nature has, after all, its own "character" to fulfil, and this is most certainly to do good. Who creates these evil natures? Why would God create a nature contrary to the "true" nature of man? The question whether one truly has an "evil" nature will be discussed elsewhere, for Philo seems to imply that one can choose his "true" nature. See H. A. Wolfson's discussion, *Philo: Foundations of Religious Philosophy in Judaism, Christianity, and Islam, Vol. I.* (Cambridge, Mass.: Harvard University Press, 1947) Vol. 1 426–456.

[6] Alan Mendelson, *Philo's Jewish Identity* (BJS 161; Atlanta: Scholars Press 1988) 117.

of the true nature of mankind (*Det.* 274). Good is conformable to man's nature, claims Philo, but evil is not (*Mut.* 197–199). Does Philo contradict himself? Is there in fact a true nature of humanity, as there is a true nature of the sun, or of salt? What is the true character, the inherent character of humankind? Or are there many?

Philo does not enter into contradiction, if the shades of meaning in Philo's understanding of the nature of humanity are maintained. Philo speaks both of the ideal nature of humankind—the true, or inherent nature—and the observable facts of man's nature—people are different and some are bad.[7] This tension is not unique to Philo in the ancient world; it was almost inevitable given the common view of each thing having its own particular nature. This was an easy view to maintain until human beings were added to the equation. For while cats and dogs seemed to have no trouble fulfilling their animal natures, humans stumbled far from the ideal. How should we account for it?

Cicero, too, stressed that people are different and unique (*De Nat. Deor.* 2.34,39). Not every good person has the same nature, and not every person is good (*De Rep.* 3.33). One is supposed to maintain one's own individual nature, if it does not involve any transgression of the universal nature, but a "bad" nature is to be rooted out. Those who have "bad" natures are still able to share in their true nature, but the way is much more difficult than for someone whose nature is good at birth (*De Off.* 1.106–113).

In Philo's thought, we can distinguish among a number of levels of human nature. At one level, some of Philo's natures are simply "types" or "characters." These can be, potentially, cast off and transcended. Though changing one's "character" is no light task, these "natures" have, finally, no true significance.

For above the "character" of a person, however difficult it is to alter, are our fleshly and spiritual natures, or rational and irrational natures, which all humankind shares (*Gig.* 30). The reason why there are evil people, who partake in less than ideal natures, is that the soul can be shaken from its proper nature (*Decal.* 142; cf. *QE* 2.106; *Legat.* 118). Humans are created and corruptible, and if thrown off course a person shares more in the fleshly, or irrational, than

---

[7] That Philo maintains a distinction in natures based on observation is clear from his claim that children imitate their father's nature (*Sacr.* 68–69).

spiritual nature of humanity (cf. *Leg.* 3.104).[8] These categories both have real meaning, and existence, but the fleshly nature is not the true nature of humankind. The true nature of humankind is the spiritual nature.

There is, indeed, only one true human nature (*Ebr.* 164–167; *Congr.* 122; *Mut.* 46,225; *Ios.* 25; *Legat.* 75). The true nature of humankind is to partake in the good; the problem is, of course, that human beings, alone among created beings, can say no to their true nature. As Wolfson says, "All men have a knowledge of the good, but some, notwithstanding that knowledge, choose by their own free will to follow the base."[9] The good is the goal, however, to which human nature ultimately strives, for nature in each case strives to maintain its true nature (*Aet.* 35–37).[10]

We can sum up our findings thus far. There is a true, inherent nature, in which all men are meant to share, and a fleshly nature, having many manifestations, in which we do share, because humanity is corruptible. Below these categories are types of human natures, some of which are good, some of which are bad, but none of which are truly decisive. A type of nature which is more suited to evil, for instance, can be led upon the path to goodness, if the right choices are made, and with the help of God; the predisposition of a per-

---

[8] Mendelson, *Secular Education in Philo of Alexandria* (Cincinnati: Hebrew Union College Press 1982) 48–51 discusses a three-pronged typology of human beings which is located in a number of places (*Her.* 45–46; *Leg.* 1.92–94; *Gig.* 60–63; *QG* 4.243). Mendelson indicates that the lowest of these types, the φαῦλος, have chosen the way of wickedness instead of the way of the μέσος. Once they have chosen the way of wickedness, they are not at liberty to change their lot (59–60).

Free will, therefore, is a limited option. "It would seem that the less gifted the individual (at the start), the less successful he will be in any endeavour to lift himself" (59). The person, like Moses, who is by nature good, is good by the grace of God. The person who occupies the middle ground can choose the good or the bad, but he can not choose to be Moses. "There can be no progress without the active aid of God" (59). Nature is a gift of God, and choice is not unlimited. "Philo was not thinking in terms of a concept of absolute free will when he charted these courses" (60).

[9] Wolfson, *Philo* Vol. 1 437. Mendelson, *Secular Education* 58–59.

[10] The ability to choose the good is, as we have seen, limited to some degree by birth and nature. The real choice for the lowest category of human beings, the φαῦλος, is the choice made to descend to the basest of natures from the level of the μέσος; once this occurs there is little chance for improvement. The choice of the μέσος, however, can also be to choose good. This is where free will enters the picture. "A member of this class alone has the free will to determine the shape of his life for good or for evil" (Mendelson, *Secular Education* 67).

son's character need not be decisive for the life which a person leads. With the proper teaching and training anyone can lead a virtuous life, for the true nature of humanity is to lead a virtuous life.

The achievement of the true nature of humanity is not a simple thing, but this does not mean one cannot improve. Everything partakes in a true nature. It is simply easier for an animal or plant to achieve its true nature than it is for a person.[11] Each passion, for instance, has a true nature (*Leg.* 3.157). So, too, does a square have a true nature (*Conf.* 87). The same is true of the soul (*Conf.* 46). The list could be extended indefinitely.[12] But the specific nature of salt, for instance, is not unconnected to nature as a whole. Nature means not simply the natural world, but the nature of all things, namely, nature as the order of the cosmos. Every particular nature shares in the nature of the whole.[13]

---

[11] Wolfson, *Philo* Vol. 1 445 claims that God also helps those who seek the good: "he will not have to rely upon his own power, that is to say, that power of free will with which God has endowed all men, for, if he proves himself worthy, God, through his thoughtfulness, will aid him." Some people, of course, are lucky; to them virtue came by nature: Noah (*Leg.* 3.24,77); Melchizedek (*Leg.* 3.25,79–81); Abraham (*Leg.* 3.27,83–84); Isaac (*Leg.* 3.28,85–87); Jacob (*Leg.* 3.29,88–89). Moses, as we will see, has an even higher nature. Of these people Mendelson, *Secular Education* 52, says, "the grace of God ... is an essential element in the original constitution of the sage." See Mendelson, *Secular Education* 47–65, for the typology of human beings and their ability to achieve virtue.

[12] Philo speaks of the true nature of almost everything: good (*Sobr.* 53); benedictions (*Leg.* 3.210); self-conceit (*Leg.* 1.52); knowledge (*Somn.* 1.6; *Gig.* 25); mind (*Migr.* 206–207); heaven (*Somn.* 1.27; *Mut.* 71); air (*Somn.* 1.20); maleness (*Spec.* 2.50–52); texts (*Contempl.* 28); salt (*QG* 4.62), etc.

[13] Since creation is the work of God, carried out by nature, which also includes the activity of the Logos, all created beings and things share in nature as a whole, as well as having their specific natures to fulfill (*Opif.* 3,16,19–22,44,46,73,130,145; *Post.* 4–5). The connection is also seen in the creation of the Forms which have their copies on earth. These copies adhere to the purpose established for them by God, whose active force in the world is the Logos. "Universal Nature ... brings forth no finished product in the world of sense without using an incorporeal pattern" (*Opif.* 130). The connection between individual human natures and universal nature was especially relevant to the Stoics. Cicero, *De Off.* 1.106–13 says that humans share in universal nature as well as human nature, as does Diogenes Laertius 7.43. Cf. Goodenough, *By Light, Light* 393–94, and Long and Sedley, *The Hellenistic Philosophers* Vol. 1 266–268, section 43; 395, section 63. This was a concern of Philo's too, but for special reasons: God's provident creation. Philo says, "God willed that Nature should run a course that brings it back to its starting-point, endowing the species with immortality, and making them sharers of eternal existence" (*Opif.* 44). Universal nature endows its creations with purpose, and these purposes share in the whole.

When Philo speaks of things φύσις, by nature, he speaks not only of things which fulfil their individual nature, but which in so doing participate in the order of the cosmos. Immoderate eating, for instance is "by nature" deadly according to Philo (*Opif.* 159). The sense is not only "inherently," by its own nature, deadly, but "by the order of nature" deadly. It is the relation of the microcosmic to the macrocosmic, in the literal sense of these terms.[14]

Philo is also directly under the influence of Greek thought on nature when he contrasts things which are by nature and things which are by habit (*Her.* 142).[15] He maintains the common Greek distinction between natural and conventional. The natural is the "stuff" which makes a thing what it is, the conventional is an unnecessary addition to nature (*Somn.* 1.167–169; 2.90; *Abr.* 52–55; *QG* 4.184). For Philo, the greatest goal for anyone, or anything, is that it "strives to maintain and conserve the thing of which it is the nature" (*Aet.* 35–37). This is true of the cosmos, too, for there exists a nature of all existence (*Post.* 182) and a nature of all things (*Agr.* 1; *Ios.* 142; *Mos.* 2.100,133–134,142; *Fug.* 14,34; *Mut.* 266).

φύσις: *The Order of the Cosmos*

Because the creation of nature was the act of a provident God, all creation, in the work of Philo, has a place in the cosmic order. Nature is purposeful and intentional. Each specific thing has purpose and intentionality, as has already been touched upon, as does nature in its entirety. Nature is not only the force of life or growth, it is the order and the purpose inherent in life.

Nature, therefore, is able to prompt people to do certain things (*Cher.* 90–92). To follow nature is the sign of strong reason (*Ebr.* 55). It is nature itself which gives us the means to follow nature by granting us the instruments of judgement (*Ebr.* 169). Nature trains people (*Ebr.* 211–212). The purpose of conforming to reasonable nature

---

[14] There are numerous examples of things "by nature": *Leg.* 3.71,3.130; *Post.* 31–32,109; *Conf.* 49,52; *Migr.* 26; *Her.* 49; *Congr.* 71; *Fug.* 120,172; *Mut.* 108,167; *Somn.* 1.114,150; 2.79,136; *Abr.* 21; *Ios.* 81–83; *Mos.* 1.97; *Decal.* 64; *Spec.* 2.122–124; *QE* 1.16; etc.

[15] Guthrie, *History* Vol. III 55; Heinimann, *Nomos und Physis* 106–108.

and the goal to which nature leads is the best possible life. Conformity with nature is equal to justice (*Her.* 95). It teaches us (*Fug.* 171–172) and reveals knowledge to us (*Somn.* 1.11).[16] Nature has an intended purpose for humankind (*Spec.* 2.48).

The Stoic colouring of Philo's view of nature is readily apparent. This is nature which guides people into reasonable and virtuous lives. This is a nature which is purposeful and moral. This is the nature of the Stoics, with one distinct difference: God created nature. God is not, as with the Stoics, the reason, the order of nature; he is not simply φύσις, he transcends his creation.

Philo does not alter the Stoic view of a world shot through with reason; he does not even alter the terminology; but he does bring to this view the Hebraic notion of the one, true God who towers over his creation.[17] Within his creation, things often seem rather Stoic. The heart of nature is truth (*Sobr.* 46–48; *Her.* 71). Nature has a never-failing wisdom (*Spec.* 2.100). It provides for humankind a champion in reason (*Cher.* 39). Right reason, ὀρθὸς λόγος, calls us to follow in the steps of nature (*Ebr.* 34). Right reason, in fact, is an infallible law created by nature (*Prob.* 46).

As with the Stoics, right reason, which is also considered the order of nature itself, manifests itself as the law of nature. The commandments are given according to nature (*Det.* 52). The ordinances of the Bible are consistent with nature (*Abr.* 5). Nature itself is the most venerable statute (*Abr.* 6). The world itself, described by the Stoic term μεγαλόπολις, has a single law: the λόγος of nature (*Ios.* 28–31).

Philo follows the Stoics in his formulations, especially in adopting the description of the order of nature as the ὀρθὸς λόγος. Reason guides nature. Philo gives us more: he is the first writer in Greek, whose work is extant, to speak so clearly and often of the νόμος φύσεως. While Philo has clearly adopted Stoic terminology, he provides the missing link: the term itself. To follow the λόγος of nature

---

[16] Cf. *Ios.* 129; *Mos.* 1.39; *Spec.* 2.239–241.
[17] Robert M. Berchman, *From Philo to Origen: Middle Platonism in Transition* (Chico, California: Scholars Press 1984) 27. Cf. with David Winston, "Philo's Conception of the Divine Nature" in *Neoplatonism and Jewish Thought* (ed. Lenn E. Goodman. Albany: State University Press 1992) 21–32.

is to follow the νόμος φύσεως.[18] It is Philo who first gives us the formulation on a consistent basis.[19]

The cosmos is ordered by laws, the manifestation of reason in the world. Although E. R. Goodenough has argued that Philo operates with two kinds of natural law, one governing the natural world, and one governing the moral world, Philo in fact makes no such distinction.[20] The world, its physical and ethical components, is one. There is an immutable law of nature (*Mos.* 2.5–7). One can live a harmonious life by following the laws and statutes of nature (*Spec.* 1.202). The laws of nature were indeed determined by God from

---

[18] Berchman, *From Philo to Origen*, 45 is especially relevant to this discussion, but refer to 35–53 to place Philo's view of nature and its relationship to Logos and the law of nature in its proper context.

[19] Philo cannot be the originator of the concept, as we argued in Chapter Two against Helmut Koester, "νόμος φύσεως." We need not, however, adopt W. L. Knox's attitude, *Some Hellenistic Elements in Primitive Christianity* (London: Oxford University Press 1944) 34 who speaks of Philo's "total lack of original thought" and the "slovenliness with which he incorporates his material." While Philo is not an originator of this concept, his treatment, we will shortly argue, is quite original and far from slovenly.

[20] Goodenough, *By Light, Light* 52–57. Goodenough distinguishes between the "Law of God, or the Law of Nature" and the "natural law of matter" in the work of Philo (54). Philo makes this distinction, according to Goodenough, to escape the attribution of the creation of evil to God (53–54). When Philo turns to the problem of evil, there is "mention of a law of material nature which seems at enmity with God's law" (54). Philo's discussion of the problem of theodicy may indeed seem an anomaly in his thought, but it does not appear that Philo has created a second form of "natural law of matter." It seems from Philo's account of creation that God is responsible for the creation of matter and the laws which govern it. If Philo has difficulty explaining the role of irrational tendencies, or evil in this creation, he is not alone, either in the ancient or in the modern world. In his "Appendix: Law in the Subjective Realm," Goodenough argues more convincingly that the "law of the nature of the whole" and "the law of the nature of the part" are sometimes in conflict (394). What a body desires, therefore, is sometimes in conflict with what reason demands. This, it seems to me, carries us back to the problem of theodicy, for the reasonable person knows, for instance, that sex is for procreation; the person who slavishly follows sexual desires without checking them with the reason inherent in him is a slave to irrational desires and, so, to sin. This is not another law of nature, though; it is a perversion of nature. The Stoics faced the same problem, in a different way. Because of their monistic view of the world and especially of the human soul—it was only reasonable—how could they explain the existence of "irrational" desires or "wrong judgements"? This they must explain, however, with a different view of the soul than Philo and without the presence of a transcendent God. See Martha Nussbaum, "The Stoics on the Extirpation of the Passions" in *Apeiron* 20/2 (1987) 129–177; Michael Frede, "The Stoic Doctrine of the Affections of the Soul" in *The Norms of Nature: Studies in Hellenistic Ethics* (eds. Malcolm Schofield and Gisela Striker; Cambridge: Cambridge University Press 1986) 93–110; Brad Inwood, *Ethics and Human Action* (Oxford: Clarendon Press 1985) 127–181.

the beginning of creation (*QG* 4.42). Nature, therefore, is governed by laws, and is itself a law. God's creation imbued the world with purpose, not only physical, but ethical.

The fact of purposeful nature means, as pointed out in the discussion of human nature, that one can act contrary to and according to nature. One can, and most people do, contravene these laws of nature (*Decal.* 150). There are activities which defy nature (*Conf.* 68). The ownership of slaves is against nature (*Contempl.* 70). Someone who kills another person undermines the laws and statutes of nature (*Decal.* 132). Impiety subverts the laws of nature (*Spec.* 2.170–173). Cutting off a part of the human body, cross-mating, and cross-breeding are all against the decrees of nature (*Fug.* 112; *Spec.* 3.45–48). In general, those who

> presume to lay hands upon nature and transform the works of nature by their own undertakings defile the undefiled. For the things of nature are perfect and full (*QE* 2.1).

While there may be no punishment for breaking the law of nature in a human court of law, one may be condemned in the court of nature (*Spec.* 3.121).

There are actions, too, which not only contravene nature, but "add" to it. The result is the same. Nature needs nothing but itself. There are no superfluities in nature (*Post.* 4–5; *Mos.* 1.117). Bad laws are "additions" to the right reason of nature (*Ios.* 28–31; *QG* 4.90,184). Homosexuals, says Philo, debase nature not only because they contravene it, but because they "add" to nature (*Spec.* 1.325). Slavery, too, is an "addition" to nature (*Spec.* 2.58; *Contempl.* 70).

The order of the cosmos, shaped by the right reason of nature, and manifesting itself in laws of nature, is not able to be altered. Nature has clear and well-defined limits (*Aet.* 57–59). Nature, the whole cosmos, is charged with reason and purpose. This is the nature of the Stoics, with one important difference: as a creation of God, it bears his ethical imprint. Above Philo's orderly and reasonable nature hovers its creator.

φύσις: *The Nature of God*

E. R. Goodenough in *By Light, Light* argued that φύσις can sometimes mean God for Philo; he has been followed or preceded by a number of other commentators.[21] Yet, as Goodenough himself acknowledges, God operates in the world through the workings of his reason, the λόγος. God transcends his creation, but controls it through his Logos.[22] The nature of God is removed strictly from the workings of the cosmos. God has a perfect, unique nature. He is uncreated and therefore his nature transcends human nature which is created and composite (*Legat.* 118).

God is prior to the universe: μόνος, ἕν, φύσις ἁπλῆ (*Leg.* 2.1–3). The transcendent nature of God means that it is unknown to humankind and that no positive assertion may be made about it (*Leg.* 3.206–207; *Congr.* 61). Philo perhaps breaks his own injunction when he claims God's nature is most perfect (*Cher.* 86), but generally Philo is true to his word.[23] Beyond the knowledge that God "is," his nature is inapprehensible (*Det.* 89). Even Moses, the greatest of men, was rebuffed when he tried to have God reveal his nature to him (*Post.* 13).

> He has driven created being far away from His essential Nature, so that we cannot touch it even with the pure spiritual contact of the understanding (*Post.* 20).

Moses could never have caught a glimpse of the pure, eternal, never-fading, never-changing nature of God (*Mut.* 7,14,140; *Plant.* 91).

There is some tension in Philo's thought on God's nature. Philo finds the chasm between humanity and God hard to accept, though he stresses it (*Mut.* 184). He often tries to blur the lines separating humanity from God. This attempt at "blurring" the separation between humanity and God occurs not only with the "borderline" nature of humanity, but when Philo introduces natures between ordinary human nature and God's nature.

Philo speaks often of the tension between human and divine nature. The mind, νοῦς, of humans has a brilliant and god-like nature (*Leg.* 2.10). There are some men who can converse with intelligible, incorporeal natures (*Deus* 55). A heavenly soul can dwell with θείων φύσεων,

---

[21] See my comments in this chapter n. 2.
[22] Berchman, *From Philo to Origen*, 27–35, 39, 42.
[23] Philo slips up a few other times, but this is due one must suspect to enthusiasm. He calls God's nature good (*Conf.* 180–181), unchangeable (*Somn.* 1.232), and sublime (*Leg.* 3.252). God is without passion of any kind (*Abr.* 202). He is, says Philo, the "best nature."

or divine natures (*Deus.* 151). Philo goes so far as to say on one occasion that the worthy man shares God's nature (*Post.* 26–28), while chastising those who believe that their nature is more than human (*Post.* 115).[24]

Humanity exists on the border of mortal and immortal nature (*Opif.* 133–135). There are human natures which are closer to God (*Mut.* 219). The High Priest has a nature midway between humanity and God (*Somn.* 1.188–189). Philo often speaks of great natures (*Ios.* 118; *Mos.* 1.2–7) and natures higher than merely human (*Spec.* 1.116). Just as man seems to be the only being who can pervert his nature, so he seems to be the only being who can rise above it and better it.

On what side does Philo finally land? Finally, it seems that Philo maintains the separation between God and mankind. The tension arises because of Philo's intense desire to see God, and his unwillingness to close the door on that possibility. When pushed, however, he is forced to admit that God is beyond the grasp of even the greatest mortal. Moses, the greatest of all, a god to men (*Mos.* 1.158), was denied a vision of God.

Philo also muddies the waters by introducing the idea of divine natures. The gulf between human and divine natures is wide; at times it seems to be bridged. In *Fug.* 163, Philo points out that divine natures are separate from human natures (cf. *Somn.* 1.135–137,143).[25] It is possible for a person to actually rise above human nature into the realm of the Logos.[26] The way beyond, however, is closed. There is no entrance to God himself.

> For nothing mortal can be made in the likeness of the most high One and Father of the universe but only in that of the second God, who is His Logos (*QG* 1.62).

This is the ultimate. Certain people do have a kinship with the Logos, because the human mind is a likeness and image of it. Those people who perfect their natures, a perfection which all people theoretically could accomplish, are able to form a relationship with the

---

[24] Refer to Mendelson, *Secular Education* 52. Cf. *Her.* 84.
[25] Mendelson, *Secular Education* 51.
[26] There is a difference between human and divine natures, however, because the human nature is partially material; a divine nature, an angel or some such being, is immaterial. Even the sage still shares in the human body.

Logos and the divine natures which reside in the realm of the Logos.

God's nature, however, is set apart: it is unknowable, simple, and indivisible. The gulf between divine natures, those of the potencies and the angels and special human beings, and the nature of God is too great to be bridged.

Philo's Scheme of Nature

Philo's scheme may be reconstructed in light of this study. There is God, whose simple nature transcends the cosmos, its order, and reason. Universal nature, the cosmos, is home of the Logos, the reason which guides and orders universal nature. Reason, the Logos, is also manifested as the law of nature.[27] Reason is also manifested in the realm of universal nature where divine natures find their home. Below universal nature is the natural world, which is ordered by the Logos. The natural world is made up of individual beings and things whose individual natures partake in the universal nature. The nature of humanity is unique in that it can bridge the gap between the natural world and the realm of universal nature, that is, humans can transcend the natural world and rise to the realm of universal nature. Human beings are alone among creatures in being able to sink below their nature and pervert it.

Nature and Law

This study of nature in the work of Philo is an attempt to situate the following discussion of law in its proper context, both in the work of Philo itself and in the broader Stoic, and Greco-Roman, context. Philo differs from the Stoics in important essentials in his view of nature: there is a transcendent God who guides his creation; and human beings, though able to perfect their nature, remain distanced from God by virtue of his transcendence.

---

[27] The relationship of the law of nature to the Logos is difficult. Goodenough claims they are interchangeable terms. André Myre, "La loi dans l'ordre cosmique et politique selon Philon d'Alexandrie" in *Science et Esprit* 24 (1972) 224–225, however, argues that the law of nature is not "le tout-près-de-Dieu." But, he does claim that the origin of the law of nature is in the Logos (223).

The law of nature, therefore, acts as a bridge through which humanity can come to know God and his workings. Purpose and intention are found in every aspect of creation, and to understand the law of nature is to come to know the purpose and intention of God and humanity's role in the cosmos.

The place of law, created from the beginning, informs Philo's thought throughout his work; the relationship of nature to law is necessary to understand the goal of the human quest and the goal of law itself. The role of written law especially plays a fundamental role in human lives, but what is its relation to nature and the laws inherent in nature? What is the purpose of the Mosaic law if nature itself contains the laws of God? How do the two relate in Philo's cosmic, and personal, scheme? How do the law of nature and the Mosaic law function in relation to human nature?

CHAPTER FIVE

PHILO AND THE LAW

The study of nature in the preceding chapter serves to demonstrate the close relationship between law and nature. An understanding of nature also allows us to understand more properly the function of law, in all its manifestations, and to understand law in Philo's larger scheme. Specifically, a study of nature allows us to place not only the law of nature and the law of Moses in their cosmic scheme, but it also allows us to understand the place of humanity in God's creation and humankind's relationship to law, nature, and God.

As with φύσις, our study of νόμος will reveal a variety of meanings and shades of meaning. This is to be expected. Yet, as with φύσις, the multiplicity of meaning in Philo's use of νόμος ultimately yields to a concept which is notable for its overarching unity. This unity of law stems not only from Philo's eclectic tendencies, the eclectic tendencies of his age, and his ability and desire to pull together a variety of Greek thought on the law, but to the very real presence in Philo's work of the one, true God, from which all true law emanates.[1]

νόμος φύσεως: *The Law of Nature*

Nature is the creation of God. It operates according to certain laws and ordinances, both physical and ethical, which God gave as unalterable (*Opif.* 61). Moses' account of creation, says Philo, gives clear evidence that the world is in harmony with the law and that the one who observes the law is regulating his actions according to the

---

[1] I use "eclectic" in a positive sense. For the rehabilitation of the term, see Pierluigi Donini, "The History of the Concept of Eclecticism" in *The Question of "Eclecticism": Studies in Later Greek Philosophy* (Berkeley-Los Angeles: University of California Press, 1988) 15–33; for its use in a positive sense for the philosophy of Philo's time, see John M. Dillon, " 'Orthodoxy' and 'Eclecticism': Middle Platonists and Neo-Pythagoreans" in *The Question of "Eclecticism"* 103–125.

purposes and will of nature (*Opif.* 3). In *De Iosepho*, Philo states that the world is the μεγαλόπολις, or great city, which has a single "polity" or rule, the λόγος of nature (*Ios.* 29). The law of nature, which is reason, or the Logos, is also the law of God, for the law of God is adjusted to the standard of nature (*Spec.* 2.37). The laws of nature, therefore, have a more solid foundation than those created by people (*Prob.* 37).

These laws of nature were determined from the beginning (ἐξ ἀρχῆς), when the world itself was created (*QG* 4.42). True law is that which is revealed by the ὄρθος λόγος and is an invention of nature not man (*QG* 4.90; *Ebr.* 142; *Sobr.* 33).[2]

The constitution (πολιτεία) of this world is the right reason of nature (ὁ τῆς φύσεως ὄρθος λόγος) (*Ebr.* 80). Philo can also claim that virtue is a law for each person (*Leg.* 3.245), because elsewhere he reveals that virtue is the law of nature (*Post.* 185). There is a deathless law engraved in the nature of the universe (*Ebr.* 141; *Spec.* 2.13). Nature was the law (θεσμός) which Abraham followed; any person who properly uses the reason with which they were endowed knows the laws and statutes of nature (*Decal.* 132).[3]

Philo, too, is more willing to spell out what exactly the law of nature contains than any other ancient writer. The problem of a law of nature was, and is, always the same: what is its content? Philo makes a number of attempts at defining it. Laws of nature guide the ordering of the planets, of numbers, and of music (*Opif.* 13,54,70). A herd needs a governor according to the law of nature (*Agr.* 31). The law of nature prohibits sleeping with a menstruating woman (*Spec.* 3.32). Passions between the sexes are recognized by the law of nature (*Conf.* 59). Philo gives many more examples and, if his examples seem unconvincing, they nonetheless demonstrate the extent to which in his view the law of nature influences every aspect of life.

---

[2] Myre, "La loi dans l'ordre moral selon Philon d'Alexandrie" in *Science et Esprit* 24 (1972) 95.

[3] This brings us to the question of the relationship between νόμος and θεσμός. There is an acknowledged difference, though it is not clear how the terms differ. There has been no study which compares the use of the two terms or the possible differences between the two terms in Philo's usage. Again, Philo is something of a gold mine when compared to other ancient sources and this vein of thought has not been exploited. According to Colson, *Philo* Vol. 9 in the *LCL*, 509 θεσμός "is more divine" than νόμος and "has a wider scope and is like a general principle." I am not certain that the distinction always holds, however, and at times the terms are interchangeable. This question will be fully examined in chapter 7.

Nothing is free from the constraints and guidance of nature. Nature guides the ethical and physical world (probably Philo would not even make this distinction: where there is life, there is law). The ὀρθὸς λόγος guides human beings no less than the planets and the moon.

In these passages Philo has given to us more explicit statements regarding the law of nature than any previous ancient author, in Greek. This ought to explain Helmut Koester's great hopes for Philo as the originator of the concept of the law of nature.[4] There is a more mundane explanation though. Philo's law of nature is the profoundly meaningful and ethical nature of the Stoics, which guides humankind with its reason, which unites humanity in one common family, and whose laws cross the borders of any given land. The only difference, and it is major, is that nature, and reason, are not the ultimate end: the ultimate end is God. Though nature is said to have invented its laws, God is the ultimate lawgiver.[5] The laws he gave cover the whole of nature's activities.

The links with the Stoic view of natural law are abundant. It is clear that Philo has adopted this view, perhaps from the Middle Platonists, while altering it in a number of ways.[6] Whether these alterations are the work of Philo remains to be seen. Whatever the case, Philo has not simply adopted this view of law haphazardly; he has made it his own. The law of nature forms an integral part of his view of nature, nature's relationship to God, and nature's relationship to other forms of law. Philo employs a view of the law of nature because Philo believes in a law of nature.

God, of course, is Philo's addition.[7] The idea of God, transcending and guiding his creation, is central to Philo's thought. Neither

---

[4] Koester, "νόμος φύσεως."

[5] *Spec.* 1.279. Myre, "La loi dans l'ordre moral" 95; Robert Barraclough, "Philo's Politics, Roman Rule and Hellenistic Judaism" in *ANRW* II.21.1, 512–514.

[6] See Horsley, "Law of Nature in Philo and Cicero" for the view that Philo and Cicero adopted this view of the law of nature from Antiochus of Ascalon. John Dillon, *The Middle Platonists* (London: Duckworth 1977) 80–81 concurs that the law of nature discussion in Cicero, *De leg.* 1 is probably from Antiochus. I am less willing to put a name to the source of Philo's view of the law of nature. If this was Antiochus' view it could very well have been borrowed from the Middle Stoics, Posidonius and Panaetius. I would like to designate Philo's, and Cicero's, view of the law of nature in general as the common view of the Middle Stoics. I do accept Horsley's contention, however, regarding the close relationship of Philo's and Cicero's views on the law of nature.

[7] Horsley argues in "Law of Nature in Philo and Cicero" that Cicero employs

God, nor the Stoic ideas of right reason, the law of nature, and the megalopolis clash in Philo's thought. Philo finds that the Stoic ideas properly explain God's work in nature, without contradicting Jewish creation accounts, and he believes that the Jewish idea of the transcendent God supplies missing information for the Stoic view of nature.

He also preserves something else: accounts of people who have fulfilled the law of nature.[8] This is interesting not only because these accounts are lacking in Stoic sources, but because of how Philo describes these wise men.[9] He differs not in his description of the reason which guides the wise man: like the Stoic sage, Philo's wise men perceive the law of nature through their unique gifts. But in his description of these wise men, he links them to other Greek forms of higher law. In so doing, Philo adds something new to Greek thought on law.

ἄγραφος νόμος: The Unwritten Law

A second form of higher law is the unwritten law. This is, in Greek thought, a vague and fluid concept, given less to definition than even the law of nature. Philo, as is customary, preserves much ancient evidence regarding this concept, in addition to information not extant in other sources.

As the study of unwritten law in the Greek tradition showed, there are two dominant concepts of unwritten law: it can refer to the unwritten customs of a people, or to a law, or laws, which are con-

---

the same idea of a transcendent God, but on this point I am not convinced. Dillon speaks of the difference between the Stoics and the Middle Platonists lying in the difference in the τέλος they chose. For the Stoics, one conformed to nature; the Middle Platonists sought after God. There is no sense of this search for God in the work of Cicero. The *mens diva* from which the law of nature came forth does not suggest a provident, transcendent God.

[8] See W. Richardson, "The Philonic Patriarchs as Νόμος φύσεως" in *Studia Patristica: Texte und Untersuchungen zur Geschichte der altchristlichen Literatur* Vol. 1 (ed. K. Aland and F. L. Cross; Berlin: Akademie Verlag, 1957) 515–525.

[9] Emile Bréhier, *Les Idées philosophiques et religieuses de Philon d'Alexandrie* (Paris: Librairie Philosophique J. Vrin, 1950) 25–26 seems to claim that Cicero (*De Rep.* 2.4) preserves accounts of Roman heroes who did the law before it was written; Cicero's passage regarding Romulus is not at all clear however. It does not speak of the law of any stripe, only Romulus ruling because of his superiority.

sidered universal, but unwritten. The category of universal unwritten law is our major concern, but we will deal initially with unwritten law as custom.

Not only does Philo speak of unwritten law as custom, he defines it for us as such. Philo says that ἔθη, customs, are ἄγραφοι νόμοι, which are in turn the decisions made or approved by the men of old (*Spec.* 4.149f.).[10] They are mores, customs, unspoken and unwritten rules, which may or may not bring punishment if broken, but which would incur for one the status of outcast. According to Philo, the observance of these customs brings praise (*Spec.* 4.150).[11]

In *Her.* 295, Philo again speaks of the unwritten law as custom. In this passage Philo defines it as a part of the law of a city; here, too, he reflects the same view as Aristotle.[12] Philo calls the instructors to sin legion, and includes among these instructors the laws of

---

[10] I. Heinimann, "Die Lehre vom ungeschriebenen Gesetz" in *HUCA* (1928) 149–171; and "Hellenistica" in *Monatsschrift für Geschichte und Wissenschaft des Judentums* 74 (1929) 441; Samuel Sandmel, "Philo's Place in Judaism" in *HUCA* 25 (1954), 226. As to whether Philo speaks of the Jewish "oral law" in this passage, the position of Heinimann and Sandmel is most convincing. (See Wolfson, *Philo* Vol. 1, 188–194 for the position that Philo here refers to the Jewish oral law. More recently Naomi G. Cohen, "The Jewish Dimension of Philo's Judaism—An Elucidation of *de Spec. Leg.* IV 132–150 in *JJS* (1987) 165–186 takes up Wolfson's position. She points out that "unwritten law" in this passage cannot be "natural law," but seems not to be aware of the Greek discussions regarding "unwritten law" as custom. See my response, "Unwritten Law in Philo: A Response to Naomi G. Cohen" in *JJS* (1992) 38–45.) Philo speaks here of unwritten laws in a general sense, not specifically of Jewish oral law. Certainly Philo knows of Jewish customs, Heinimann, "Die Lehre" 159, and he may even have had them in mind at times (see *Legat.* 115); but Sandmel, "Philo's Place" 226, is right to point out that in *Spec.* 4.149 Philo speaks specifically of ἔθη. Is this strong enough to stand for *Halakhot*? It seems not. When Philo is clearly referring to the customs of the Jews, he speaks of the ἄγραφα ἔθη (*Legat.* 115; cf. also with *Hypoth.* 7.6). This is a phrase Philo uses perhaps with the specific intent of referring to Jewish customs. But I am still not convinced that Philo is referring to Palestinian custom and not Alexandrian custom. See also E. Mary Smallwood, *Philonis Alexandrini: Legatio ad Gaium* (Leiden: E. J. Brill 1961) 208–209. Cohen has revised and updated her argument in her 1995 book *Philo Judaeus: His Universe of Discourse* and no longer claims that "unwritten law" must refer to the law of nature. She has, however, brought forward more evidence for the connection between Palestinian *Halakhah* and Philonic interpretation and Alexandrian Jewish practice, though I am not convinced that this *Halakhah* is what Philo refers to when he speaks of "unwritten law." See further discussion in *Appendix 2*.

[11] Sandmel, "Philo's Place" 227, points out the close connection to Aristotle, *Rhet.* 1.14,7. Philo seems to be reliant on this passage. Sandmel seems to be off track, though, when he claims that Philo is here speaking of the law of nature; he is still discussing the ἔθη of the previous passage.

[12] Aristotle, *Rhet.* 1.14,7; cf. also *Rhet.* 1.10,8, 1.13,1–7, 1.13,18.

cities, written and unwritten. This division was defined by Aristotle, and the presence of the division in this passage removes this mention of unwritten law from consideration as universal law, as does, quite obviously, Philo's claim that these unwritten laws lead to sin.[13]

On two occasions Philo speaks of the ἄγραφα ἔθη (*Legat.* 115; *Hypoth.* 7.6) as a part of the law by which the Jews are guided.[14] These may indeed be the oral laws of the Jews, but it is doubtful that Philo has in mind particular Rabbinic or Palestinian laws. He is most likely referring to Alexandrian Jewish customs, or Jewish customs in general. His intention in both these passages is probably apologetic, namely, he wants to demonstrate that the Jews too follow the customs of their elders. Philo uses the term ἔθη in both passages and it is not an accident; had Philo intended to state that these practices were the equivalent of law he would have designated them as νόμοι (or perhaps θεσμοί). Custom should not contradict nature (*Ebr.* 18), though it can (*Decal.* 136), but it does not occupy the same level as law.

Philo does use unwritten law to denote eternal, or divine law, but his uniqueness in this respect has not yet been fully noted and stressed. Philo is unique in two major respects: he links the unwritten law directly to the law of nature; and he claims, in an idiosyncratic use of the term, that certain people *are* unwritten laws. Though scholars today, beginning with Rudolph Hirzel, often connect the law of nature with the unwritten law, and it is clear there are connections between the two concepts, only Philo did so explicitly in the ancient world. He, too, is the only one who designated people as "unwritten laws."

The patriarchs followed the law of nature (*Prob.* 62; *Abr.* 5–6,276; *Mos.* 2.13). This is the highest and the best law. They followed this law without need of instruction: they relied upon reason. Following Aristotle (*Pol.* 3.8,1–2) and the Stoics (Diogenes Laertius 7.125), Philo

---

[13] I doubt that it ever even crossed Philo's mind that the Mosaic law could lead to sin, yet it remains interesting that Philo claims that law in general could lead to sin. Is it only coincidence that Paul and Philo claim that law leads to sin? Or was this a *topos* in the Greco-Roman legal tradition? In the same passage Philo lists παιδαγωγοί as a cause of sin. Paul links the παιδαγωγός and the law when he discusses the sin which the law leads to (Gal. 3:23–26). Was either of these men the first to do so?

[14] Cf. *supra*, 17. The *Rhetorica ad Alexandrum* also contains the phrase ἄγραφον ἔθος, but there it refers to eternal law.

claims that there is no reason to give laws to the perfect man (*Leg.* 2.94).¹⁵ Virtue is a law itself (*Leg.* 3.245). These perfect men are basically laws themselves. Philo, however, gives them a title: those who have followed the law of nature *are* unwritten laws (ἄγραφοι νόμοι). They follow the unwritten law, but more than that, they become the unwritten law. An "unwritten law" is the product of following the law of nature. *De Abrahamo* is called the first book on unwritten law, that is, on Abraham himself (*Abr.* 1–5).

Men such as Abraham are the originals of which the laws are copies (*Abr.* 3); in the same way, Philo calls the written laws copies of the law of nature (*Mos.* 2.13,51). Abraham is the law of nature, for which Philo uses the term unwritten law in a unique way. The enacted laws are memorials to these men, these ἄγραφοι νόμοι or physical representations of the law of nature (*Abr.* 5–6).¹⁶ By following unwritten nature (ἀγράφῳ τῇ φύσει),¹⁷ Philo says that Abraham became a law himself and a θεσμὸς ἄγραφος (*Abr.* 276).¹⁸ In two other passages Philo concentrates on this sense of unwritten law. In *De Decalogo* Philo introduces the tractate by stating that he will now concentrate on the written laws, since he has already discussed the patriarchs, or unwritten laws (*Decal.* 1). Philo describes the lives of those who follow virtue, elsewhere described as the law of nature (*Leg.* 3.245), as unwritten laws (*Virt.* 194).

---

¹⁵ Cf. Dio Chrysostom, 76.4.

¹⁶ Hirzel, *Agraphos* 17, is the only one who mentions the oddness of Philo's usage of ἄγραφος νόμος. He believes it may stem from Stoic influence, but it is not clear how. Perhaps he intimates that the Stoic sage embodied the law of nature, but it is not clear how this leads to a similarity with Philo's designation.

¹⁷ This is an odd phrase, "unwritten nature"; it is probably influenced by ἄγραφος θεσμός later in the passage. It may parallel the "law of nature" = "nature" conception, namely, "unwritten law" = "unwritten nature."

¹⁸ Θεσμός ἄγραφος, which can only be translated as "unwritten law," deserves a word. Victor Ehrenberg, *Sophocles and Pericles* 169 has said that one never sees this phrase because of the divine connotations of θεσμός, yet here it is. Philo uses θεσμός often, and often to refer to divine laws, or laws from God (*Prob.* 3; *Her.* 168; *Congr.* 120). Horsley, "Law of Naure in Philo and Cicero" claims that the use of θεσμός at this historical juncture was influenced by the Middle Platonists. Was this phrase borrowed from the Middle Platonists? Or is this Philo's creation? It is hard to imagine that it can mean anything more than ἄγραφος νόμος. The same is true of θεσμός φύσεως (e.g., *Legat.* 68; *Ios.* 30; *Spec.* 1.202; 2.233), the phrase must be the equivalent of the νόμος φύσεως. While Philo seems on occasion to observe distinctions between θεσμός and νόμος, in terms of the higher law the distinctions must have been broken down. The question is explored at length in chapter 7.

Philo gives to us the second meaning of unwritten law in *De Abrahamo* too. He says that there are those who are led to hopefulness by unwritten law, a law which is given by nature, not by written law.

> Great indeed are the efforts expended both by lawgivers and by laws in every nation in filling the souls of free men with comfortable hopes; but he who gains this virtue of hopefulness without being led to it by exhortation or command has been educated into it by a law which nature has laid down, a law unwritten yet intuitively learnt (*Abr.* 16).

Philo makes clear the obvious implications from other passages: the unwritten law is not only the physical representative of the law of nature, but it is the law of nature itself. Of course, a physical representation of the law of nature is the law of nature, but here the connection is made explicit.

Philo has given a number of twists to the concept of the unwritten law. He ties unwritten law directly to the law of nature; by describing the patriarchs as unwritten laws he makes the connection even tighter. These two forms of higher law seem to make sense together, at least to us, but they were developed discretely and no one in the ancient Greek world found a way of bringing them together. Of course, it may simply be that no one in the Greek world had a need to bring these two concepts together. Philo did have a need, which we will argue more explicitly in the next chapter, and he found a way.

The law of nature remains the dominant concept, unwritten law becomes an adjunct to it. Unwritten law, a vague concept which usually denotes one or two eternal laws in Greek discussions, becomes a concrete idea, whose content is determined by the law of nature. An unwritten law is the law of nature, but more importantly for Philo, a person who has followed the law of nature. Two discrete concepts have subtly overlapped: when Philo speaks of men who are unwritten laws or of eternal unwritten law, the content of these laws is determined by the law of nature.

νόμος ἔμψυχος: *The Living Law*

There is a third category of higher law which may also undermine the ascendant character of the law of Moses, or material law in general; this is the concept of the νόμος ἔμψυχος. This Hellenistic

Pythagorean ideal contrasts the king, the friend of God, with the written law. For his subjects, the king replaces the law and becomes the law himself. Philo is, again, both a source and an originator. As a source, he gives us much information on the living law concept; as an originator, he again draws the concepts of higher law together, in this case connecting the unwritten law and the law of nature with the living law ideal.[19]

Νόμος ἔμψυχος appears in *De Abrahamo* 5. This passage makes clear the close relationship between all forms of higher law in Philo's work. The patriarchs have already been described as unwritten laws and men who live according to nature, when Philo describes them as ἔμψυχοι καὶ λογικοὶ νόμοι (*Abr.* 5). By living in conformity with nature, that is, by following the law of nature, one becomes a νόμος ἔμψυχος.[20] The terms of higher law have become in the hands of Philo almost interchangeable.

There is another result. Whereas Philo gave the unwritten law more form by connecting it to the law of nature, by connecting the living law ideal to the law of nature, Philo drains the powerful kingship concept of most of its power. The king, who was once the unique creation of God, becomes in Philo's hands the one who follows the law of nature.

Yet the concept of the living law has all the implications it has in the Hellenistic fragments, at least in the case of Moses. The "kingly" and unique aspects of the ideal are not lost on Philo. Moses was a king, and more specifically, he was the νόμος ἔμψυχος.[21] Long before he became a lawgiver, he was a νόμος ἔμψυχος τε καὶ λογικός (*Mos.* 1.162). He was a king because of his goodness (εὔνοια) (148); he was a hater of evil (μισοπόνηρος) by nature (149) and his goal was to benefit his subjects (151). He enjoyed, too, a close relationship with God. The kingly office was an office which God bestowed upon him (148). It was bestowed because of his justness (δικαιοσύνη)

---

[19] Archytas (*Stob.* 4.1.132) makes at least one connection which Philo may have drawn upon through intermediaries. He speaks of the unwritten law influencing the law on earth, which may either be the written law or the king. In this case, however, the unwritten law and the living law are not the same concept.

[20] This connection could have been influenced by the Stoic conception of "every good man is king," which was then adopted to the Pythagorean model of kingship. Whether this connection was first made by Philo remains to be seen.

[21] Goodenough, *Politics* 90–100; Bréhier, *Les Idées* 18–19; Meeks, *The Prophet-King* 109–111.

(154). He was considered a partner (κοινωνός) of God (155; cf. 158). The elements obeyed him because he was a friend of God (156). His closeness to God made him a model for other men (158), "beautiful and godlike," to imitate (μιμέομαι) the better (159). His subjects also are said to emulate (ζηλωταί) him (160).[22]

The passage in *Mos.* 1.148–62 is Philo's greatest example of the Hellenistic kingship ideal. Every element of the νόμος ἔμψυχος ideal, but one, is present in Philo's portrayal, as well as a smattering of what may be categorized as Cynic-Stoic kingship traits.[23] The only thing missing is the contrast between the king as law and the written law. This is no accident. It is partly due to the fact that Moses has yet to be described as the lawgiver, and partially because Philo has found a way to solve the contrast.[24]

When Philo does describe Moses as the lawgiver in *Mos.* 2.4 a part of the puzzle which was missing is revealed. Since it is the king's duty to command right and wrong, Philo says, and since this is the function of the law, it follows for Philo, and the νόμος ἔμψυχος ideal, that

> the king is a living law, and the law is a just king.[25]

---

[22] On another occasion Philo calls Moses θέος (*Sacr.* 9). This is probably inspired by the designation in the Hebrew Bible. Meeks, *The Prophet-King* 104–105 claims that in this passage Moses appears to share consubstantiality with God. Goodenough, *Politics* 99–100 rightly insists that Moses is not the supreme being and likens Philo's view to Ecphantus. I would liken it to Diotogenes' (and Aristotle's) view that the king is a "god to men." Meeks does later say that Moses' "godhood" appears to be only figurative (105). Cf. *Mos.* 2.288–292; *Virt.* 73–75; *Det.* 161–162. See also Mendelson, *Secular Education* 54.

[23] Ragnar Höistad, *Cynic Hero and Cynic King: Studies in the Cynic Conception of Man* (Uppsala: Lund, 1948) 181–201.

[24] Meeks, *The Prophet-King* 111,130 points out that Moses as a prophet and mystic is found only in Philo's portrait of Moses as king, and not in Hellenistic portraits. This is certainly true of Moses as a prophet, but I believe the living law ideal paints its kings as mystics. Goodenough, *Politics* 97 says Moses as the high priest is also an innovation. We must, however, consider Diotogenes' passages (*Stob.* 4.7,61–264,1; 265,1–12) in which he describes the king, in Doric, as θεραπεύειν θεώς (264,1) and θεραπεύεν τὼς θεώς (265,1). This may be translated as "one who does service to the gods" or "one who worships the gods." The king is referred to in these passages as a θεραπεύειν θεώς in the context of a description of his official roles, i.e., military leader and judge, and so one can consider this role as official too. In this case it may refer to the king as priest.

Meeks also points to the contacts between Hellenistic kingship and the Biblical portrait of kings (131). This contact is certainly present, but contacts exist among all forms of ideal kingship in the ancient world.

[25] Compare this language to Diotogenes in *Stob.* 4.7,61–263,15–19 and Plutarch,

For Philo, if not for Diotogenes and Plutarch, whose descriptions of the king are similar to Philo's linguistically, this means that the king also fulfilled the law of nature, for the living law lived in conformity with the law of nature. Even more, as we shall see, there is no contradiction between the living law and the written law because in Philo's unity of law there is only agreement. This is the other part of the puzzle, but it is a piece that cannot yet be put into place.

Philo describes Moses as the true King.[26] Were there any others? It is clear that everyone who fulfilled the law of nature, who was an unwritten law, was classified as a νόμος ἔμψυχος.[27] In Philo's scheme of the unity of law this was only necessary. The living law as the embodiment of the law of nature was Philo's creation, and there existed more than one such embodiment. Nevertheless, when Philo describes Moses in terms of the "living law" ideal, as a king, the specific kingship language he uses is reserved only for Moses.[28] That is, in terms of the full ideal, only Moses meets the requirements of the Hellenistic king, or is described in terms of such a king.[29]

Ad Principem Ineruditem. 780e. I. Heinimann, *Philons griechische* 195 points out the similarity between the portrayals of kingship in Philo and Plutarch.

[26] God of course is the "true" King in Philo's work, as in the νόμος ἔμψυχος fragments. Cf. Goodenough, *Politics* 90–91.

[27] Barraclough, "Philo's Politics. Roman Rule and Hellenistic Judaism" in *ANRW* II 21.1 520–521 says that four men are called kings: Moses; Adam (*Opif.* 148); Melchizedek (*Leg.* 3.79); Abraham (*Virt.* 212–218). Only Moses fits the unique role of the νόμος ἔμψυχος. Abraham is not described by one of the terms of the living law ideal of kingship.

Goodenough has argued that Joseph incorporates the Pythagorean ideal of kingship (see Barraclough, "Philo's Politics" 449), but the entire ideal is certainly not present.

W. Richardson, "The Philonic Patriarchs" is able to uncover very little material that coincides with the Pythagorean ideal beyond Moses. Philo's kingship in general is based upon Hellenistic models (Heinimann, *Philons griechische* 182–186) and the idea of the Stoic-Cynic sage, who is also the king, is also present (D. L. Thiede, *The Charismatic Figure as Miracle Worker* (SBLDS 1; Missoula, Mont.: Scholars Press, 1973) 119–125), but only Moses is the unique living law king. (The superiority of Moses in relation to the other patriarchs is stressed by Meeks, *The Prophet-King* 102–103.) The "living law," which every sage is by definition, is a watered down version of the ideal when it is not applied to Moses: it basically means the one who fulfils the law of nature. Only Moses is the kingly living law.

[28] Francesca Calabi, *The Language and the Law of God: Interpretation and Politics in Philo of Alexandria*. South Florida Studies in the History of Judaism 188. (Atlanta: Scholars Press, 1998), 7–10.

[29] The special portrait of Moses as the living law, of course, agrees with the portrayal in other contexts of Moses as the most perfect sage (*Sacr.* 8–9). Moses' special status must in part be due to the fact that he alone was the lawgiver. It is in

The living law ideal speaks of a man, a king, a special being existing between man and God: only Moses has this rare status.³⁰ Only Moses is described according to the full details of the νόμος ἔμψυχος ideal. Philo seems to maintain a distinction between the living law as the sage who fulfils the law of nature, and Moses as the living law, the true king, the friend of God.³¹ This distinction speaks not only of Philo's high regard for Moses, but, more importantly for our purposes, of Philo's awareness of how he is using and changing the concepts of higher law.³² He maintains the distinctiveness of the unique king in his portrait of Moses, but reduces the νόμος ἔμψυχος to the sense of sage in his portraits of the other patriarchs.

The important additions that Philo has made to the νόμος ἔμψυχος ideal, apart from casting the "living laws" all in the past,³³ are the connection to the unwritten law and the law of nature, completing his unity of all forms of higher law, the claim that every sage is a νόμος ἔμψυχος, and his silence on the major component of the living law ideal: the conflict between the written law and the living law.

These considerations obtain at almost a theoretical level, but his thought on the relationship between these higher forms of law and

---

the context of the discussion of Moses as the lawgiver (*Mos.* 2.4), that Philo refers to him as the living law. No other Patriarch was a lawgiver. Mendelson, *Secular Education* 53, stresses Moses' superiority to the other Patriarchs.

³⁰ From the fragmentary discussions of Isaac in Philo's work—a treatise on Isaac is not extant—it is clear that Isaac had a special status between man and God. Goodenough, *By Light, Light* 153–166, reviews the evidence. Nevertheless the fragmentary discussions do not describe Isaac as a νόμος ἔμψυχος and it is difficult to argue from silence that his possible status as a νόμος ἔμψυχος rivals that of Moses.

³¹ Abraham is also described in kingly terms, but even he seems to lag behind Moses. In the description of Abraham as the perfect proselyte, he is twice called a king (*Virt.* 211–219), which the LXX also does. His perfection is more than human (217), and he was granted his sovereignty by God (218), but he appears to be less than Moses. Of course, he is in some way a king, and he is a living law; the distinction between Moses and the others lies not with the weakness of the other patriarchs, but with Moses' unique closeness to God. He is the one Philo describes as the νόμος ἔμψυχος in full and the only one described as king and living law in the same passage. For instance, none of the terms of the Pythagorean kingship ideal are found in this description of Abraham. This ought to be somewhat surprising. Cf. D. L. Thiede, *The Charismatic Figure* 120.

³² One remembers the uniqueness of the living law in the Hellenistic Pythagorean fragments; he is like the rest of humanity only in bodily form.

³³ That is, Philo is not writing for actual or present-day kings. Though he would, of course, desire that all kings follow the example of Moses.

material law enters the world of daily practice with a passion. How did higher law relate to the law of Moses? How did the higher law relate to other forms of material law? What was the relationship between the law of Moses and, for instance, the law of Rome? Greek discussions of all these terms implied an inferiority of the written law. Does Philo imply such? Philo is far from only a theoretical thinker when he answers these questions. His answers tell us not only about the theory of law he created, but the practical reasons as to why the unity of higher law is so important to him.

The Law of Moses

Law comes from God. God is the true lawgiver (*Sacr.* 131; *Det.* 68; *Mos.* 2.48; *QE* 1.42; *Spec.* 2.129).[34] In saying this, Philo claims something no other Greek writer could, or dared to do. The lawgiver of a given city was looked upon with honour and respect,[35] but however highly they esteemed their law, and claimed for it even nourishment from the gods, no one would claim divine authorship for their legal code.[36] This allows Philo to claim something else as well: an eternal law, given by God, which was the model for the Jewish written code.[37] This eternal law in its highest manifestation is the law of nature.[38]

---

[34] Myre, "Les caractéristiques de la loi mosäique selon Philon d'Alexandrie" in *Science et Esprit* 25 (1973) 37, 67; Adele Reinhartz, "The Meaning of νόμος in Philo's *Exposition of the Law*" in *SR* 15/3 (1986) 340.

[35] There is a sense of divine inspiration in the giving of Greek law, but it does not reach the level of the Mosaic law's divine origin. Lycurgus, for instance, the Spartan lawgiver, was found to be inspired at the Oracle at Delphi and his laws were given divine imprimatur, but they were not given by the gods. In fact, both Plutarch (*Lycurgus* 4.1) and Herodotus (1.65,66) share the notion that his laws may have come from Crete. Draco's laws were overthrown, except for the law of homicide, by the introduction of Solon's laws (Aristotle, *Athen. Const.*, 7.1). Solon hoped his laws would be obeyed for 100 years (Aristotle, *Athen. Const.*, 7.2; Plutarch, *Solon*, 25.1). Plutarch says that when someone asked Solon if he had "enacted the best laws for the Athenians, he replied, 'the best they would receive'" (Plutarch, *Solon*, 15.2). Bréhier, *Les Idées* 16, 18.

[36] Myre, "Les caractéristiques de la loi mosäique" 37, 67.

[37] Ibid., 67. The primary characteristic of the Mosaic law is its divine origin.

[38] Cicero, *De Leg.* 2.10 claims that law came into existence at the same time as the divine mind. In Cicero's view, the law of nature holds equal status with Philo's law of nature. They differ in the relation of the law of nature to written law.

The Mosaic law, therefore, as E. R. Goodenough,[39] Samuel Sandmel,[40] André Myre,[41] and others have pointed out,[42] seems to exist below the law of nature in Philo's hierarchy of law. The law of nature exists in the realm of the Logos, and is, in some ways, the Logos.[43] This gives it an ontological status somewhat higher than the law of Moses, for the law of Moses, a written law and a law which exists in corruptible nature, is a copy, albeit a true one, of the law of nature.[44] What this actually means for Philo in practical terms has never truly been determined. What is the place of the Mosaic law? Is it, as Goodenough has argued a law which is finally to be transcended? A law which is ultimately superfluous? A law which can even be called "bad"?[45]

Two things should be clear: the law of Moses is the only law that the vast majority of people would ever need; and it is the best written law by far. The discussion of the relationship between the law of Moses and forms of higher law is not theoretical, but it is limited. Philo did not foresee a great number of people who could fulfil the law of nature; in this he is at one with his Greek sources. The material law, the law of Moses in this case, is the law which the ordinary person must observe; and in observing it, the ordinary person is performing the best written law that Philo could imagine.

In Philo's scheme of law, the performance of the law of Moses means something unique and special. While Cicero complained that the Roman civil law was only an outline sketch of the law of nature (*De Off.* 3.69), Philo claimed something else: the Jews had an actual copy of the law of nature (*Opif.* 3,69,71; *Abr.* 3; *Mos.* 2.11,13,48).

---

[39] Goodenough, *By Light, Light* 73–96.
[40] Samuel Sandmel, "Philo's Place" 225–228.
[41] Myre, "Le Loi de la Nature" 176f.
[42] Kleinknecht and Gutbrod, "νόμος" in *TDNT* IV, 1052–1054; Charles Bigg, *The Christian Platonists of Alexandria* (Oxford: Clarendon Press 1913) 49.
[43] Myre, "La loi dans l'ordre cosmique et politique selon Philon d'Alexandrie" in *Science et Esprit* 24 (1972) 222–224.
[44] Myre, "La loi de la nature" 168.
[45] Goodenough, *By Light, Light* 92–93: "Only in comparison with 'acute and seeing Nature' could Philo have called any great body of racial laws 'bad.' But in contrast with the higher reality, even the Jewish Code would become an impediment, a thing to be run away from, and bad." Goodenough also uses terms such as "inadequacy" (88), "to be transcended" (92), "inferior" (95) to describe the Mosaic law in relation to the law of nature. Even with his qualification of these terms, his choice of words is unfortunate.

Not for Philo an outline sketch. Philo's world could admit no such contradictions. God gave the law to Moses; God also created the world and with it the law of nature. The law of Moses, divinely given, could in no way contradict the law of nature, divinely implanted in the world at creation.[46] Philo is thus able to claim more than any Greek or Roman author could or would. Cicero was compelled to say that

> the civil law is not necessarily also the universal law; but the universal law ought to be also the civil law. But we possess no substantial, life-like image of true Law and genuine Justice; a mere outline sketch is all that we enjoy (*De Off.* 3.69).

Philo was given leeway which the Stoics, for instance, did not possess. He was able to argue that the world was in harmony with the law of nature, and the law in harmony with the world. So far, Philo is in line with Stoic claims. Philo could add, however, because of the role of a transcendent God in the giving of the written law something the Stoics could not, namely, that the law of Moses, a particular written law, is in full agreement with the law of nature.[47] Moses' account of creation in Genesis implies

> that the world is in harmony with the Law, and the Law with the world, and that the man who observes the law is constituted thereby a loyal citizen of the world (κοσμοπολίτης), regulating his doings by the purpose and will of Nature, in accordance with which the entire world itself also is administered (*Opif.* 3).

The law of Moses is, therefore, a written code unlike any other.

Philo's mighty claims for the Mosaic law do not stop here. God's role in giving the law of Moses also allows Philo to place its prominence above other laws.[48] Philo echoes at one point the long-standing debate in Greek circles concerning law and nature. He claims that

---

[46] Bernhard Lohse, *Askese und Mönchtum in der Antike und in der alten Kirche* (Munich: Oldenbourg 1969) 110.

[47] Myre, "Les caractéristiques" 67 points to the tension of this claim when he says, "la caracterè historique de la révélation s'oppose à sa préexistence." This is, indeed, Philo's greatest problem with the relationship between the forms of law, even if we accept, as I will argue shortly, that the greatest difference between the two laws does not rest with the laws so much as with the people who do the law. Cf. Federico Pastor, "Libertad helénica y libertad paulina" in *Miscelanea Comillas* 37 (1979) 232.

[48] Cf. Mendelson, *Philo's Jewish Identity* 130–131,134.

the current view is that man created laws, that is, that they are conventional, arbitrary, and not based in the real nature of things (*Leg.* 3.3). The odd thing is, Philo would agree with this statement in regard to almost any form of material law but one: Moses' law is special. It is stamped with the seals of nature and is, therefore, immortal (*Mos.* 2.13). Moses' laws are given by the voice of God (*Mos.* 2.34). His laws are oracles of God (*Decal.* 15; *Legat.* 210). The most faithful picture of the world polity (*Mos.* 2.51), the law of Moses is a law for the whole world (*QE* 2.42).

Because Philo traces the law directly back to God he can say not only that the Mosaic law is the best law, but in truth the only law worth following.[49] This allows Philo not only to tout the virtues of the law, but to deride other forms of law.

Moses' law, he says, embraces the multitude of particular laws, all other state and city codes (*Congr.* 120). Anything which is correct about any other code of law, therefore, is already found in the Mosaic law. To put it another way, if it does not agree with the Mosaic code, it is not really law.[50] At the same time, the rules of the Jews run counter to those of other nations (*Mos.* 1.87). The differences between the law of Moses and other law codes is not a matter of preference, or relative to the culture; only the Mosaic law contains the truth, or the full measure of truth. Philo claims, rather hopefully, that the acknowledged truth of the Mosaic law has won it wide respect.

Moses' laws won fame (*Mos.* 1.1; 2.20) and he was the best of all lawgivers (*Mos.* 2.12). Almost every other people honours and respects the Mosaic law (*Mos.* 2.17,43).[51] The law leads those who follow it to be kind to neighbours (*Spec.* 2.104). The proselyte who obeys the Mosaic law, much like the Stoic wise man, becomes immediately temperate, continent, modest, etc. (*Virt.* 182). In short, he obtains the virtues.

Some of these claims certainly answer polemic directed against the Jews, that they are misanthropic for instance (*Legat.* 353; *Contempl.* 24),[52] or indulge in apologetic on behalf of his people (*Legat.* 115–117;

---

[49] Bréhier, *Les Idées* 11,16.
[50] Myre, "La loi dans l'ordre cosmique" 233–236.
[51] Philo also knew the truth: in *Spec.* 4.179 he states that few accepted Jewish law.
[52] A full list of the types of anti-semitic charges brought against the Jews in Philo's day is found in Josephus, *Contra Apion*, 1.223–320, 2.1–296 (esp. 1.309 and 2.148 on the specific charge of misanthropy).

Prob. 75–87). Who could blame Philo, given the precarious position of the Jews in Alexandria in his day? Yet Philo is not only dealing in a game of philosophical one-upmanship, an attempt to prove that the Jewish law is better than other codes of law, which was a common enough practice in his day,[53] he is involved in the logical, and necessary outcome of his philosophical thought. The Mosaic law, as the true and reasonable copy of the law of nature, must be superior necessarily to those laws which are not. Now, as Philo says in *Legatio ad Gaium* 277, all peoples love their own laws; it is just that their own laws fall short of the ideal.

What Philo claims for the Mosaic law is something special, but it is dependent upon his view of a transcendent God and his role in the creation of nature and law. Philo's grand claims for the law of Moses have far-reaching implications: other law codes are reduced not to Ciceronian sketches, but mere scribbles.

Other Codes of Law

Philo observes that laws, customs, and ways of life are not regarded universally (*Ebr.* 193). In *De Iosepho* 29–31, he goes into some depth explaining the differences among peoples and their laws and notes again that laws among various peoples are not identical. Philo's observances are not great insights. His conclusions, however, are quite distinctive. These law codes are "additions" to nature and inventions. These additions to nature keep people and states apart, for covetousness for their own law leads them to call "laws" whatever is advantageous to them. These laws of various states are additions to the right reason of nature, a copy of which is located in the Mosaic law.[54]

Not every single law is an addition, of course, for some single laws agree with the law of Moses.[55] This, however, is the criterion: they must agree with the law of Moses. Zeno, for instance, according to Philo, drew some of his laws from the law of Moses (*Prob.*

---

[53] Thiede, *Charismatic Figure* 101.
[54] Myre, "La loi dans l'ordre cosmique" 236–238, 245. A law, if it is real law, must agree with the law of nature. All people are subject to this law. Cicero said the same thing, but how could he tell which law was truly law?
[55] Cf. *Abr.* 16. In this passage Philo acknowledges the benefits of law in general.

57). So, too, did Heraclitus (*QG* 4.152) and Socrates (*QG* 2.6; *Spec.* 4.61). This kind of claim was common among the Greeks themselves, but it allows us to surmise that a law was only a law to the extent that it agreed with the Mosaic law.[56] This exception shows how far Philo's rejection of the law of others went.[57]

Conclusions

There is a hierarchy of law which mirrors the hierarchy of nature. Nature is the guide by which we measure law. The law of nature is, in fact, the dictates of nature, otherwise expressed as the Logos or Right Reason. The Logos guides all nature, plants and animals as well as man.

The one who follows the law of nature is called both a living law and an unwritten law. The unity of all these forms of law is unique to Philo. Also unique are the altered meanings these forms of law have in Philo's hands. Part of the alteration is simply the result of the synonymy of these terms in the work of Philo, but part is the result of his originality and his need for unity among concepts of law.

The law of nature was created before the Mosaic law and it is higher than the written law, although it is still not clear what this means. One may follow nature, guided by reason, and so fulfil the law of nature, or one may follow the law of Moses.

Yet, human beings, alone among the creation, have the ability to "add" to or pervert their nature.[58] Philo is not unique in the ancient world in claiming that this is so, but he is unique in his ability to say what exactly is and is not according to the law of nature. This

---

[56] Goodenough, *The Jurisprudence of the Jewish Courts in Egypt* (New Haven: Yale University Press, 1929) 214; Barraclough, "Philo's Politics" 485. There is no disputing Goodenough's claim that in practice Philo actually borrowed from Gentile law. Even Goodenough admits, however, that Philo himself would have never admitted it (214–215). I doubt he even thought of it consciously.

[57] Mendelson, *Philo's Jewish Identity* 27–28 points out the ambivalence Philo had, in fact, for the law of others. He refers specifically to *Ebr.* 36–37, 80–81 in which Philo seems to accept, or tolerate, for practical purposes other people's laws. Mendelson observes: "this is the reasoning of a man who has made his peace, possibly after a long struggle, with harsh realities."

[58] Calabi, *The Language and the Law of God*, 14.

is because the law of Moses, given by God, is the true copy of the law of nature. As a result, Philo is also able to judge other law codes wrong-headed and misguided on very specific grounds. The yardstick, the Mosaic law, is the rule to which all other forms of law must measure up.

Philo creates his unity of law, first by relating all forms of higher law to one another, and second by connecting the law of Moses tightly to the law of nature. How they relate, what it means in practical terms, is still not clear. Negatively, it means that any form of material law other than the law of Moses is no law at all, or only law insofar as it agrees with the law of Moses.

The unity, of course, is a result of Philo's use of all three forms of higher law in Greek legal thought. He alters "unwritten law" to signify one who follows the law of nature and who becomes its embodiment. The "living law" comes to mean not only one who is the king, but the one who follows the law of nature. These forms of law find their content in the law of nature.

What becomes of the law of nature? Philo has claimed it is found in the law of Moses. What does this mean in practical terms? Does it mean that the law of Moses is a substitute for the law of nature? That the person who follows the law of Moses observes the law of nature? Or does it in fact reduce the worth of the law of Moses? Does the law of nature become the way to the exclusion of the law of Moses? Should the law of Moses be cast off? Is it finally superfluous?

Philo is, naturally, not explicit on the topic, but he preserves two forms of information which may help to determine the truth. He preserves claims of people who have actually followed the law of nature. This is interesting not only for the claim itself, but because it allows us to study the relation of the law of Moses to the law of nature. If you have one, do you need the other? He also preserves information on all forms of higher law, which may be successfully compared to the law of Moses. What does it actually mean that the law of nature is "higher" than the law of Moses? Does it imply a change in the law? Or a true understanding of the law of Moses?

CHAPTER SIX

THE UNITY OF THE LAW

It is true, many commentators agree, that the law of nature is a higher form of law than the law of Moses in the work of Philo.[1] While these commentators admit readily that Philo speaks of the harmony between the law of Moses and the law of nature (*Opif.* 2–3; *Decal.* 1; *Abr.* 4–6; *Mos.* 2.12,14,48,51–52,211; *Spec.* 2.163; 4.164,179; *QE* 2.42) and the superiority of the Mosaic law in relation to other human codes of law (*Spec.* 4.179), they point to other statements, or implicit claims within the statements which reflect the harmony of the law of Moses and the law of nature, which, they believe, reflect its inferiority. The inferiority, or secondary status, of the law of Moses, they say, stems from the superiority of the law of nature (*Migr.* 94; *Abr.* 4–6; *QG* 4.184; *QE* 2.19), the inherent inferiority of any "copy" of an "original" in the work of Philo (*Opif.* 130; *Mos.* 2.11,14,51–52; *Spec.* 4.164; *Praem.* 29; *Plant.* 132; *QE* 2.42), and the ability of some special people to follow the law of nature without a written code (*Leg.* 1.94; 3.144; *Abr.* 4–6; *Spec.* 2.42–48), an ability which is superior to the act of following the written code (*Det.* 66–68; *Migr.* 46–52, 174–175; *Somn.* 1.191; *Virt.* 94; *QE* 2.19). It is also true that the inferiority of the written law is implied in Greek discussions of higher law.

Yet, Philo claims, the law of Moses is the true copy of the law of nature. In what way is the law of nature "higher" than the law of Moses? In what way is it different and more desirable? How can commentators claim that the Mosaic law is ultimately to be transcended by the special few? Or that such transcendence is desirable? Such transcendence follows from Greco-Roman discussions of the law of nature, but how does one transcend the law of Moses?

---

[1] There is a long history of this reading in modern Philonic scholarship: Charles Bigg, *The Christian Platonists of Alexandria* 49; E. R. Goodenough, *By Light, Light* 73–96, esp. 87f.; Sidney Sowers, *The Hermeneutics of Philo and Hebrews* (Richmond, Virginia: John Knox Press 1965) 44–48, esp. 48; Sandmel, "Philo's Place in Judaism" 109; André Myre, "La Loi de la Nature" 176f.; Kleinknecht and Gutbrod, "Νόμος" in *TDNT* IV 1052–1054.

The question, if limited, is not theoretical: Philo knew of people who fulfilled the law of nature, and the continuing existence of the law of nature and the example of the Patriarchs imply that there could always be more. It is also true that in Greek sources the written law may be discarded if one follows the law of nature; moreover, the "living law" was able to replace the written law. The question, then, bears asking: did Philo consider the law of Moses superfluous for some people in some instances?

Who Follows the Law?

The Mosaic law was the way for almost everyone; the law was to be observed, its precepts followed. While Philo could soar when he spoke of nature, or God, or even of law, he could also plant his feet firmly on the ground. In *Legatio ad Gaium* Philo says that penalties are good for the morals of the multitude who (presumably) keep the law because they do not wish to suffer penalties for disobedience (7).

The best reason to follow the Mosaic law, according to Philo, is because one understands the purpose of the law, even loves the law, and realizes that the law dictates what is best according to our nature. The law should be in one's heart, not only on one's lips (*Praem.* 82). Philo would rather have the law performed because it is good and just, not because observance is compelled. But if worst comes to worst, compulsion is not without merit.

Philo does not reduce the law to one or two commands. He maintains the unity of the Mosaic law:

> The legislation is in some sense a unified creature, which one should view from all sides in its entirety with open eyes and examine the intention of the entire writing exactly, truly and clearly, not cutting up its harmony or dividing its unity (*QG* 3.3).

While Philo is also capable of distinguishing between the letter of the law and the inner meaning of the law (*Agr.* 157), and the inner meaning is clearly more important,[2] Philo does not reduce the law

---

[2] Sandmel, *A Jewish Understanding of the New Testament* (New York: KTAV 1974) 66 says that Philo "has a feeling of condescension, bordering on contempt" for those who only perform the literal law. This may be too strong, but there is definitely a pronounced sense of the superiority of those who follow the law of nature. This problem will be discussed throughout this chapter.

to its "inner" meaning. He fights against such a reduction (*Migr.* 92–93). One must follow the law.

The good fortune of the Jews is that they have a true copy of the law of nature (*Mos.* 2.13,51). For the vast majority of people, this copy would have been sufficient. Cicero could claim that "we can perceive the difference between good laws and bad by referring them to no other standard than nature" (*De Leg.* 1.44), but this method was unavailable to most people. The Greeks and Romans had to perceive in each case what the content of the law of nature was, the average Jew simply had to follow the law of Moses.[3]

Yet, it is also true that there is a degree of elitism in Philo's thought: those who only follow the literal laws may do what is good, but they do not represent the best.[4] Better is to understand the "inner" sense of the laws; but it is best not even to need the laws. What people did not need the law in its written form? How did they fulfil the law? What role did the Mosaic law, after all, play?

Higher Law and the Law of Moses

There are a number of ways to approach the relationship between the law of Moses and the higher forms of law. At no point is Philo explicit about the relationship, other than to call the law of Moses a copy of the law of nature, but in his descriptions of the higher forms of law and how people fulfil these forms of law there is information which illuminates his understanding of the relationships.

The Law of Nature and the Patriarchs

As far as Philo was concerned, his discussions of those who followed the law of nature were factual. Philo could point to the past and name his sages, those who had followed the law of nature. Even

---

[3] Cf. Vander Waerdt, *Natural Law* 231–263. He claims that Antiochus had already begun to move in this direction by offering *praecepta* through which all could follow the law of nature. Cf. *supra* 28 n. 69.

[4] Montgomery J. Shroyer, "Alexandrian Jewish Literalists" in *JBL* 55 (1936) 261–284 has an excellent discussion, especially 263,267,272. He also speaks of people (he terms them "literalists") who were unable to accept the law literally and who, therefore, rejected it (277–279,284).

better, he had a record of how they followed the law of nature in the Torah, something the Greeks and Romans, even the Stoics, could not claim.

The law of nature was Philo's answer to how the Patriarchs followed the law of Moses before the law of Moses was given; it was a problem which concerned Paul and the Rabbis as well. Philo's answer is somewhat different from theirs: the Patriarchs fulfilled the law of nature, which was given before the law of Moses. One could claim that this was simply Philo's way of worming out of a sticky exegetical corner, if the law of nature were not so fundamental to his thought. It provided the answer to some difficult historical questions for Philo, but it also is, in many ways, the centre of his philosophy: his views of nature and law are integral to his philosophic system. The law of nature existed in the past, and this explains easily how the Patriarchs followed the law of Moses before it was given by God; but the law of nature exists still and is connected to other forms of higher law.[5] It can continue to be a way of guidance, and must in some sense co-exist with the law of Moses.

Philo is vague when he discusses the way in which the Patriarchs are said to have followed the law of nature. The Patriarchs followed nature and became the archetypes for the written law (*Prob.* 62). If we want to know what they did, however, we are led into a kind of tautology: what they did, the law of nature, is found in the law of Moses, the copy of their lives. If so, how can the law of nature be a better way?

The answer seems to rest with *how* the law is done and *how* the law is understood. The law of nature, it seems, is not higher because it contains "better" laws, or different laws; the content seems to be the same, if draped in symbolic language in the Torah. The higher quality of the law of nature lies with the observer of the law: the Patriarchs follow the law guided only by reason, not a material code, and they follow the law because they perceive it is good and right. The content may not differ.[6]

Whether the Patriarchs follow the "inner" sense of the Mosaic law or the actual laws is not obvious. There is no doubt that Philo would

---

[5] If Philo was interested only in using the law of nature to explain how the patriarchs did the law of Moses, there would be little reason to connect it to these other forms of higher law.

[6] Koester, "νόμος φύσεως" 536.

have argued that they would have fulfilled the "inner" meaning these laws point to, but can one argue that the letter of these laws was also observed? The Mosaic law would not be contradicted by the actions of the Patriarchs, but could all its dictates have been followed?

It is possible, from the few clues that Philo gives us, that he might have argued that the Patriarchs actually observed the law of Moses.[7] The "originals" of the particular laws are the men who "lived good and blameless lives" (*Abr.* 4). They are "living and reasonable" laws (*Abr.* 5). Moses writes of them for two reasons: to show that the "enacted ordinances are not inconsistent with nature"; and to demonstrate that the written law is not difficult to follow because earlier generations followed the unwritten law (*Abr.* 5). The enacted laws, therefore, "are nothing else than memorials of the life of the ancients," "preserving to a later generation their actual words and deeds" (*Abr.* 5).

For Philo, the Patriarchs, the actual embodiments of the law of nature, are the model for the enacted ordinances. The enacted ordinances are not only consistent with nature, they "preserve" the actual ἔργα καὶ λόγους, οἷς ἐχρήσαντο of the Patriarchs. This may imply only that the stories of the Patriarchs are preserved in the Torah, but the clear sense seems to be that the law of Moses contains the deeds and words of the Patriarchs. This is solidified by the use of the verb χράομαι (make use of, employ), which points to the actual behaviour of the Patriarchs.[8] When the Patriarchs followed the law of nature, therefore, it seems that they also complied with the law of Moses. Their words and deeds are the basis for the enacted ordinances, which are, indeed, the Mosaic law. How this relationship can be said to function practically is difficult to comprehend, to say the least, but Philo intimates, in the following passages, that it exists.

Again, in *Abraham* 275–276, Abraham is said, following Genesis 26:5, to have *done* "the divine law and all the divine commands."

---

[7] Goodenough, *By Light, Light* 74 rejects the view that the Patriarchs were "bundles of commands which were written down by Moses ... there is no thought of deducing the specific commands from the incidents of the lives of the Patriarchs." This sounds eminently sensible, but I believe that the opposite view may be exactly what Philo intended.

[8] It is used by Josephus, for instance, in *Antiquities* 16, 27 to indicate "living in accordance with the laws." Cf. Walter Bauer, *A Greek-English Lexicon of the New Testament and Other Early Christian Literature*, trans. William F. Arndt and F. Wilbur Gingrich (Chicago and London: The University of Chicago Press 1979) 884.

The verb is significant: Philo says that Abraham did (ἐποίησεν) these laws, not that he somehow "fulfilled" or "modelled" or "guarded" them.[9] If we agree that Philo is here referring to the law of Moses, and we know that Abraham has done the law of nature, it should also be clear that there exists no difference between them. Indeed, Abraham was not νόμιμος, "lawful" according to a legal code, he was a "law himself and an unwritten law" (*Abr.* 276); but being "lawful" and becoming a "law" are not contradictory: Abraham became a law because he did the things which the law required. The difference is, he followed the dictates of the law of nature, without having the written laws.

This interpretation is borne out by *Migr.* 130. Philo takes up his interpretation of Gen. 26:5 once again. Again, too, Philo says that Abraham "did (ἐποίησεν) all my {God's} law (πάντα τὸν νόμον μου)." He replaces φυλάσσω with ποιέω in this instance too, and he is more explicit about Abraham's actions.

> "Law" being evidently nothing else than the divine word enjoining what we ought to do and forbidding what we should not do, as Moses testifies by saying, "he received a law from His words" (Deut. 33:3f.). If, then, the law is a Divine word, and the man of true worth "does" (ποιεῖ) the law, he assuredly "does" (ποιεῖ) the word: so that, as I said, God's words are the wise man's doings (πράξεις).

Here is Philo's clearest statement: the Patriarchs do the law of Moses.

Philo also contrasts the Patriarchs as "unwritten laws" with the written laws (*Decal.* 1). Philo does not state differences in content between the two forms of law. He stresses only that he has spoken of unwritten law and now must speak of written law. The way of the Patriarchs is a better way to observe the law, the way of reason and truth, but it is nowhere clear that in content it is a different way.

The difference between the written law and the law of nature, including the other forms of higher law, seems not to rest on the

---

[9] The verb used by the LXX, φυλάσσω, translates the Hebrew *shamar*. Both of these verbs can be translated as "watch," or "keep guard." Φυλάσσω does not have the same intimations of "performance" as ποιέω. That Philo is aware of the change in the verb is shown by his use of φυλάσσω in *Her.* 8, where he follows verbatim the text of the LXX. The verse is also discussed in *QG* 4.184, where it is found in an abbreviated form in Armenian. Πάντα is used in both *Migr.* 130 and *Abr.* 275 to describe the extent of Abraham's observance; the word does not appear in the LXX or in the Hebrew text. Νόμος is used to signify the "law" which Abraham follows in *Migr.* 130; νόμος does not appear in the LXX.

content of the law itself. It may be that the law of Moses "hides" its truths in the language of metaphor, but when the truth is revealed it does not differ from the higher forms. The one who follows the law of nature by the reason within him alone, without relying upon rewards and punishments, indeed without needing the guidance of a law code, has the ability to understand what one is truly obeying and why one ought to be obedient. That the content of what one obeys differs from the law of nature is not likely, at least not in Philo's scheme.

The transcendence of the written law by the Patriarchs does not seem to imply the transcendence of the contents of the written code, as it does in Greek and Roman natural law thought, it implies only the transcendence of the limited understanding of the one who must rely upon the written law. The Patriarchs, of course, provide the models and patterns for the laws and indicate conformity and agreement with the law of Moses. The Jew, therefore, who does only the written law does to a limited degree an "inferior" law. This "inferiority" is not found in the Mosaic law, but in the literal-minded follower of the law who is unable to understand the truth of the law and to whom this truth points. A help in understanding the relationship between the (material) written law and the (intelligible) natural law, and its correlates, might be forthcoming in grasping Philo's use of arithmology in his work. Arithmology, Philo's symbolic use of numbers, is dependent upon Philo's view of the cosmos, a view infused with his view of the Platonic forms, which exist in the intelligible world, whose realm for Philo is the Logos, and their copies here in the sensible world.[10]

As Horst Moehring states, Arithmology allows Philo to stress two points:

    a. the cosmic and human order described by Moses is *of universal validity* (my italics), as is made most obvious in Philo's universalistic interpretation of the sabbath;

---

[10] Horst Moehring, "Arithmology as an Exegetical Tool in the Writings of Philo of Alexandria" in *The School of Moses: Studies in Philo and Hellenistic Religion: In Memory of Horst R. Moehring*. Brown Judaic Studies 304. Studia Philonica Monographs 1. Ed. John Peter Kenney (Atlanta: Scholars Press 1995), 151. See *Timaeus* 27D, 53B for significant references, as mentioned by Moehring. Cf. also Robert Berchman, "The Categories of Being in Middle Platonism" in *The School of Moses: Studies in Philo and Hellenistic Religion: In Memory of Horst R. Moehring*. Brown Judaic Studies 304. Studia Philonica Monographs 1. Ed. John Peter Kenney (Atlanta: Scholars Press 1995), 98–140 for the background on Philo's view of Being, esp. 115–119.

> b. this order is represented most clearly and purely in Jewish law, liturgy, and tradition; the Jewish religion is, therefore, the most natural religion."[11]

Further, according to Moehring, "the superiority of the Jewish tradition is not esoteric in character; as can be shown through arithmology, it is reasonable and demonstrably so."[12]

Arithmology, though not our dominant concern here, does point to the universality of truth in Philo's cosmos, especially as expressed in Jewish law and tradition, and to the relationship of the material to the intelligible world. Jewish law represents true law here on earth, everywhere, as the numbers employed by human beings here on earth represent their intelligible counterparts; in Moehring's words, numbers have a "λόγος-character" in the work of Philo.[13]

The cosmic order which is expressed through numbers also helped Philo "to explain the sacred texts of the books of the law in terms that were universally understood, even though not universally accepted."[14] While the specific use of numbers by Philo is not of significance here, though let is be said that seven has pride of place, his view both of the intelligible world they represent and the harmony of the world inherent in them, spill over into all his thought. This is particularly so in his view of the relationship between the material and the intelligible world and the universal nature of the true copy of reality. One is one, as seven is seven, because they truly represent the reality of numbers in the Logos, or intelligible world; so, too, the law of Moses is truly the law because it perfectly represents in material form the reality of Law, the natural law, which exists in the realm of the Logos, the intelligible world. The harmony of the cosmos demands that there is a connection between the Torah and the cosmos as all reality is perfectly mirrored in truth. The law of Moses, therefore, can be nothing but the reflection of the true law of the cosmos for Philo.

---

[11] Moehring, "Arithmology," 176.
[12] Ibid., 176.
[13] Ibid., 145.
[14] Ibid.

The Living Law and Present-Day Rulers

If, though, the Patriarchs followed the law of Moses, as the scanty evidence indicates, what of Philo's own day? Could one follow the law of nature without relying on the law of Moses? Our discussion begins with the living law ideal and the rulers of Philo's day. At a number of places, Philo seems to suggest that the rulers constituted the law of their given land, that they were, in fact, living laws.

Philo does in principle extend the living law ideal to Gentile states, for he claims that rulers are living tablets, contrasting them with the written law (*Det.* 141; cf. *QE* 2.6). This contrast is clear to us now: the king is the law, or the law is written. What, however, are the implications in Philo's thought? Moses, the true living law, lived his life in agreement with the law given to him on Mount Sinai. And since Philo links the living law ideal to the law of nature, could a Gentile king fulfil the law of nature, in fact be a representation of the law of nature, and not observe the Mosaic law? Would the king of a Gentile land, who is himself the law, observe the Mosaic law? Could a Gentile king contradict the law of Moses and still be lawful?

As odd as it seems the answer appears to be that a king who truly was the law would, indeed, do the Mosaic law. Philo may be stating the *de facto* truth when he says the king is the law in his land—but this is only half of the story. Any king may indeed be the law of his land, but this may only signify that he is a bad law, a tyrant. What constitutes "good" law, law in fact, is only the law of nature which has its copy in the law of Moses.

The truth of Philo's claim, that rulers are living tablets, is seen only when the proper law is in view. All future rulers, says Philo elsewhere, would find a law to guide them by looking to Moses as their archetype and model (*Virt.* 70). A true "living law" would do nothing which was not in agreement with the law of Moses. What this means in practice, probably, is that only a Jew could be a living law.

For when Philo does speak of the living law ideal in his own day, as E. R. Goodenough and Wayne Meeks have shown, he speaks of its perversion.[15] Gaius, who considered himself a law, is the model of perversity par excellence (*Legat.* 119), a model of perversity not

---

[15] Goodenough, *Politics* 103–113; Meeks, *The Prophet-King* 49,51,61 #6.

only for Philo, but for the Roman historians as well.[16] Goodenough asks at one point why Philo did not grant that a Roman emperor was the living law, but surely the answer is obvious: no one fulfilled the requirements.[17] In principle they could have; in reality they did not; in all probability only a Jew would.[18] At any rate, Philo would have recognized the living law by his actions—they would have conformed with the prescriptions of the law of Moses.

Philo is to some degree saved by the unity of law in his thought. Whereas in Greek sources the law and the king are separate legal entities—if one rules, the other is not necessary—in Philo the separation between forms of law does not exist. The living law is the law of nature, and the law of nature is the original of the law of Moses: written and unwritten law are in this way one. Every king is the law of his land, it is true, but that does not imply that anything the king calls law is true "law," though it may function as such. In name it may be law, it may function as such, but unless it compares favourably to the law of nature/law of Moses, it is in reality no law. For Philo, there is only one law, and the king is the law only insofar as he follows it.

One cannot, therefore, render the Mosaic law superfluous by being a living law, because the true living law would follow the Mosaic law. Moses was the living law, which means he lived in conformity with the law of Moses. Gaius' claims to be the law are ridiculed by Philo because they are unwarranted claims, not because Philo does not believe in the ideal itself.[19] A real νόμος ἔμψυχος would be much like Moses (*Virt.* 70). This would be quite impossible for a Gentile ruler.

All forms of law, in Philo's work, combine to create a tightly woven system. While Greek and Roman writers on the living law ideal only attempt to grasp what such a ruler would be like, or how he may embody justice and equality, or how he would relate to the present written law, Philo knows what such a king would be like.

---

[16] Dio Cassius 59; Suetonius 4. Barraclough, "Philo's Politics" 458–460 claims, however, that Philo's portrait of Gaius is exaggerated.

[17] Goodenough, *Politics* 112–113.

[18] Goodenough, *Politics* 112–113; cf. Heinimann, *Philons griechische* 190 who points out that Deut. 17:15f. forbids a foreigner from being king of the Jews. The implication of the living law ideal, for Philo at any rate, is that a true νόμος ἔμψυχος would be king of all the lands, and therefore king of the Jews.

[19] Goodenough, *Politics* 107; Meeks, *The Prophet-King* 51.

He has an exemplar, the original as it were, of the living law. If everyone else is scrambling to find his footing, Philo can place his feet on solid ground.

A king may claim to be the living law, he may abolish the law of Moses, he may institute laws which mock the law of Moses, but his law would be a sham and the king would be a phoney. The true νόμος ἔμψυχος will not contradict the law of nature, and it is this law which supports the law of Moses. Philo is weaving the seamless garment: the law is of one piece.

The Law of Nature in Philo's Day

Is it still possible that an individual could follow the law of nature without knowing of the law of Moses? If a Stoic wise man fulfilled the law of nature would he naturally do the law of Moses? Could a Greek do the things to which the law of nature points, but not perform the physical requirements of the Mosaic code? Could a Jew disregard the law of Moses for the higher law?

The question must have been a real one for Philo:

> This theory about the unwritten Torah being available to the men of old before the legislation of Moses does not serve as merely a convenient stopgap for that period in history between Creation and Moses... It produces the extremely momentous insight that a true law of nature is in fact an ultimately superior criterion for the life of the truly wise man.[20]

And if the law of nature is still operative in Philo's day, does not the chance exist that it may, in fact, be followed (*Prob.* 72–75)? Philo says that

> these people often ask "Who have there been in the past, and who are there living now of the kind that you imagine?" An excellent answer is that in the past there have been those who surpassed their contemporaries in virtue, who took God for their sole guide and lived according to a law of nature's right reason, not only to free themselves, but communicating to their neighbours the spirit of freedom: also in our own time there are still men formed as it were in the likeness of the original picture supplied by the high excellence of sages (*Prob.* 62).

---

[20] Koester, "νόμος φύσεως" 535.

The giving of the Mosaic law opened up the way for more to follow the requirements of nature's right reason—the Mosaic law is the codification of reason—but the law of nature still exists in its own right.

In the previous passage, Philo seems to imply that the law of nature is still being followed, and it seems that he intends to say that these special people are Jews. The Patriarchs surpassed their contemporaries in virtue; in Philo's own day such people existed too. Philo says of the wise men that "this small body though scanty is not absolutely non-existent" (*Prob.* 72; cf. *Mut.* 35–37). The *crux interpretum* in *Prob.* 62 is, how are these people formed in the likeness (εἰχών) of the original picture (ἀπὸ ἀρχετύπου γραφῆς)? Indeed, what *is* the original picture? Does it imply people following the law of nature, or attempting to, or simply following the Torah?

The original picture must be the lives of the Patriarchs, the unwritten and living laws, the men who fulfilled the law of nature (*Abr.* 3–6). The copies are the written laws, the ἀρχετύποι are the Patriarchs. Do those who follow the Patriarchs, though, guide themselves by following the right reason of nature, or does Philo simply mean that they follow the original picture preserved in the Torah, whose pages contain the lives and actions of the sages?

Philo is responding to a question of who in the past were virtuous and who now are most virtuous, so it seems likely that Philo is speaking of people in his own day who followed not merely the written ordinances, but the "original pictures," the embodiments of the law of nature, themselves.

Yet, even here, it is the Patriarchs who are taken as the measure of the law of nature, nature's right reason, and as we have seen repeatedly, they do not contradict the law of Moses. The law of nature is the model for the copy. Even if the people of Philo's day are following the law of nature, there is no indication that they oppose the law of Moses; in fact, the opposite is suggested. If Philo knows of sages in his own day, they are patterned after the Patriarchs, and one must suspect that their ability to follow the law of nature rests in their ability to understand what the law truly is, and to keep it through the dictates of reason.

There is still one distinction to be drawn. The follower of the Mosaic law should not abandon the literal commands of the Mosaic law (*Migr.* 92–93) and neither it seems should the Jewish sage (*Prob.*

62).²¹ What of the Greek who follows the law of nature? Would he too observe the law of Moses? The question is not as alien as it may initially appear (*Prob.* 72–75). Philo is dependent upon Greek discussions of higher law, which he alters and supplements, and the question of how Gentiles might follow the law crosses his mind.

The Gentile, like the Jew, shares in the reasonableness of nature, having, as it were, the same natural ability to find God and to share in nature's right reason as the Jew. True, the Jew has the advantage of having the superior law of Moses (*Ios.* 29–31; *Mos.* 2.12–13,17, 26–27,34,43–44,51) and proselytes to the law immediately achieve some higher level of virtue (*Virt.* 182), but the Greek is not a priori without hope, not if the universality of the law means anything.

Philo, in fact, admits that there exist Gentiles who follow the law of nature. The clearest case of Gentiles observing the law of nature comes in *Spec.* 2.42–48, in the midst of a discussion of the Sabbath. Philo begins his discussion of the fourth commandment, under which he includes a discussion of the festivals, the laws regarding the seventh year, and the year of the Jubilees, in *Spec.* 2.39.

Philo includes as a festival the feast of "every day" (ἡμέρα ἅπασα). This feast appears to be based on Numbers 28,29 and the instructions regarding the "continual" offerings.²² Philo understands these verses to mean that "every day" is a feast for the special few virtuous people (cf. *Sacr.* 111). By establishing this feast, the Mosaic law

> accommodates itself to the blameless life of righteous men who follow nature and her ordinances (*Spec.* 2.42).

If vice had not wrought such destruction among the majority of humanity, Philo says, all would be able to celebrate this festival. As it is, only a few do celebrate it.

Surprisingly, some of the few who do celebrate this festival are Greeks and Barbarians (*Spec.* 2.44). Philo says,

> they are the closest observers of nature and all that it contains ... true cosmopolitans (κοσμοπολίτας) who have recognized the world to be a city having for its citizens the associates of wisdom, registered as such

---

²¹ Mendelson, *Philo's Jewish Identity* 20–21.
²² The LXX understands the sense of the "continual" offering. The word the LXX uses, e.g. Numbers 28:3, is ἐνδελεχῶς, "continually."

by virtue to whom is entrusted the headship of the universal commonwealth (τὸ κοινὸν πολίτευμα) (*Spec.* 2.45).

These Greeks and Barbarians must be followers of the law of nature. Recall Philo's words regarding creation in *De Opificio Mundi*:

> that the world is in harmony with the Law, and the Law with the world, and that the man who observes the law is constituted thereby a loyal citizen of the world (κοσμοπολίτης), regulating his doings by the purpose and will of Nature, in accordance with which the entire world itself also is administered (*Opif.* 3).

Philo says, these people, these Gentile "cosmopolitans," "naturally make their whole life a feast. These are indeed but a small number left in their cities like an ember of wisdom to smoulder, that virtue may not be altogether lost to our race" (*Spec.* 2.46,47). If everyone was as virtuous as this small number of Gentiles, every day in the world would indeed be a feast (*Spec.* 2.48).

There is no doubt that in this passage Philo introduces us to Gentiles, a very few, who follow the law of nature. Could these Gentiles be said by Philo to follow the law of Moses? The discussion does take place within the context of a passage on Jewish festivals, and the festival these Gentiles are said to follow is a "Jewish" festival. But Philo, whether by chance or foresight, does not settle for us clearly the question of whether Gentiles who follow the law of nature also follow the law of Moses.

The festival which Philo claims they observe is vague and indeterminate in terms of performance. It is kept in the soul, it would seem, not through a body of practices enjoined by Moses or the Hebrew Bible. Would these Gentiles, for instance, follow the other festivals Philo has listed? It seems impossible that they could actually follow these festivals, but further on in the discussion Philo states that

> those who are not of the same nation he describes as aliens, reasonably enough, and the condition of the alien excludes any idea of partnership, unless indeed by a transcendency of virtues he converts even it into a tie of kinship, since it is a general truth that common citizenship rests on virtues and laws which propound the morally beautiful (*Spec.* 2.73).

This indicates that the virtuous Gentile can indeed follow the law of nature, and even the law of Moses. If Philo does not intend to say that the virtuous Gentile somehow follows the law of Moses, the way to superfluity of the Mosaic law is a real possibility.

There is limited confirmation elsewhere that virtuous Gentiles follow the law of Moses. When Philo speaks approvingly of the Stoic founder Zeno and of one of his laws, he later states that Zeno probably found this law in the Jewish law book (*Prob.* 57). The same is said of Socrates and Heraclitus, as we have seen. Claiming someone else's, or some other school's, thought as one's own, is a common enough ploy among Greek thinkers, but for Philo it supports the centre of his thought: any law worth following must be from the Jews. If Zeno or Socrates knew something of the "right" law, it must be because they knew the Jewish law.

E. R. Goodenough has built a rather strong case that Philo has actually at times borrowed Gentile law: Greek, Roman, and Egyptian.[23] In doing so Philo sometimes even contradicts Jewish law. The significant point, however, as Goodenough himself admits, is that Philo would never have admitted to such borrowing.[24] Not because he wanted to hide the reality, but because he did not believe he was doing such a thing. If Philo said he saw a law regarding poisoning in the Jewish scriptures, which in fact comes from Gentile law, he probably did see such a law.[25]

What this means is that the Greek who fulfilled the law of nature, or who knows part of it, borrowed it from Moses, in one way or another. Failing that, reason would not guide one against the dictates of the Mosaic law. As strange or unbelievable as it may seem, any sage, any "unwritten law," any "living law" must in the course of obeying the law of nature also obey the law of Moses. How this would have been accomplished is a mystery, as it is also for the Patriarchs, but Philo's thought leaves no alternative.

It seems clear that a Greek sage would resemble no one so much as a Hebrew Patriarch. A Greek audience would have, indeed may

---

[23] Goodenough, *Jurisprudence* 75–76,100–102,106–107,111,155,193. These serve as examples, the book contains many more such examples. Cf. also Barraclough, "Philo's Politics" 517–518. I. Heinimann, "Jüdisch-hellenistische Gerichtshöfe in Alexandrien?" in *MGWJ* 74 (1930) 363–369 attempts to show that Goodenough's examples do not point to actual practice in the Jewish community; on this point, he convinces. He believes that Philo is drawing on ideal Greek or Roman legal forms. The case that Goodenough has built, though, that Philo draws on Gentile law, still holds, at least for our purposes.

[24] Goodenough, *Jurisprudence* 214–215.

[25] *Spec.* 3.93–98; Philo speaks of putting the poisoner to death in this passage, which appears to be based on the injunction in Ex. 22:18 to put a sorcerer to death. Cf. Goodenough, *Jurisprudence* 106.

have, found this incredible, perhaps even insulting, but Philo is certain of it and saved to some degree by Stoic agnosticism: they are not certain of the content of the law of nature and they are not sure if anyone has followed it.[26] Philo's boldness is supported by Stoic timidity.

He has no doubts. He knows of people who have followed the law of nature and he has a record of how they followed it. If there was a sage, Philo would recognize him. If the thought of the Greek sage being circumcised or following the dietary laws seems odd to us, it would not have seemed so to Philo. Philo was certain of the truth of Judaism, and this claim was necessary to his identity and to his community. Apart from that the scarcity of the sage meant that no one could truly contradict his claims, although if Gentiles read his work there would certainly have been enough people to dispute them. Philo's legal thought is driven, though, by his conviction that the Jew has a record of the law of nature: the Jews had the truth, for which the Gentiles were searching, and Philo invited those who wanted to know to follow the one, true law.

The Law of Nature and the Law of Moses

Greek discussions of the law of nature brooked no wholesale abandonment of the written law, even by the sage, but it was a possibility that certain laws could be overturned. If the material law did not reflect the higher law, why should one who knows the truth not abandon the transcended written law?

Goodenough believes that Philo is implicitly acknowledging the secondary status of the Mosaic law when Philo refers to it as a copy. He says it "would have been natural, in view of the general trend, for Platonists and Pythagoreans to have developed a theory that the written law was only a reflection or image of the Idea-Law."[27]

---

[26] This is not to suggest that the Stoics had nothing to say about the wise man and how he would live. As we saw in Chapter Two, the Stoics were quite willing to describe the sage and his life. The καθήκοντα would also give us the ground rules whereby a sage would live, and could thereby be noticed. But the problem of Stoicism, if indeed they considered it a problem, is that only the sage knows how he would act in a certain circumstance and only the sage can act correctly (according to the κατορθώματα). Philo is willing to be much more definite and specific.

[27] Goodenough, *By Light, Light* 87.

Goodenough can find no such example from Philo's day and draws on the fifth century C.E. Neo-Platonist Proclus to explain Philo's view of the relationship. Goodenough insists that Proclus' view of the law shows how Philo regarded the written law as inferior. Apart from Proclus' late date, I am not convinced that Goodenough interprets Proclus correctly,[28] but there is far more damaging evidence against Goodenough's view: Cicero.

Cicero, whose view of the law of nature probably comes from the same source as Philo,[29] does preserve a statement on the relationship between the written law and the law of nature. In *De Off.* 3.69 Cicero says that the written law is a shadow (*umbra*) and appearance (*imago*) of true law (*veri iuris*); he states further that "we do not possess a whole (*solidam*) and distinct (*expressam*) copy (*effigiem*) of the true law." This is significant evidence.

Cicero says that there is no "whole and distinct copy" of the law of nature. Philo's claims that the Mosaic law is an εἰκών of the law of nature (*Abr.* 3; *Mos.* 2.51), or that the laws are μιμήματα, true imitations, of the laws of nature (*Mos.* 2.11), or stamped with the seals of nature (*Mos.* 2.14,48) go far beyond Cicero's claims that the civil law is a shadow or mere appearance of true law. Whereas Cicero is preserving the consensus regarding the inferiority of the written law, Philo is arguing that in fact a true copy of the law of nature exists. Moses' laws

> are firm, unshaken, immovable, stamped, as it were, with the seals of nature herself... secure from the day when they were first enacted to now, and we may hope that they will remain for all future ages as though immortal, so long as the sun and the moon and the whole heaven and universe exist (*Mos.* 2.14).

Therefore,

> whoever will carefully examine the nature of the particular enactments will find that they seek to attain to the harmony and of the universe and are in agreement with the principles of eternal nature (*Mos.* 2.52).

---

[28] See Goodenough, *By Light, Light* 87-88 for his translation of the relevant passage. I am not sure the translation does justice to the text. Proclus calls true laws an εἰκών of the cosmic laws, and by this intends to speak of their superiority vis-á-vis bad laws and customs. Though Platonism regarded the copy as inferior to the original, that is not Proclus' intention here. See Proclus, *In Rem Publicam* II (ed. W. Kroll; Amsterdam: Hakkers 1965 repr.) 307, 11.15f. for the Greek text.

[29] Horsley, "The Law of Nature in Philo and Cicero" 35-59.

Philo does not devalue the law of Moses by speaking of it as a copy; he is stressing its value.³⁰

Philo may have heard the argument from Hellenistic Jews in Alexandria that the written law of Moses is only an inferior law, but he saves himself from the potentially anti-Mosaic results to which the law of nature, and other forms of higher law, could lead without abandoning the higher forms of law. He does this by tying the horse more firmly to the cart. He claims his material law is the perfect copy of the law of nature.³¹ The law of Moses cannot, therefore, be abrogated, even in part, or improved.³² The divine origin of the law allows Philo to claim that the written law and the law of nature have the same source and the same content. This unity and continuity which Philo maintains without fail saves him from degrading the written law and at the same time allows him to affirm the existence of a "higher" law.³³

---

³⁰ Valentin Nikiprowetzky, *Le Commentaire de l'écriture chez Philon d'Alexandrie* (Leiden: Brill 1977) 122.

³¹ Bréhier, *Les Idées* 30 claims that this is the only argument with which Philo can defend the law of Moses.

³² Mendelson, *Philo's Jewish Identity* 53 says that "Philo must have held... that not every prohibition or command of the Torah is equally important." Theoretically, though, if not in practice, he maintained the unity of the Mosaic law.

³³ Philo protects the law of Moses in another way, which has not been noted by Philonic scholars. Philo devalues and downplays the role of the ἀδιάφορα and καθήκοντα in the life of the ordinary person; in their place he substitutes the law of Moses. The καθήκοντα were those appropriate actions which were to be chosen among the indifferents (ἀδιάφορα). Not every καθῆκον act, however, was always according to nature, and only the wise man could truly perform good acts, or perfectly virtuous acts (κατορθώοματα). This meant, in effect, that only the sage could live a life according to nature. Philo's claim that anyone who can follow the law of Moses is following nature is a much broader claim than the Stoics would make. Also, Philo would not claim that the actions prescribed by the law of Moses are only sometimes preferable. In this way the actions which the ordinary person is to follow are fixed and not given to deliberation. This is much different than the theory of the indifferents. Cf. Vander Waerdt, *Natural Law* 231–263 who claims that the law of nature became the καθήκοντα with the revisions of Antiochus. I do not see that such an argument is found in the work of Cicero. The move to make the law of nature applicable to the life of the ordinary person seems to have been underway, but I do not think the outlines of the law of nature were codified (cf. *De Leg.* 1.42,44; 2.11). If in fact they had been, it would give Philo more impetus to claim that the law of Moses was the law of nature; the urgency would have been real.

Philo does know of the Stoic theory of indifferents (*Opif.* 74; *Leg.* 1.56; 2.17; 3.165,210; *Sacr.* 19–20,99; *Det.* 122; *Plant.* 100; *Prob.* 61,81). He knows of the division between good, indifferent, and bad acts (*Prob.* 60). He knows, too, that it is the disposition of the sage which makes his acts truly good (*Leg.* 3.210). Philo even

How the two are related, however, still remains unclear; Philo is never explicit. André Myre affirms that the law of nature is primary and that of Moses secondary, but admits that the discussion is nuanced and does not lend itself to generalizations.[34] What is the place of the law of Moses?

Philo's Contribution: The Unity of Law

To answer this question finally, we need to ask two questions of Philo. We need to ask why Philo presents three discrete forms of higher law as one. In no other ancient source do all three forms of higher law appear, and in no ancient source are any two forms of higher law as tightly connected as all three forms are in Philo's work. Many sources which may have contributed to our knowledge of higher law in this period are missing or only partially extant, but this should not detract from Philo's contribution. A second question is closely related: whether Philo created this unity of law or borrowed it, was it used in order to protect the Mosaic law from superfluity? Every Greek notion of law which could potentially render the Mosaic law, or any form of written law, superfluous is not rejected and ignored but co-opted and altered. Why? Unwritten law, the law of nature, and the living law find a welcome home with Philo, but all with changed meanings.

The Living Law

The idea of the living law, as we know it from the fragmentary sources, is contained in full in Philo in the discussion of Moses, with one major exception: the king as the law is not contrasted with the written law. Instead of replacing the law, the king in Philo, preeminently Moses, is the pattern for the written law. Any other living

---

knows that not all καθήκοντα are always appropriate in every circumstance (*Cher.* 14–15). But he never speaks of these acts in conjunction with the law of nature. His true feelings come to the fore in *Leg.* 3.126 when he links human virtue (κατ' ανθρώπους ἀρετῆς) and laws by convention (θέσει νομίμνω) to καθήκοντον and κατορθώματον (!). Philo labels these all "human opinions" and believes that knowledge of God transcends them all. See the *Excursus* after Chapter 7.

[34] Myre, "La Loi de Nature" 176, 180–181.

law would also follow the law of Moses; there would be no disagreement. Philo also adds to the concept in two ways: he links the living law ideal to the law of nature; and he extends the concept to people in the past who were not actual kings.[35]

If Philo adopted the νόμος ἔμψυχος ideal from the Middle Platonists, then it is possible that the link between the law of nature and the Hellenistic Pythagorean living law took place among them. The connection makes sense. If the king was to be just, by what measure was he to be just? The Pythagorean fragments offer no external measure,[36] they simply claim that the king is to be most just and the best man. The law of nature ideal may have seemed both obvious and necessary. Obvious because the king had to be just according to some objective, though admittedly unknown, measure; necessary because the measure could not be arbitrary.

More important, the ideas fit nicely together. In an age in which philosophical "unity" among the schools was claimed by some philosophers, and without much alteration, the living law ideal could breathe real life into the Stoic maxim that the wise man, the best man, was king. The living law ideal provided an apologia for why, and how, this was so; the Stoics provided the claim that the king need not be, after all, a king. This could have influenced Philo. Though Moses is truly presented as a living law, even he was not a king in the true sense of the word. The other Patriarchs were even less so. Philo's use of the living law ideal often means, simply, sage-king: the Stoic wise man who follows the law of nature. This new understanding of the living law ideal would serve Philo's purposes perfectly.

The connections between the living law ideal and the law of nature could have come from elsewhere.[37] We have argued, however, in "Appendix 1: The Date of the Pythagorean Kingship Tractates" that

---

[35] This is the pattern, of course, of the Stoic-Cynic view of kingship (every wise man is king: Diogenes Laertius 7.122), but not the Pythagorean.

[36] By that I mean they offer no code of law; the king is just by reference to his imitation of God. Archytas, *Stob.* 4.1.135 offers that the unwritten divine law nourished the written law or the king, but this is not adopted by the other writers.

[37] In defense of Philo's originality on this point, Plutarch, another thinker influenced by the Middle Platonists, does not connect the law of nature to the νόμος ἔμψυχος. It is true, however, that he calls the king a λόγος ἔμψυχος. It is possible that the term λόγος was influenced by the Stoic tradition through the Middle Platonists. Philo, who calls his wise men ἔμψυχοι καὶ λογικοὶ νόμοι, may borrow from both traditions: the Pythagorean νόμος ἔμψυχος tradition and the Middle Platonists.

Philo may be dependent on the Pythagorean texts themselves. Philo's own concerns supply us with motive enough to suspect that Philo is responsible for the synthesis of the law of nature and the living law. His purpose would seem to be to claim the Patriarchs as the true wise men, in every possible form, while at the same time eliminating claims that there are higher forms of law which threaten the written law. Even if the connection between the law of nature and the living law came from elsewhere, it is doubtful that the elimination of the contrast between the living law and the written law came from someone other than Philo. The law of nature in Greco-Roman thought always maintained the contrast between the higher law and the written law; this was the raison d'être of the higher law. Only Philo could have eliminated the contrast, because only Philo had a written law whose protection mattered as much as the higher law.

The Unwritten Law

This is a more difficult category to consider. Unwritten law, after Aristotle, is not found in many Hellenistic discussions, and never in Stoic discussions, of law. The new discussions of the law of nature seemed to relegate this older and vaguer concept to the sidelines. Philo brings it back into play.

It is likely that this is Philo's own addition. The claim that the one who fulfils the law of nature is an unwritten law is found only in Philo; the claim is an odd one and does not readily suggest itself. The links between the living law ideal and the law of nature would have been easy to forge given the parameters of both discussions, specifically the concentration on the king/sage, but what in the unwritten law discussions suggests that someone who follows the law of nature is an unwritten law? The explanation for the connection seems to require the need to account for all forms of higher law.

Since the law of nature is the over-arching form of higher law in Philo's work, what is the place of the unwritten law? It is, in fact, easy to understand why the concept of the law of nature would relegate the idea of unwritten laws to the sidelines in Greek thought in general: the law of nature offers a systematic explanation of what true law is. Law, even if not written, is not arbitrary and not simply one or two "unwritten" laws. The law of nature is inherent in the universe, not dependent on the unknown whims of gods. The impetus to take account of the unwritten law, instead of ignoring it, as most do in the Hellenistic period, must depend upon the need to leave no loose ends, no opportunity for someone to ignore their written law in the service of a higher law. It is probably Philo who connected the unwritten law to the law of nature, and probably Philo who claimed the one who does the law of nature is, in fact, an unwritten law.

Philo is, indeed, often an eclectic thinker, so it is possible these connections came from elsewhere. Still, since they serve his purposes so well, and since it is hard to imagine a purpose other than his that would lead to such connections, Philo was likely the one who created the links among these various forms of law.

The unity of the higher forms of law would seem to be Philo's contribution to Greek legal thought. There are a number of factors which suggest that this is the case. First, it is found nowhere else in the ancient sources. This is not decisive because of the fragmentary nature of the sources, but it is a weighty consideration. Second, the unity of the higher law demonstrates the unity of all law in Philo's thought, and supports his view of God's provident creation, both of the world and of the law of Moses. All forms of law are present and accounted for. Third, the unity of the higher law fits Philo's syncretistic philosophical style. It may be that the connections were more apparent to him than to a member of one of the rival schools. Finally, it helps Philo be rid of a thorny problem regarding the arbitrariness of the written law. This thorny problem dogged the Greeks since the time of the Sophists. Philo protects the law of Moses by claiming it is intimately related to all forms of higher law. These forms of law, therefore, cannot undermine the law of Moses.

In his hands, the disparate and discrete parts of Greek legal thought become the interlocking pieces of a cosmic puzzle. The law is a grand picture: the living law had to fit in this scheme, as did the unwritten law, because the pieces had to form a unity. Why did Philo put this puzzle together? He was probably the only one looking for the pieces.

The Law of Nature and the Law of Moses

The tight connection between the law of nature, and by extension the other forms of higher law, and the law of Moses must be Philo's legacy too, though it could have come from another Jewish thinker.[38] Greek discussions obviously would not have made the specific connection between the law of nature and the law of Moses, but it is difficult to imagine a Greek thinker making the connection between the law of nature and any form of written law. Which law would they have chosen? Which law did the Greeks agree was the best: that of Athens or Sparta? Which law could claim to be from the hand of God? Cicero, whose natural law thought may have the same source as Philo, calls Rome's law, which he considered the best possible written law, a "shadow."[39] This is an evocative phrase, especially contrasted with Philo's "true copy," but it probably has a mundane source: the consensus view.[40] And why would this not be

---

[38] On the general connections between the law of Moses and nature/virtue/wisdom see 4 Maccabees 1:8–9,15–18,28–30,34–35; 2:6,23; 3:17–18; 5:17–26; 6:31–35; 7:7–9; 13:1–6,16–18; 16:1–3; 18:1–3 and Wisdom of Solomon. On the purpose of the defense of the law of Moses in 4 Maccabees see Stephen Westerholm, "Law and the Rule of Reason: The Argument of 4 Maccabees," presented at Torah/Nomos Seminar *Canadian Society of Biblical Studies Annual Meetings* May 1987. He claims that the author was concerned with protecting the law of Moses by claiming in it the true embodiment of reason. In general, then, Philo did have predecessors.

In no other extant Jewish text, however, do we find such philosophically knowledgeable and mature (not to mention extensive) arguments as in Philo; I believe that in most particulars he is responsible for his synthesis. He was not, of course, the first to attempt to protect the law of Moses by linking it to Greco-Roman thought, but I believe his thought is in large measure original.

[39] Marcia L. Colish, *The Stoic Tradition from Antiquity to the Early Middle Ages* Vol. 1 (Leiden: E. J. Brill 1985) 96–101 argues that, in fact, Cicero considers the law of Rome to be the law of nature in *De Leg.* 2.26. But this he does, as far as I can tell, only for some specific instances. He would not, and does not, claim Roman law, in its entirety, the law of nature. She is correct, however, in saying that Cicero begins the transformation of the law of nature as a cosmic law to that of a higher law. Cicero starts what Philo finishes. Vander Waerdt, *Natural Law* 231–263 has attributed this move to Antiochus, especially as it relates to the καθήκοντα. It may be, however, that it was indeed Cicero who was concerned with the relationship between the law of nature and the civil law. Antiochus was interested in finding a guide for all humans through the καθήκοντα, but Cicero, the lawyer, would have had abundant reason to wonder how the law of nature was to be related to the civil law and a system of law.

[40] John Dillon, *The Middle Platonists* 81 says of the dispute over who is responsible for Cicero's view of the law of nature that "what the champions of the various views do not seem to recognize is that the theories of these three men {Panaetius, Posidonius, Antiochus} are almost bound to be identical." I am not certain that identity among the various views can be maintained, though there must have been similarity. Vander Waerdt, *Natural Law* 234 clearly opts for Antiochus, but he too recognizes the probable changes wrought by Panaetius and Posidonius. In the specific instance of who introduced the move from κατορθώματα to καθήκοντα as a guide

the consensus? Was this not the point of the law of nature? That there was an eternal law which transcended the sometimes arbitrary, sometimes bad law of the cities? This was the very point upon which the origin and the development of the law of nature rested.[41]

Only a Jew, one is tempted to say only Philo, could have tied their material law so tightly to the law of nature. Only the Jews could have wanted to.[42] If the law of nature was the salvation of the meaning of law for the Gentile, could it not easily become the undoing of the law of Moses? Would there not be, after all, a law which transcends the law of Moses? The divine character of the law of Moses, the importance of the law for the life of the community, could not allow the law of Moses to be simply another law.[43] While the idea of the law of nature, and other forms of higher law, may have posed no real threat to the law of Moses, theoretically it did, and some in the Alexandrian community might have argued for its transcendent nature. It may be that Philo's designation of the law of Moses as the "true copy" of the law of nature was a direct response to the consensus view, the view propounded by the Middle Stoics and their followers. But whether or not the term itself is a response, the ideas certainly are.

Conclusions

Why create this unity of law? Answers have already been suggested. First, Philo believed in the truth of the higher forms of Greco-Roman law. He was convinced that truth could be found in Greek philosophy, in this case Greek legal theory, filtered through his Jewish perspective. He was convinced, that is, not only of the truth and reality of the law of nature, but of its connections to other, discrete forms

---

to the law of nature, Vander Waerdt is convincing in his claim that it is Antiochus, though such a move may have been made by Cicero himself. Nevertheless, I do not see, as he does, that there was a code of *officia*. A number of passages speak against such a move, as we have discussed earlier. See the Excursus following chapter 7 for further discussion regarding this question.

[41] Reinhartz, "The Meaning of νόμος" 344 says "from the tenor of his arguments, it would seem that no such claims were being made for other specific law codes. For example, Philo does not find it necessary to argue that other law codes do not embody the law." In some way he does, but the point holds: no one else could have conceived the need to argue that their written law was the law of nature.

[42] Helmut Koester, "νόμος φύσεως" 533.

[43] Mendelson, *Philo's Jewish Identity* 24.

of higher law. Philo was also convinced of God's provident creation, God's action in creation, and God's giving of the Mosaic law. There were many possibilities for contradiction in Philo's melding together of Greek and Jewish law, there was only one possibility for success: there could only be one, true law, to which the law of nature, the unwritten law, the living law, and the Mosaic law belonged.

There may be, of course, a second, more practical reason: the good of the community. Philo believed in the truth of the law of nature, but he probably realized, at the same time, the danger the notion could present to his community. Perhaps he even faced the danger from proponents of these higher laws. The law of nature, in the hands of Apostates or extreme Allegorists, could be used to undercut the written law: why should we follow this national law of the Jews? We follow the one, universal law. Paradoxically, then, the connection between the higher forms of law and the law of Moses, in the hands of Philo, probably saved the law of Moses from loss of status or non-observance. Philo rejected the possibility that the law of Moses might be transcended by higher forms of law; while he distinguished between the "inner" and the "outer" law, a "higher" and "lower" way to follow the law, the law of Moses remained untouched. The reality must be faced: the law of nature, except for its quality of preexistence, is contained in full in the law of Moses in Philo's work. The person with true understanding is able to see the law of nature in the law of Moses. The Greek sage in the work of Philo would act much like a Hebrew patriarch.

What then of the superiority of the law of nature in Philo's work? The Greeks and Romans do not offer us a valid comparison. They sought a superior law. Philo sought to protect his written law. The superiority of the law of nature in Philo is only relative: it goes to the heart of how people observe and understand the law, not the law itself.[44] The law of Moses is a guide for the weak and the ordinary, the majority of people, but it is not a weak and ordinary law. Philo attacks literalists, not for literally following the law, but for not understanding the law they follow.[45] The superiority of the law of

---

[44] Nikiprowetzky, *Le commentaire* 122f. Against, also, Yehoshua Amir, "Mose als Verfasser der Tora bei Philon" in *Die Hellenistische Gestalt des Judentums bei Philon von Alexandrien* (Neukirchen-Vluyn: Neukirchner 1983) 96,100. He implies that the law of Moses is only quantitatively better than the laws of others.

[45] Shroyer, "Literalists" 263–265. Mendelson, *Philo's Jewish Identity* 4–5.

nature tells us more about the state of those who fulfil it than about the relative merits or demerits of the Mosaic law in relation to it.[46]

If the written laws "hide" allegorical meaning, indeed, the true meaning, this does not imply a degradation, in principle at least, of the written law. The true nature of law could be found without these written guides, reason could guide the way; so technically a written code is not necessary. But without a written law, the results would be disastrous. The majority of people, ordinary and somewhat dull, could not observe the law.

Kleinknecht and Gutbrod have argued that Philo's attachment to the law of Moses was a contradiction because he would not give up the centrality of the law, even though it had nothing to do with the "sources of his religiosity."[47] Goodenough claims that finally the law of Moses is to be abandoned.[48] However close Philo comes to such conclusions by toying with Greek discussions of higher law, he never accepts them. He protects the law of Moses so that all people have access to this great code of law, without which they would be lost.[49]

Philo, of course, could have ignored Greek discussions of the law, but that would have left the field to the extreme allegorists, a group who in fact could easily have become antinomists. Apart from that, Philo believed in the law of nature. He saw his chance to keep the Mosaic law strong by tying it to all forms of higher law so tightly that they became in practice, and almost in theory, one.[50] In attempting to protect the Mosaic law from superfluity, a real possibility, he produced a vision of law unique in the ancient world.

In the final analysis, Philo's unity of law seems to be not only a way to express God's creation of law and unity of purpose, but an attempt to protect the law of Moses from Hellenistic assaults, by

---

[46] As Barraclough, "Philo's Politics" 509 says, Philo wants people to live a life according to nature.

[47] Kleinknecht and Gutbrod, "Νόμος" in *TDNT* IX 1054.

[48] Goodenough, *By Light, Light* 54–71, 73–96.

[49] Mendelson, *Secular Education* 61 says that "Philo often speaks of the path on which progressive men find themselves as 'second best.' Yet he does not view this alternative pejoratively." Cf. *Abr.* 123, *Somn.* 1.44, *Fug.* 146, *Migr.* 171, *Spec.* 1.36–40.

[50] Myre, "La loi de la nature" 167. Myre says they are not identified, probably because the law of Moses is historically promulgated (Myre, "Les caracteristiques" 67) and so not pre-existent. The tension between the preexistence of the law of nature and the historical creation of the law of Moses cannot, I believe, be resolved. Nikiprowetzky, *Le commentaire* 126, says, however, "Mais ce caractère temporel n'implique nullement dans la pensée de Philon que la Loi n'a qu'un caractère contingent."

Jews or Gentiles.[51] He recognized the danger to which allegorical understanding of law led, to which his own thought could have led. The way to superfluity was a possibility. In the famous passage in which Philo scolds the allegorists (*Migr.* 89–93), he has no more impressive argument to bring than that it is good for the community to observe the law.[52] Perhaps Philo had no other argument to bring, perhaps he believed that "true" knowledge leads to transcendence of the written law, but Philo was more than a theorist. If the "true" knower could ignore the law, who was to stop the lax follower?[53] Where do you draw the line? Philo drew the line at the observance of the law: it must be followed.

If Philo did see the Mosaic law as inferior, or not related to his chief source of religiosity, it is only in the sense that the law of Moses pointed beyond itself to the true nature of law and, therefore, his chief source of religiosity, namely, God. But as God was the author of all true law for Philo, we must be careful even in claiming that Philo believed the Mosaic law ought to be transcended. What, indeed, could that mean? To transcend is to rise above, and in rising above the Mosaic law, Philo did not intend it to be superfluous, he intended the law to be truly understood. That did not mean leaving the law of Moses behind, it meant grasping it for what it truly was.

In taking over Greek views of law, Philo particularized a universal view of law, the law of nature, and universalized a particular law, the law of Moses.[54] Philo was intent on convincing the Hellenistic world that the law of nature had been uncovered, that the true law could be followed.[55] He extends Judaism to the world in Greek dress. In the words of André Myre:

---

[51] Shroyer, "Literalists" 281.

[52] Reinhold Mayer, "Geschichtsfahrung und Schriftauslegung—zur Hermeneutik des frühen Judentums" in *Die hermeneutische Frage in der Theologie* (eds. Oswald Loretz and Walter Strolz; Freiburg: Herder 1968) 316–317. Mayer stresses the difficulty Philo faced in strengthening the role of the law of Moses. He points out "wie schwierig... die wörtliche Gebotserfüllung theoretisch zu fundieren war."

[53] Mendelson, *Philo's Jewish Identity* 13.

[54] Helmut Koester, "νόμος φύσεως" 534.

[55] Wolfson, *Philo* Vol. 2 374–378 makes an important observation. Plato and Aristotle despaired of an ideal state because they had no ideal law; Philo had that law.

> Il y a comme une tendance chez les commentateurs à présenter Philon comme un Juif timoré, rempli de complexes d'infériorité, qui voyait s'écrouler le judäisme dans la diaspora et voulait désespérément essayer de le sauver en l'hellénisant. Cette façon de voir ne peut tenir. D'abord Philon n'était certes pas conscient d'être hellénisé. Ensuite, il n'essayit pas de sauver le judäisme. Au contraire, il voulait sauver le paganisme qu'il voyait se perdre dans une multitude mortelle de systèmes alors que la sagesse révélée... les différents systèmes.[56]

Philo is unique and often original in his thought on the law.[57] And far from becoming a subverter of the faith in his work on the law, he is, indeed, a protector.

---

[56] Myre, "Les caractéristiques" 66.
[57] John Dillon, *The Middle Platonists* 143: "the work of Philo... deserves to be ranked as one of the more considerable *tours de force* in the history of thought."

CHAPTER SEVEN

THESMOS IN PHILO OF ALEXANDRIA

A fair amount has been written about Philo and the law (νόμος), including in this study, not only in regard to the law of Moses, but in regard to Greco-Roman forms of law, such as ἄγραφος νόμος, νόμος φύσεως, and νόμος ἔμψυχος. The common thread which has joined these various studies has been the term νόμος. There is, however, an analogous term used by Philo, but by few of his contemporaries, which has not received due attention; this is the term θεσμός.

Not only does Philo use the term θεσμός in a variety of contexts, long after the word had passed out of common usage, but he uses it in ways in which the remaining literary evidence, at least prior to Philo, suggests is unique. Specifically, he combines θεσμός with the adjective ἄγραφος, and he pairs θεσμός with φύσις in the genitive case; that is, he speaks of θεσμὸς ἄγραφος and θεσμὸς φύσεως. These last two phrases are confined to the work of Philo until later Christian Patristic authors, and even there only θεσμὸς φύσεως is found.

This chapter is concerned with Philo's use of θεσμός in all of its contexts, and especially concerned with whether Philo intends subtle and nuanced differences when he chooses θεσμός instead of νόμος. We will also inquire into Philo's use of the terms θεσμός ἄγραφος and θεσμός φύσεως, with the specific intention of determining the difference, if any, between these phrases and those with νόμος. We will seek the influences in Philo's use of θεσμός—which might indeed offer us a clue as to its meaning in his work—if it is not indigenous to his work and his own concerns, or, indeed, simply an example of a varied vocabulary. Finally, some suggestions will be made concerning Philo's place in the study of θεσμός itself, including the need to consider Philo in lexical discussions of the term.

Thesmos and Nomos

Any study of the terms νόμος and θεσμός demands an overview of their history and development; though the terms came to be considered cognate, their origins reflect different ends of the universe. Νόμος, according to Felix Heinimann, has its root in the verb νεμεῖν, which means to distribute or to pasture and to graze.¹ The verb gave birth to two substantives, νομή and νόμος. Νομή came to mean a pasture, field, or grazing, though it also had the sense of a division or distribution. Νόμος, however, took as its primary meaning a certain sense of distribution and division, but as Heinimann puts it, "das Wort bezeichnet also nicht mehr die Handlung des νεμεῖν selbst, sondern ihr Ergebnis."² That is, νόμος came to reflect not simply division and distribution, but proper and just allotment and apportionment.

In Hesiod (*Works and Days*, 276f.), and in Herodotus (4,106) νόμος is not necessarily a reflection of δίκη.³ Νόμος does, however, reflect an order in the lives of humans and animals. Νόμος is a reflection of the order of nature in Hesiod, an order bequeathed by Zeus. While it is a "law" for animals to eat each other, humans have a "law" of δίκη from Zeus, and this is far better than the νόμος given to the animals. The order of nature is also seen in agriculture in Hesiod (*Works and Days*, 388f.), for it is a νόμος on the plains, by the sea, and in the mountain valleys to begin the harvest in early May and to plow in November. This, too, is an order created by Zeus.

So although νόμος is not concerned with legal edicts, it is concerned, initially, with an order created by Zeus, and with that which is proper and allotted to each within that order; justice is a part of the order created for humanity. From the beginning, it is clear, the idea of νόμος was also linked to the divine. This link is strengthened in the work of Heraclitus.

In the important passage of Heraclitus, fragment 91, Heraclitus speaks of human laws (οἱ ἀνθρώπειοι νόμοι) and divine law (ἑνὸς τοῦ θείου, or "one (law) of God". Heinimann, for one, does not see a contrast implied between human and divine law, but rather the relation of divine law and human law.⁴ Human laws seek nourishment from divine laws, but are considered binding upon their subjects. The sense of the divine origin of νόμος is seen, according to Heinimann,

---

[1] Heinimann, *Nomos*, 59.
[2] Ibid., 61.
[3] Ibid., 62.
[4] Ibid., 66.

in Pindar, fragment 169, in which νόμος, he says, is a personification of Zeus.[5]

Side by side, then, grow two senses of νόμος. Νόμος came to mean the binding, written laws of the πόλις, those which had authority over their subjects. But even here, lawgivers, such as Solon and Draco sought out the advice of oracles; the divine was never far from νόμος. This is seen, as well, in the phrases ἄγραφος νόμος and νόμος φύσεως which indicate that law never became merely a human enterprise, but functioned within either the will of the gods or the order of nature. Written law, written by human lawgivers, expressed, however incompletely, divine and natural order. Although νόμος grew from the earth, it had heavenly connotations.

The earliest word used to describe the laws of humans, however, was not νόμος, but an ancestor of θεσμός, θέμις. Both words are based on τίθημι, to put, place, lay, or set up, and have the sense of that which is laid down or established. This word, and its cognates, found its origin in heaven. Homer spoke first of the θέμιστες, or ordinances, which kings received with their sceptre from Zeus.[6] Θέμις never rose from the ground up as did νόμος, but the Titan Themis was the child of Earth and Heaven: a fitting description of Greek law. Zeus took Themis as his wife and she bore for him "the Hours, Order, Justice, Peace, and the Fates."[7] These were the progeny of Θέμις.[8]

At some point, the word used became θεσμός, and this took on the same sense as νόμος. The θεσμοί were the laws used to govern the πόλις. Draco's laws for the Athenians were called θεσμοί, while Solon's were called νόμοι.[9] One could be a νομοθέτης, just as one could be a θεσμοθέτης: a lawgiver. Both θεσμός and νόμος came to refer to the written laws of the πόλις, but both also had connections to the divine. Law, in its earliest stages in Greece, was never simply a matter of human invention.

---

[5] Ibid., 69. Cf. Guthrie, "The Nomos-Physis Antithesis" in *The History of Greek Philosophy* Vol. III, 133–34, where he claims that Zeus, too, is subject to this law.

[6] Werner Jaeger, "Praise of Law," 353–54.

[7] Michael Grant, *Myths of the Greeks and Romans* (New York: A Mentor Book, 1962), 89.

[8] Rudolf Hirzel, *Themis, Dike, und Verwandtes* (Hildesheim: Georg Olms, 1966), 7–22. Hirzel states that to speak of Zeus or of Themis was to speak of one and the same thing.

[9] Cf. however Heinimann, *Nomos*, 72, who claims that both Solon and Draco called their laws θεσμοί.

If both words came to mean much the same thing, and both exhibited elements of divine influence, it is true to say that at some point θεσμός passed out of common usage and νόμος came to be the dominant term.¹⁰ Νόμος came to mean a written law, but its divine origins came to be expressed by terms such as ἄγραφος νόμος and νόμος φύσεως. Θεσμός carried with it the same meanings: written law, but, perhaps more prominently, law which came from the divine. Why it fell from favour is not clear, for it expressed meanings similar to νόμος, but fall it did.¹¹

Others have issued different opinions as to the origins and meaning of θεσμός, however, and before moving to the work of Philo, it is these opinions as well as a number of occurrences in the literature of θεσμός which we must consider. I have argued that θεσμός, though its origin was divine, came to express written law just as νόμος did. Victor Ehrenberg and Frank Colson have offered more specific views of θεσμός.

Ehrenberg argues that θεσμός "means by itself written law" and is thus "distinct from law by usage, or νόμος."¹² Νόμος, Ehrenberg says, in a phrase such as ἄγραφος νόμος means either eternal laws of gods or the custom of a given community. In both cases the law is not written. "It is in the nature of a θεσμός," though, "to be written."¹³ On the other hand, Colson is able to argue, with regard to Philo in particular, but with the whole of θεσμός in mind, that "besides being more divine the θεσμός has a wider scope and is like a general principle."¹⁴

Does Philo intend, when he uses θεσμός, to differentiate it from νόμος because he intends to say a certain law is written in character or because it is divine in character? Or does it share in both aspects, written and divine, as we have argued? Does θεσμός mean

---

[10] Martin Ostwald, *From Popular Sovereignty, From Popular Sovereignty to the Sovereignty of Law: Law, Society, and Politics in Fifth Century Athens* (Berkeley: University of California Press, 1986) 87 associates the replacement of θεσμός with νόμος to the democratic reforms of Cleisthenes in Athens.

[11] Martin Ostwald, *From Popular Sovereignty*, 509 suggests that θεσμός came to have a sense of "imposition" upon the will of the people, while νόμος referred to laws chosen freely (cf. 27, 85–89).

[12] Ehrenberg, *Sophocles*, 169.

[13] Ibid., 169.

[14] F.H. Colson in *Philo* IX, *LCL*, 509.

anything other than νόμος in the work of Philo? If not, why does he use the term so often, and, as we will find, in so many odd formulations? If so, what exactly does θεσμός express which νόμος cannot? Why does Philo revive the term? In Philo, the richest repository of θεσμοί lays untapped, and its recovery may aid us in understanding θεσμός and νόμος not only in Philo, but in general.

Θεσμός *in Greek Literature*

The use of θεσμός in earlier Greek literature establishes no defined meaning to which we can simply contrast νόμος, even while acknowledging their distinct etymological origins. As used in Greek literature, it is synonymous with νόμος in almost every respect. It seems that any subtlety of meaning in general terms is lost to us or did not exist. Θεσμός is to νόμος as law is to statute or as law is to ordinance: what is the difference? We acknowledge the etymological differences amongst all three terms, we may even have in mind particular meanings for each term, but it is difficult to distinguish specific meaning confined to each term. Whether each term refers to different concepts of law or types of law seems almost a quibble. In particular circumstances, ordinance might denote a specific type of rule—a municipal as opposed to federal rule—but it might not. Law might always be used when referring to the rulings of a Supreme Court, but we cannot assume that every reference to a law indicates such an august and significant statute. This is the situation we find when we come to examine θεσμός: each usage of the word must be determined in context, but in general there is little, beyond etymology and origin, which separates θεσμός from νόμος.

This survey of the literary evidence takes us back to the fifth century B.C.E. The speaker in Sophocles' *Ajax* 1104 is Teucer, who asks rhetorically of the king of Sparta, Menelaus, what gives him the right to rule over the Athenians. Teucer states that no θεσμός has given Menelaus the right to rule. There are no clues within the text as to whether this θεσμός would be established by human or divine fiat, but it can certainly be translated as "law." If this θεσμός is seen as divinely enshrined, it might lend the term a taste of its heavenly origins, but there is no allusion to such origins in the text, beyond, perhaps, its reference to kingship itself. The fact that the question is asked, however, why the king of Sparta deigns to rule over the

Athenians indicates that the θεσμός in question is related to the will of the human subjects.

The passages found in Plato—and the one passage in particular which is later cited by Plutarch (*Phaedrus* 248 c)—do seem to reflect the divine origin which some scholars have maintained is at the root of θεσμός. In the *Phaedrus*, it is said that a soul which accompanied a god, but saw nothing of reality, "shall suffer nought until the next revolution, and if able to do so ever, it {the soul} shall go unscathed." This, says Plato, is a θεσμός of the goddess Adrasteia. Here the term is related to the goddess Adrasteia, who is associated with Nemesis, and the subject of the sentence, the soul, is itself a divine element.

In *Epist.* 355 c, Plato uses the terms θεσμός and νόμος as synonyms. In this passage both terms refer to laws which will edify the soul, body, and possessions, in that order. Just prior to this passage, in 355 b, Plato uses the term νόμος (in the accusative plural) as a synonym for θεσμός. In this instance, both words refer to the natural order of the human being, "a law and an ordinance" which reflect reality.

The last literary appearance from the fifth century is found in Democritus *Fragmenta* 266.7. In fragmentary form, and so difficult to read, the passage contrasts the behaviour of the ruler with the law, which guarantees or preserves his righteousness. The king, or ruler, is compared to the law, θεσμός, against whose justice and power he is measured. While this passage does not indicate the king and θεσμός as opposed forces, but rather the law as a check and balance on the king, it also does not indicate that the θεσμός has a divine not human origin.

There are only two examples of θεσμός from the literary records of the fourth century B.C.E. The first to consider is from Aristotle, found embedded in the work of Philo and attributed to Aristotle in *Fragmenta varia* 1.1.20.21. The citation reads as follows:

> for all things that perish, then, this is the law (νόμος) and this is the rule (θεσμός) prescribed—when the parts that have come together in the mixture have settled down they must in place of their natural order have accepted disorder, and must move to the opposite places, so that they seem to be in a sense exiles; but when they are separated they turn back to their natural lot.

"This" law and "this" rule refer to a citation of Euripides, who states that after death a dissolution occurs in which each element of a thing does not die but returns to its natural state. Νόμος and θεσμός are used in this case as complementary and interchangeable terms, much like "law and ordinance" or "rule and regulation." Here, it is true, that θεσμός refers to the natural and divine order of the cosmos, as in Plato, but so, too, does νόμος.

A fragment of the comedian Alexis contains a dialogue between a cook, who represents the Sophists, and a Milesian. The cook says,

> the fire-god's (Hephaistos') hounds, to whom it is given alone, by some unseen law of necessity (ἀνάγκες), leave to combine their birth and death in one, leap thick and fast into the sky.

It is generally considered that Hephaistos' hounds are the sparks of fire which illuminate and burn out (their birth and death) simultaneously. It is this act of the natural order of things which is termed a θεσμός. Possibly "unseen law" approaches the meaning and import of "law of nature" or "unwritten law," at least as reflected in the natural world.

The third century leaves us only one example of θεσμός, according to the *TLG* and von Arnim, and it too is embedded in the work of Philo. The identification of this passage as Chrysippean is fraught with difficulty and, finally, untenable. Von Arnim attributed this passage to Chrysippus in *Fragmenta Moralia* 337.7 (*SVF* 3), though Philo nowhere does. The *TLG* simply has adopted von Arnim's attribution.

The passage appears in Philo's *De Opificio Mundi* 143, where Philo's discussion of Adam is attracted to the Stoic ideal of the first man, the cosmopolitan who lived according to ὄρθος λόγος, which is a θεσμός, or a divine law (νόμος). Without doubt, this replicates Stoic ideals about the first man, such as those found in Seneca's *Epist.* 90.5, and perhaps even ideals known as those of Chrysippus, though it is not clear why the attribution to Chrysippus is made by von Arnim.[15] Certainly, the connection made in this passage between Adam and the Stoic sage must have been made first by Philo, or some other Jewish writer, not by Chrysippus. If this is the work of Chrysippus, or some other Stoic writer, then a clear connection has been made to Philo's use of θεσμός, here and elsewhere, and Stoic

---

[15] Brad Inwood has stated in private correspondence (June 12, 2000) his belief that von Arnim simply made an assumption based on the common Stoic ideas in this passage, but there exists no external or internal evidence to attribute this passage to anyone but Philo.

thought on the law, even on the law of nature. But no such direct connection has, or can be made. Philo's source, or sources, may be any one or number of Stoic thinkers, even Chrysippus. At this time, though, we cannot claim Chrysippus as the source, and it is fair to say that no third century source refers to θεσμός to our knowledge.

Many of the references to θεσμός that might be dated to the second century B.C.E. are found in Hellenistic Jewish literature and will be dealt with later in the chapter; the only remaining citations dated to the second century are found in another Jewish source, *The Sibylline Oracles*, and refer in each case to the word ἄθεσμός, "illegal" or "illicit," to designate particular behaviours. *Sibylline Oracles* 5.166 and 5.430 both refer to paedophilia as ἄθεσμός, while 8.9 and 13.31 refer to the "lawlessness" of the Italians and kings respectively.

The first century B.C.E., apart from Philo's work, leaves us with one passage from Dionysius of Halicarnassus, *Rhet.* 5.118. In this passage he refers to a particular law as a θεσμός and a νόμος. This pairing again alerts us to the complementary and interdependent meaning of these two terms, i.e., "law and statute."

Plutarch, writing in the first century C.E., uses θεσμός five times, but only in two passages. Two occurrences are found in *Solon* (19.5.1 and 19.5.8) and three in *De Fato* (568, 570, and 570). Both instances of the word in *Solon* refer to the publication of the law in Athens by Solon, which is called θεσμός and which reflects accurately the historical designation of Solon's law. In *De Fato*, Plutarch's treatise on fate draws on a number of Plato's works. One of the passages Plutarch cites is from the *Phaedrus* 248c. The passage is cited in 568.c.7 and more fully in 570.a.8. These direct quotations account for two uses of θεσμός in this text. The third usage, in 570.b.5, pairs νόμος and θεσμός to describe the legislative quality of fate. The pairing is not unusual, indeed, we have seen it is fairly common, and the terms again are used in a complementary or like manner.

Another Jewish author of the first century C.E., Flavius Josephus, uses θεσμός in *The Jewish Wars* 4.386.2, a passage in which the phrase "laws of nature" also occurs. Josephus denounces the Zealots as annulling the laws of nature (τοὺς τῆς φύσεως νόμους) in their treatment of the dead, among other things. He claims they have trampled "every human ordinance (θεσμός)" and "every dictate of religion," including the words of the prophets. In this case, θεσμός is contrasted to divine laws and stresses that human laws, laws of religion, and the laws of nature, though separate categories, have all been abrogated by the Zealots.

Two other references are found in the first century C.E. One, found in Appollonius' *Lexicon Homericum* 87.22 describes θεσμός as a law. The second occurrence, from the *Harpocration Grammaticon*, speaks of a θεσμός as particular law or statute as opposed to a νόμος, which indicates the general category of law, that is, it refers to a θεσμός of the laws. The second half of the passage, though, describes that θεσμός could also refer to the constitution of the state according to Aristocrates. This description is significant, for it points to the fluidity of meaning even in the ancient context, that is, such fluidity is not being imposed from without by modern scholars, and cautions us from seeing θεσμός (or νόμος) too rigidly.

Usage after the first century does not differ much from what we have seen prior to this period. Where θεσμός is used in ways which reflect the distinct Philonic terminology, it is in Christian authors of the patristic period, whose dependence upon Philo is likely. The terms θεσμός and νόμος in centuries we have examined suggest terms which are often synonymous and which are, if both are used, difficult to distinguish one from the other, unless the specific author makes such a distinction between the terms. It seems impossible to suggest that an occurrence of θεσμός indicates much more than νόμος, certainly it does not seem to indicate divine as opposed to human law, and the clear implication of this survey is that the word had, indeed, dropped from common usage. By the time of the first century B.C.E. and on, Jewish authors seem to refer to θεσμός as a group more than any one else. What this might indicate will be examined shortly. It is time now to turn to Philo himself and his uses of the terms θεσμός and νόμος.

Νόμος *in Philo*

Νόμος in the work of Philo has a wide variety of meanings and shades of meaning. While it is impossible to review the range of the uses of νόμος in Philo here, one must at least mention the most important ways in which νόμος is regularly used.

Philo employs νόμος in the same ways that other Greek authors use the term. Philo uses νόμος to refer to written law, most often to the laws of Moses. He also uses νόμος when he refers to the criminal or civil law of other people or states; in these cases, he often speaks negatively of the law(s) in question. For Philo, not everything which is called a law deserves to be revered as one. Nevertheless, Philo knows of the mundane uses of law. Νόμοι are enacted as a series of commands and prohibitions, even if they do not reflect the truth.

For Philo believes that the law of Moses was given by God and reflects ideal patterns of the law. This is not an innovation of Philo; as we have seen, the link between human law (νόμος) and the divine was common in Greek thought. Philo need not have travelled that far however: the divine role played in the formation of the law of Moses is clear in the Hebrew Bible. It is also no innovation to claim that one's own written law is the best representation of the divine law. Philo made such claims regularly, but strengthened them by claiming that only the law of Moses reflected the divine law.

The names Philo fastened to the divine law were names common from Greek literary and philosophical thought. The law of nature and unwritten law were important concepts in Greek legal philosophy, as we have examined in depth, expressing the belief in an order inherent in nature (φύσις) itself or in the will of gods. Philo also uses ἄγραφος νόμος to refer to the customs which a people come to consider as law. Philo knew, too, as has been discussed at length, of the νόμος ἔμψυχος, the perfect king who embodied the law of heaven, and found such beings in the models of the patriarchs, foremost in Moses.

Our purpose, here, is simply to set the stage for a study of θεσμός. Philo thinks of "true" law, written or divine, as something revealed uniquely to the Jews, but this does not detract from his understanding of νόμοι as those written laws which pertain to any given people nor from his knowledge of a variety of forms of "higher" law. Though Philo's understanding of what constitutes the law of nature, or a living law may not be in line with other Greek understandings, his use of νόμος is ordinary in every sense.

This is the important, if expected, result: Philo uses νόμος in all of the anticipated situations. Νόμος means law in Philo in all of its variety. How, then, does Philo use θεσμός? That the terms νόμος and θεσμός once were interchangeable does not adequately explain why Philo uses the word so often when others have ignored it.[16] What led to the fall from favour of θεσμός is not clear, but if we

---

[16] Michael Gagarin, for instance, in private correspondence (October 25, 1999) states that he is unaware of any resurgence in the use of the term prior to Philo, only that it began to fall out of common usage in the classical period.

are able to ascertain how Philo uses the term, we may be able to determine why it gained favour with Philo. It may be that this is a quirk of Philo's vocabulary, or evidence of certain archaic tendencies in his thought; it may be that there is nothing to choose between νόμος and θεσμός in the work of Philo, but it still leaves us to ask why?

Thesmos in Philo: θεσμός

Colson has claimed not only that θεσμοί are "more divine," but that they have "a wider scope" than νόμοι.[17] A number of passages seem to bear out his contention. These passages are concerned with the decalogue.

The ten commandments, divine in origin if nothing else, are called by Philo θεσμοί: each commandment is a θεσμός (*Decal.* 32; *Her.* 168–172; *Congr.* 120). In *Congr.* 120 the θεσμοί are said to be the general heads under which are subsumed the particular laws (ἀπείρων νόμοι). Philo states in *Her.* 168 that the ten commandments are legitimately (κυρίως) called θεσμοί, and then lists them. He has earlier said that God is the θεσμοθέτης.[18]

The wide scope of the θεσμοί, and their divine origin, are in these cases obvious; differentiating them from νόμοι on these two counts, even in the contexts defined by these same passages, is somewhat less obvious. The passage in *Decal.* 32, for instance, calls the "ten words or oracles" νόμοι or θεσμοί. Likewise, *Her.* 167, which precedes the definition of the "legitimate" θεσμοί, calls the ten commandments νόμοι. Colson also supplies νομοθεσίαν, legislation, in *Congr.* 120 as a description of the ten commandments.[19]

---

[17] Colson in *Philo* IX, *LCL*, 509.
[18] Colson, *Philo* IV, 366, n. 1 surmises that the lawgiver intended may not be God, but Moses. The passage reads, ὑπὸ τοῦ θεσμοέτου μόνου, but Colson suspects that the proper reading may be θεμοθέτον θεοῦ. That is, "by the only lawgiver," God, may be, "by the lawgiver of God," Moses.
[19] This is supplied by Colson, *Philo* IV, 518, n. 2 as a substitute for ἐκκλησίαν. He calls it a "very drastic alteration," but sees no way for ἐκκλησία to stand, for it is modified by ἱερὰν and θείαν. He says the congregation can be called "holy," but not "divine." Could Philo intend, however, to call the body of legislation an ἐκκλησία?

It is true, though, that not every use of θεσμός indicates a wide range or special, divine sense. In *Spec.* 3.30, 61, 63, the laws noted all have to do with marriage and divorce. In *Virt.* 112, a captured woman, who is taken as a wife, ought to have all of the rights of all θεσμοί pertaining to wedlock. Finally, as one further example, Philo states that proselytes follow the laws (θεσμοί) of goodwill (*Virt.* 104).

The θεσμοί are often both divine in nature and wide in scope, but it is not true to say that νόμοι are not equally divine and wide in scope, even on the basis of the three passages examined above. This is seen throughout his corpus. In *Decal.* 16 Philo states that people "should not wonder if laws (νόμοι) were the pronouncements of God." He says in *Mos.* 2.34 that the νόμοι were "given by the voice of God." There is also no way to differentiate the ten commandments as θεσμοί from the later commands and prohibitions which make up the νόμοι of the law of Moses, because Philo is capable of calling the ten commandments νόμοι, as we have seen, and the other laws θεσμοί.

Philo refers to many laws, other than those which comprise the Decalogue, as θεσμοί. In these instances, Philo often refers to θεσμοί or a θεσμός as sacred, divine, or from God. He claims that "every good man is free" is a law (νόμος) or a super law (μᾶλλον δὲ θεσμὸν) (*Prob.* 3). Philo claims that the constitution of the world is "the right reason of nature," which he goes on to call a νόμος θειος or θεσμός (*Opif.* 14). Elsewhere, the words of God are described as "oaths" (ὅρκοι), "laws of God" (νόμοι τοῦ θεοῦ), or "sacred laws" (θεσμοὶ ἱεροπρεπέστατοι (*Leg.* 3.204). Those who have forsaken God have been false to the the "most sacred" θεσμοί (*Det.* 142). The scope of these divine laws is broad: both the angels (*Conf.* 174) and the lowest person (*Decal.* 42) follow θεσμοί, called in *Decal.* 41 the θεσμῶν ἱερῶν or sacred laws.

If any difference can be discerned at this point between Philo's use of θεσμός and νόμος it is simply this: θεσμοί are never said to be false or inadequate. They may be broad in scope and divine in character most of the time, but so, too, can νόμοι be broad in scope and divine in character. What is missing from Philo's use of θεσμός, though, is the claim that they can be false. True νόμοι, those which come from God, those which share in the Logos, those such as comprise the νόμοι of Moses, are from God; but it is true to say that not every νόμος comes from God, as we observed in the last chapter. Some νόμοι are the creation of human design, those of cities, for instance, which do not have the divine stamp. This is not said of θεσμοί. A θεσμός is always true law.

Thesmos Physeos: θεσμὸς φύσεως

Perhaps the most peculiar use of θεσμός in Philo is in combination with φύσις. Victor Ehrenberg claimed that this pairing is never seen. Other than Philo's work, I know of no other instance of this phrase in earlier or concurrent literature.[20] The phrase νόμος of nature is rare, but θεσμός of nature is unique to Philo. Why this is so is a matter for our analysis, and perhaps speculation, but the meaning of the phrase itself should be found in the texts themselves. The phrase appears numerous times in Philo's work, sometimes in a basic formulation (θεσμός φύσεως) and sometimes equating the two terms in a sentence or paragraph (i.e., nature is a θεσμός). The phrase can also refer either generally to *the* θεσμός of nature or specifically to *a* θεσμός of nature.

Philo calls θεσμός the "right reason of nature" and a "divine law" in *Opif.* 143, which is clearly the equivalent of the law of nature. In *Abr.* 6, the Patriarchs are said to have followed nature as the "most venerable θεσμός." Philo also refers to the νόμοι and θεσμοί of nature, on a number of occasions, though there is no sense of how the two terms for law might differ in this context—indeed, it seems they do not (*Opif.* 172; *Somn.* 2.174; *Decal.* 132; *Spec.* 1.202). The translation for these four passages, in English, is as "laws and statutes," which strikes me as wholly reasonable, rendering the different terms in functionally indistinguishable English.

The classical formulation of the noun with the genitival noun also appears: as there is a νόμος φύσεως, so too is there a θεσμός φύσεως. In *De Iosepho* 30, in the midst of Philo's clearest statement of the law

---

[20] It appears at least once in Methodius, *Symp.* 3.2 (Migne, Vol. 2, 18.64B), where Christ is said to transform the first θεσμός φύσεως to another rule; it perhaps also appears in Pseudo-Dionysius Areopagita, *d.n.* 2.9 (Migne, Vol. 3, 3.648A), where it is said that Christ was another θεσμός contrary to nature and in Procopius of Gaza, *Comm. In Proverbs*, *6:20* (Migne, Vol. 87, 1276A), where a similar, not identical locution (τοὺς τεθέντας ἐν τῇ φυσει), is used. In these cases, I would seek influence from Philo.

of nature, he says that the nations refuse to accept the θεσμοί φύσεως. According to Philo, everyone who follows the θεσμοί of nature should also follow the Sabbath (*Mos.* 2.21). Philo asks at one point, what are the νόμοι and θεσμοί but the ἱεροὶ λόγοι φύσεως (Spec. 2.13). Giving birth is according to the φύσεως θεσμοῖς (*Spec.* 2.233). A tree bears fruit κατὰ τοὺς τῆς φύσεως θεσμούς (*Spec.* 4.215). Finally, sovereignty, according to Gaius Caligula, cannot be shared and this, too, is a θεσμός φύσεως (*Legat.* 68).

It is also the case that behaviours can be in opposition to the truth of the θεσμός φύσεως. Philo states that the practices of the Egyptians serve to subvert the φύσεως θεσμοί (*Spec.* 2.170), as do those who commit infanticide (*Virt.* 132) or engage in slavery (*Prob.* 79). The usage here is also in line with the common descriptions of the law of nature by the Stoics and Philo: practices are not only according to nature, but contrary to the laws of nature.

But can a θεσμός φύσεως or θεσμοί φύσεως be anything other than the equivalent of the term νόμος φύσεως? The law of nature covers all true law for Philo, so it seems that whether νόμος or θεσμός precedes nature, it cannot cover more or less law than the corresponding term. They must be equivalent in scope. This reading is cemented by Philo's claim that the "immutable statutes" (θεσμοὺς ἀκινήτους) are the νόμοι of nature (*Aet.* 59). While this equivalency of meaning seems clear, it is not clear why Philo has adopted this term alone among his peers or predecessors.

Thesmos Agraphos: θεσμὸς ἄγραφος

The phrase θεσμός ἄγραφος, or unwritten law, occurs only once in Philo's work. This is the only occurrence of this combination in any literature of which I am aware. The meaning of θεσμός ἄγραφος in this one instance is also used in a particularly Philonic sense. On a number of occasions in Philo's corpus, he refers to the Patriarchs as νόμοι ἄγραφοι; as we have discussed earlier, this sense of unwritten law is unique to Philo. Philo's one use of θεσμός ἄγραφος is identical to this use of unwritten law, as he calls Abraham a law himself (νόμος αὐτός), or a θεσμός ἄγραφος. It seems likely that this is Philo's own construction, particularly given its uniqueness to his work.

Understanding Thesmos in Philo

Part of the problem in determining Philo's use of θεσμός is the lack of guidance, even basic information, from other sources in Philo's day. The word is not in regular use at all.[21] Colson, it seems to me, is in general correct when he states that θεσμός in Philo reflects its roots in θέμιστες, the divine ordinances given to the king in the work of Homer. Θεσμός indicates laws which have a divine origin. Of course this does not take us too far, as so, too, does νόμος reflect the divine law in the work of Philo. We are stepping forward, though, with the observation that no θεσμός is said to be false by Philo, which is not the case with νόμος. Θεσμός always is the image of true law, while νόμος can be either true or false.

Martin Ostwald suggests some of this difference in his work on Nomos *and The Beginnings of The Athenian Democracy*.[22] Without turning the two terms into academic caricatures of their actual application, or ignore the closeness in meaning, I would like to focus on the differences Ostwald locates in his examination of θεσμός and νόμος. In general, Ostwald finds that θεσμός does reflect its earliest usage, and has a sense of being imposed from the heavens onto humans. It is imposed by those standing apart from or higher than those on whom the θεσμοί constitute an obligation.[23] The sense of obligation Ostwald also finds in the νόμοι, but the obligation is less motivated by the authority of the agent who imposed the laws and more by the fact that the obligation is recognized and accepted by those who live under the laws.[24] The two terms approach "law," then, from opposite directions: θεσμός is imposed by a lawgiver upon the people, while νόμος is an expression of what people regard as a valid norm for their community.[25] Ostwald suggests that the change in terminology occurred suddenly in Athens and was a deliberate attempt to move from the concepts underpinning θεσμός to those

---

[21] Kurt Latte, "θεσμὸς" in *Pauly-Wissowa Realenzyclopädie der classischen Altertumswissenschaft* (ed. August Friedrich Pauly, Georg Wissowa, Wilhelm Kroll, and Kurt Witte; Stuttgart: J. B. Metzler, 1894–1982), 32.

[22] Martin Ostwald, *Nomos and The Beginnings of The Athenian Democracy* (Oxford: Clarendon Press, 1969).

[23] Ostwald, *Nomos*, 55–56.

[24] Ibid., 55–56.

[25] Ibid., 55–56; cf. 33–54.

underpinning νόμος.²⁶ If we grant, as I am willing to do, that Ostwald is correct and that θεσμός passed out of common usage as democracy arose in Athens; and if we grant, as I am willing to do, that θεσμός reflected always its earliest formulations as the divine law and was so considered to a greater degree than νόμος, how does this impact upon Philo's use of the term? Indeed, why did Philo revive the term? Why did he feel it necessary to incorporate θεσμός in his work to such an unprecedented degree? There are really only two options for why Philo might have adopted θεσμός: either he is relying on some other author's or school's work, or he feels that θεσμός meets an internal need in his own work that he feels νόμος cannot fulfil alone.

It cannot be that νόμος does not have divine providence in the work of Philo, for it does as numerous evidence has been adduced to just that effect. In *Sacr.* 131, Philo says,

> He Himself is the lawgiver (νομοθετική) and the foundation of laws (πηγὴ νόμων), and on him depend all particular lawgivers.

There is no sense, therefore, in Philo's work that true νόμοι are degraded in any sense or do not share a divine origin; whatever the history of the terms in Greek thought, Philo treats all true law, νόμος or θεσμός, as the creation of God, manifested through the Logos.

The difference in the work of Philo is that all θεσμοί are from God, but not all νόμοι are divine in origin. As mentioned earlier, some νόμοι are only "so-called laws." In this sense, Philo might imply the understanding of νόμος as convention, which is found negatively in the Sophists, but which positively might simply reflect the law of a certain town or city.²⁷ For Philo, however, it might have been a ready-made argument against the validity of certain νόμοι and support for his contention that all real law comes from God and all accurate positive law is reflected in the code of Moses. Θεσμός, therefore, could be seen as a word reflecting the stability and reality of God's law here on earth, without qualification. Νόμος had been challenged, from the Sophists on, and Philo might have felt that the term was always in need of either qualification or defence.

On a number of occasions a νόμος is compared to a θεσμός and θεσμός does seem to be the weightier term. This seems to be true

---

[26] Ibid., 55.
[27] Ibid., 33–40, for both responses to νόμος.

of *Prob.* 3, where a νόμος is said to be better described as a "super law" (μᾶλλον δὲ θεσμὸν). Elsewhere, along the same lines, a θεσμός may be described as a νόμος θεῖος, or "divine law" (*Opif.* 141). In these instances, θεσμός seems to retain a hint of its past: its superiority is located in its divine origin.

When the terms are paired, however, it is not clear to me that Philo intends two separate categories of law: one divine (θεσμός), the other human (νόμος). Far from a νόμος being the creation of human beings, except, of course, where they do not represent God's order and creation, but are additions to nature, Philo is insistent upon the divine origin of νόμοι. Philo seems to group the phrases together in order to express the all-encompassing nature of God's law: there is nothing beyond it, no term which is not found in its fold.

For it is clear that θεσμός φύσεως and θεσμός ἄγραφος have the same sense as νόμος φύσεως and νόμος ἄγραφος. Abraham, called θεσμός ἄγραφος and νόμος ἄγραφος, embodies the same law of God in both terms. Likewise, there is no distinction between θεσμός φύσεως and νόμος φύσεως. They are phrases whose meaning is identical and which point to the identical content. The laws of nature, θεσμοί or νόμοι, refer to both physical and ethical laws, included within, of course, the Logos.

We return to our two options: I am not aware of any other use of the terms θεσμός φύσεως and θεσμός ἄγραφος though it remains a possibility that some other philosopher or thinker was using them; if this is so, it cuts against the grain of current and common usage at the time, for θεσμός was not in favour in any form, and νόμος φύσεως remained a rare locution let alone θεσμός φύσεως.

There is a possibility that Philo was influenced in his use of θεσμός itself by its appearance in the Septuagint or that the term was in use in the Jewish community in Alexandria. Some examples follow. In LXX Proverbs 1:8 and 6:20, the passages reproduce a similar parallelism:

> Listen, Son, to the teachings of your father and do not abandon the laws (θεσμοὺς) of your mother (1:8);

> and

> Son, guard the laws (νόμους) of your father and do not abandon the laws (θεσμοὺς) of your mother (6:20).[28]

---

[28] My translations.

It is impossible to know if their appearance in the LXX gave Philo the impetus to use the word—it is a possibility—but it does not match the manner in which Philo utilizes the term in his work. The parallelism of Proverbs 6:20 calls for a term distinct but similar to νόμος and this might have influenced its further use in 1:8, which renders an identical second clause to that of 6:20. A related term occurs in 2 Maccabees 6:20 and 12:14, θέμις, but its use in both cases refers to things which are "not right" and does not impinge upon any particular view of law. One further use of the term, in Wisdom of Solomon 14:23, is not particularly relevant to Philo's usage, though it does indicate that the word itself was used, even if irregularly. Interestingly, the use in Wisdom of Solomon contrasts with the positive qualities θεσμός seems always to have in Philo's work; here it is used with respect to the depraved rites of idolatry. David Winston translates 14:23 as follows:

> (23) For either performing ritual murders of children or secret mysteries or frenzied revels connected with strange laws (ἔξαλλων θεσμῶν), (24) they keep neither their lives nor their marriages pure.[29]

I do not see that this passage could have influenced Philo, unless to rehabilitate the term, but given his own antipathy to idolatry, why would he have wanted to rescue the word in this context?

Two other passages suggest that perhaps the term was used positively with respect to the Jewish community in Alexandria, which may have influenced Philo himself in adopting and renewing its usage. One occurrence of θεσμός, that of 3 Maccabees 6:36, is of more than passing interest, for it speaks of a κοινὸν θεσμόν, a common law, established to mark a festival for the whole Jewish community in Alexandria to end a persecution. The RSV translates the phrase as "public rite," which might not get to the heart of the phrase; it might indeed be better seen as a common law, one for the whole community, though it runs the risk of being confused with κοινὸς νόμος, a phrase, which we saw earlier, can refer to something similar to the law of nature. It is possible, though, that with this phrase we are moving to a place in which it is likely that θεσμὸς was a word which was used by the Alexandrian Jewish community.

---

[29] David Winston, *The Wisdom of Solomon: The Anchor Bible* (New York: Doubleday, 1979), 269.

It does not have any of the sense of "higher" law, with which it is imbued in Philo's work, but it does relate to the common life of the Alexandrian Jewish community, and it might be one more piece of the puzzle which answers why Philo even used this term. A second important usage occurs in 4 Maccabees 8:7, in which the seven noble brothers defy Antiochus Epiphanes during his persecution of the Jews. Antiochus promises the brothers positions of governmental authority if they renounce "the ancestral law of their community" (τόν πάτριον ὑμῶν τῆς πολιτείας θεσμόν). Whether this is a conscious attempt to recall an older word is difficult to determine, but in both 3 and 4 Maccabees the word θεσμός is used to refer to a Jewish community law. Perhaps it was this usage, if it reflects actual community practice, which inspired Philo to take note of the term, but it cannot explain how Philo uses the word. For this, only Philo himself offers an explanation.

We are left, I believe, with another piece of Philo's cosmic puzzle and Philo's use of θεσμός must stem from internal needs. These internal needs relate both to his philosophic desire to create One Law, given by God, and to include under this rubric all manifestations of Greco-Roman law and to his apologetic desire to protect his community from attempts to undermine or minimize the importance of the law of Moses. Philo does this with respect to θεσμός, to my mind, even though the word is no longer being used in a Greek context, and only sporadically in a Jewish context, and even though the phrases θεσμός φύσεως and θεσμός ἄγραφος were never used before him. Philo's Unity of Law did not simply encompass all known terms of Higher Law, it lead to the creation of new terms of law. No matter what law you consider, it is law, θεσμός or νόμος, only with respect to its relation to its source, God, and God's true copies, the Patriarchs or the law of Moses. Philo's innovation reflects once again his devotion to the Jewish law.

EXCURSUS

PHILO AND THE STOICS ON THE καθήκοντα AND THE κατορθώματα

Scholars of Stoicism have long noted the paucity of the appearance of the term νόμος φύσεως in early Stoic sources. Until Cicero, writing in Latin, the term "law of nature" is quite rare in Stoic sources, or sources sympathetic to Stoicism. This we have noted throughout the study. Philo is an exception to this rule amongst writers in Greek: the term νόμος φύσεως appears often in his work, as does his own locution θεσμός φύσεως as we have just examined. Richard Horsley has suggested, in fact, that Cicero and Philo share a common source for their view of the law of nature.[1]

Yet, care must always be taken in evaluating the law of nature in the work of Philo and not just with respect to the actual phrase νόμος φύσεως; Philo has a number of major concerns which deviate from those of Stoicism. This is seen in his use of the terms καθήκοντα, which are appropriate actions, a Stoic technical term, and κατορθώματα, the perfect actions of the Sage.[2] These two terms, unlike νόμος φύσεως, do appear in many Stoic sources before Cicero and they are important in defining an ethical life in Stoic thought. Appropriate actions are those actions which are according to nature, but sometimes subject to violation. Only the actions of the Sage, the κατορθώματα, are perfect and not subject to modification, for only the Sage is truly able to follow the dictates of nature. Both of these terms are central to the moral world of the Stoics. Philo, however, plays down the importance of these terms, and, indeed, denigrates them in a way a Stoic never could; although a number of scholars have argued that a move was afoot to replace the κατορθώματα as a rare guide to behaviour which only the Sage could fulfil with the καθήκοντα which the major-

---

[1] "The Law of Nature in Philo and Cicero," 35–59.
[2] For a discussion of the terms cf. I. G. Kidd, "Moral Actions and Rules in Stoic Ethics," 247–258; "Stoic Intermediaries and the End for Man," 150–172; Rist, *Stoic Philosophy*; Inwood, "Commentary," 95–101; *Ethics and Human Action in Early Stoicism* (Oxford: Clarendon Press, 1985).

ity of humankind could attain, Philo suggests a much more concrete basis for the law of nature.

This excursus examines Philo's purposes in his treatment of these two terms, and compares his treatment to that found in the Stoic sources. This study also treats the importance of these terms for the Stoic view of the law of nature, and suggests reasons as to why Philo finds them peripheral in his treatment of the law of nature. Finally, I propose that Philo's view of the law of nature be used with care in comparison with Stoic or Middle Platonist texts.

The questions concerning κατορθώματα and καθήκοντα in Philo and the Stoics come down to the content of the law of nature and for Philo, the law of nature had material content, of which the law of Moses was its exact copy. For the Stoics the law of nature was contentless, since only the Sage knew right reason and, therefore, only the Sage was capable of aligning his activity with the κατορθώματα, or the perfect actions. There is no code because the appropriate actions (καθήκοντα) do not in every instance allow for the proper course of action in a given situation.

For this reason, the καθήκοντα are only guides to behaviour, appropriate actions which may or may not be correct depending on the situation. It is one of the reasons καθήκοντα are not laws, and why they are finally not concerned with the final or ultimate Good.

The law of nature surpassed human laws, as we saw in chapter two, and the καθήκοντα would, finally, be considered superfluous in the same way, made extraneous in some cases. The law of nature was completely reasonable and just; it perfectly reproduced nature in a way that no written code could do. The written law was second best as numerous ancient and modern scholars have noted.[3] Brad Inwood is clear in arguing for the necessity of true law in early Stoicism to be considered nothing other than the actions and thoughts of the Sage, the Wise Man.[4]

Others have claimed that in later developments, something else was afoot: the desire to call a written code, generally the Roman code, the

---

[3] Ludwig Edelstein, *Meaning*, 83; Vander Waerdt, *Natural Law* 85, 95–98; Inwood, "Commentary," 97–98. Cf. al, n. 38 in chapter 2 for Edelstein's quotation regarding the relation of positive and higher law. Diogenes Laertius, 7.125.

[4] Inwood, "Commentary," 101; cf. with "Rules and Reasoning in Stoic Ethics" in *Topics in Stoic Philosophy* (ed. Katerina Ierodiakonou; Oxford: Clarendon Press, 1999), 95–127 for a more thoroughgoing account of Inwood's treatment of this entire question, though unchanged in his conclusions; I. G. Kidd, "Moral Actions and Rules in Stoic Ethics," 247–258.

representation of the law of nature. Marcia L. Colish argues that, in fact, Cicero considers the law of Rome to be the law of nature in *De Leg.* 2.26,[5] and that the situation by the time of Cicero had become untenable for those who argued that only the Sage could follow the law of nature. This passage lies at the heart of the argument, as I mentioned earlier:

> the civil law is not necessarily also the universal law; but the universal law ought to be also the civil law. But we possess no substantial, life-like image of true Law and genuine Justice; a mere outline sketch is all that we enjoy (*De Off.* 3.69).

But that Cicero considers some laws of Rome to embody laws of nature for some specific instances should not be a surprise. The law of nature *was* to be enacted in codes of law, ideally, even though it could never be done so completely. Cicero would not, and does not, claim Roman law is the law of nature:

> just as that divine mind is the supreme Law, so, when [reason] is perfected in man, [that also is law; and this perfected reason exists] in the mind of the wise man; but those rules which, in varying forms and for the need of the moment, have been formulated for the guidance of nations, bear the title of laws rather by favor than because they really are such (*De Leg.* 2.11).

The Sage still embodies the law of nature, but Colish is correct in saying that Cicero begins the transformation of the law of nature as cosmic law embodied in reason to that of a higher law which influences the civil law; Cicero only starts, though, what Philo finishes.

Peter Vander Waerdt has attributed this move to someone other than Philo; he states that a "codification" of the natural law was undertaken by Antiochus of Ascalon, especially as it relates to the καθήκοντα.[6] It may be, however, that it was indeed Cicero who was concerned with the relationship between the law of nature and the civil law, given his profession and practical philosophic bent. Antiochus was interested in finding a guide for all humans through the καθήκοντα, but Cicero, the lawyer and politician, would have had abundant reason to wonder how the law of nature was to be related to the civil law and a systemic code of law.

---

[5] *The Stoic Tradition from Antiquity to the Early Middle Ages* Vol. 1 (Leiden: E. J. Brill, 1985), 96–101. See 125, n. 39 in chapter 6 for further discussion of Colish's position.

[6] *Natural Law*, 231–263. See n. 34 in chapter 6.

John Dillon sounds a note of caution in attributing to one person genesis for Cicero's view of the law of nature: he believes that the views of Panaetius, Posidonius, and Antiochus "are almost bound to be identical."[7] Vander Waerdt chooses Antiochus, but he too acknowledges the roles which Panaetius and Posidonius likely played in the continuing growth of this concept.[8] In the case of determining who was responsible for placing more emphasis on καθήκοντα instead of the Sage's κατορθώματα as a guide to the law of nature, Vander Waerdt is probably correct that it is Antiochus, though we must not rule out the fact that Cicero, too, could have modified and developed his sources.

Nevertheless, the significant issue for a study of Philo is, did the middle Stoics or Cicero move toward a view of the law of nature embodied in a code? Was Philo influenced in his view of the law of nature existing in the law of Moses by previous Stoic discussion? I do not see, as Vander Waerdt does, that there was a code of *officia* in the work of Cicero. A number of passages speak against such a move, as we have discussed earlier (*De Leg.* 1.42,44; 2.11; *De Off.* 3.69).

Vander Waerdt claims in an important discussion that Antiochus, followed by Cicero, knows of a code of laws, or *officia*, which contain the content of the law of nature.[9] Antiochus replaces, therefore, the κατορθώματα of the sage for the καθήκοντα, which even the ordinary person could follow. This is an important distinction, but while I think it is true that Antiochus, or Cicero, made this move to increase the significance of the καθήκοντα, I do not think that Antiochus or Cicero had a code of *officia*. I also do not think that the wise man's ability to follow the law of nature completely falls by the wayside. In a passage significant for Vander Waerdt's claim that there was a code of *officia* (*De Leg.* 2.8–11), it is still admitted by Cicero that "divine mind is the supreme Law, so, when [reason] is perfected in man, [that also is law; and this perfected reason exists] in the mind of the wise man" (*De Leg.* 2.11). Cicero also says in *De Off.* 3.69 that we have no true representation of the law of nature. How do we determine which laws are just? By referring them to the standard of nature, says Cicero (*De Leg.* 1.44). This implies that one can "determine" how to act according to nature in individual circumstances,

---

[7] John M. Dillon, *The Middle Platonists* (London: Duckworth, 1977) 81.
[8] *Natural Law*, 234.
[9] *Natural Law*, 235–263.

but it does not imply to me that it had been accomplished and set down in a code of *officia*, nor does it imply that anyone but the sage could do this perfectly and so truly follow nature. If all this seems to undercut Vander Waerdt, I still agree in general that the move had been made by Antiochus to try and find general rules to guide the ordinary person; I do not believe that such rules had been codified or that the role of the Sage as embodiment of the law of nature had been cast aside.

It is at this point that the differences between Cicero and Philo become apparent. Philo is willing to be much more definite and specific about the content of the law of nature. There are also a number of passages in Philo's work in which he treats the terms κατορθώματα and καθήκοντα, or related terms. For the most part these terms are used as the Stoics or Cicero would use them, they appear neither as unique nor out of line with common usage, but on a number of important counts Philo dismisses these terms and shows how significantly he has moved from Stoic views of the law of nature.

That Philo knows the terms is demonstrated by his careful usage. Philo appears in most modern compilations of Stoic primary sources, specifically with respect to the term καθῆκον.[10] In the example given by Long and Sedley, Philo explains how a proper function (or appropriate action) may be done improperly, and how an improper act may be done properly (*Cher.* 14–15). His language recalls the category, of which the Stoics spoke, of proper functions which depend upon circumstances. Circumstance matters when determining the content of an appropriate action. So the Sage who gives false information to save his country is performing an action which is καθῆκον. The disposition of the actor counts (*Leg.* 1.56). This is Stoicism.

So, too, is it Stoic to draw the distinction between perfect virtues, which belong only to the Sage and the middling virtues of the καθήκοντα, which only the Sage can perfect (*Sacr.* 43; *Plant.* 100).

So in what way does Philo differ? In one major passage dealing with Greek virtue Philo tips his hand in a way to be expected from him. However deep the influence of Stoicism is buried in Philo, it takes second place to the law of Moses and its Creator. To whatever extent κατορθώματα and καθήκοντα are virtues, they do not reach to the heights of their role amongst the Stoics or Cicero.

---

[10] Long and Sedley, *The Hellenistic Philosophers*, 59H, 362–363.

Philo devalues and downplays the role of the ἀδιάφορα (indifferents) and καθήκοντα in the life of the ordinary person; in their place he substitutes the law of Moses. The καθήκοντα were those appropriate actions which were to be chosen among the indifferents (ἀδιάφορα). Not every καθῆκον act, however, was always according to nature, and only the wise man could truly perform good acts, or perfectly virtuous acts (κατορθώματα). This meant, in effect, that only the Sage could live a life according to nature. Philo's claim that anyone who can follow the law of Moses is following nature is a much broader claim than the Stoics would make. Also, Philo would not claim that the actions prescribed by the law of Moses are only sometimes preferable. In this way the actions which the ordinary person is to follow are fixed and not given to deliberation. This is much different than the theory of the indifferents. I do not see that such an argument is found in the work of Cicero, nor such a fixed code given or considered. The move to make the law of nature applicable to the life of the ordinary person seems to have been underway, but I do not think the outlines of the law of nature were codified (cf. *De Leg.* 1.42,44; 2.11). If in fact they had been, it would give Philo more impetus to claim for apologetic purposes that the law of Moses was the law of nature; the urgency would have been real.

Philo does know of the Stoic theory of indifferents (*Opif.* 74; *Leg.* 1.56; 2.17; 3.165,210; *Sacr.* 19–20,99; *Det.* 122; *Plant.* 100; *Prob.* 61,81). He knows of the division between good, indifferent, and bad acts (*Prob.* 60). He knows, too, that it is the disposition of the sage which makes his acts truly good (*Leg.* 3.210). Philo even knows that not all καθήκοντα are always appropriate in every circumstance (*Cher.* 14–15). But, remarkable to note, he never speaks of these acts or terms in conjunction with the law of nature.

Philo's true beliefs are stated in *Leg.* 3.126 when he links human virtue (κατ' ἀνθρωπείους ἀρετῆς) and laws by convention (θέσει νομίμων) to Καθηκόντων and Κατορθώματον. In language no Stoic could ever muster, Philo labels these all "human opinions" and suggests that knowledge of God transcends them all. For all of Philo's knowledge of these technical terms—and this impeccable knowledge should alert us to how deadly serious he is about discounting this central aspect of Stoicism—he relegates them, especially the κατορθώματα, to a place of indifference in his philosophical scheme. To call the κατορθώματα "human opinions" is to suggest that the apex and crux of Stoic thought is an afterthought in the world of Philo.

The law of nature was not to be located in any existing written code of law for a Stoic thinker, at least not in its ideal or complete form. Cicero himself said that the law of nature placed Roman civil law in a "small and narrow corner" (*De Leg.* 1.17). It was a foolish notion, he said, to consider that everything which every nation considers law is just (*De Leg.* 1.42). There are, in fact, evil statutes which should not be called laws (*De Leg.* 2.13). A code of written law was to the law of nature "a mere outline sketch" (*De Off.* 3.69). Philo says that some written laws are not law in the true sense of the word at all. Epictetus, likewise, writes of the laws which come from God as worthy of following, not those from human legislators (4.3,11–12).

The law of nature, as has been stated with some degree of browbeating, was for Stoics the wise man's reason.[11] Everyone, everyone with reason, which theoretically includes us all, has the ability to follow the law of nature. The chances of actually doing so were meagre. It was difficult to know how many wise people there had ever been— not many, all agreed—or if there had ever been a wise man. Cicero shared this understanding of the wise man, as was discussed in chapter 6. The wise man was a perfect human being.

The perfection attributed to the wise man makes it apparent why no one was certain if there had been one in the past or when there would be one in the future. This meant that the ultimate ideal for the Stoics was something of a theoretical construct; practically, it left everyone grasping for the ideal.[12] Why? In reality, everyone was, technically, foolish. As was discussed earlier, this was the source of much mockery by the critics of Stoicism (Plutarch, *Stoic.Repug.* 1048e; *Virt.Sent.Prof.* 76a). Later Stoics, it is true, particularly Seneca (*Epist.* 90.27–28,34–46,94.21,29,37–40,95.36–37,40), devised a system of progress to lend hope to the great mass of fools, but the system remained intact. Unless one was to suggest that there could be a code of law which all could follow, and if only the rare wise man fulfilled the law of nature, those who were not wise were still fools. The idea of progress might have warmed Seneca's heart, but those who are progressing are still not and never can be truly happy. What is progress if you can never reach the safety of shore?

---

[11] Vander Waerdt *Natural Law*, 234.
[12] Rist, "The Stoic Concept of Detachment," 260; Long and Sedley, *The Hellenistic Philosophers*, 384–385.

Philosophers, such as Cicero, were left to suggest that *some* laws might embody the law of nature, but ultimately the law of nature existed apart from written laws. As Lapidge put it:

> one looks in vain for how man was to live in harmony with universal nature.[13]

What answer could there be to the one who was not the Sage?[14] The law of nature was finally the domain of the wise man alone.[15]

To this, Philo ultimately could not agree. Though a Stoic in so many respects, Philo lays his cards on the table for all to see. That which the Stoics considered most central, Philo defines as "human opinions." This demands necessary attention: the κατορθώματα, the embodiment of the Sage's reason, the Stoic law of nature *par excellence*, are called by Philo, "human opinions." Careful study of Philo always reveals a careful Philo. In one passage, *Leg.* 3.126, Philo plays his hand: the law of nature, revealed in the law of Moses, has little to do with the ultimate virtue of the Stoics and everything to do with the God of the Jews.

However close Cicero or Antiochus of Ascalon came to moving the goal away from the κατορθώματα to the καθήκοντα, and creating a code of law—which may, perhaps, have influenced Philo's thought—he was studious in avoiding any false identification of his code, the law of Moses, with any Roman code (a list of καθήκοντα) or with any Roman Sage (the embodiment of κατορθώματα). Whether the κατορθώματα or the καθήκοντα remained the goal for the Stoics, Philo was clear in saying that the goal for him remained God, the source of "human opinions," and their transcendent creator. Philo's law of nature, once again, is Stoic on the surface and Jewish to the core.

---

[13] Lapidge, "Stoic Cosmology," 162.
[14] Kerferd, "The Image of the Wise Man," 27.
[15] Rist, "The Stoic Concept of Detachment," 267.

CHAPTER EIGHT

CONCLUSIONS

In Philo the Greco-Roman concepts of higher law are prevalent; not only are they prevalent, but Philo has mastered them. Philo, though he has adopted the language and the conceptual framework of Greek legal thought which could potentially undermine the law of Moses, adapts these potentially troubling Greek concepts of higher law, and by so doing strengthens the place of the law of Moses. If there is an underlying similarity in Philo's and the Greco-Romans' conception of the law, it is that they both were spurred on by problems they had regarding the place of the written, or positive law.[1] This leads to some general similarities, but many more differences in their reflections on the law.

In terms of Philo's views of the law, encompassing simply the law of Moses and more complexly the Greek forms of higher law, he had to come to terms with his faith and its law in the Hellenistic world, a world of universalistic tendencies. His work serves as a valuable indicator of the struggles and hopes of the Judaism of the day. Philo was both a philosopher and an apologist, but his allegiance, far from being split with Hellenism, was with Judaism. The purpose of much of his writing is to convince wayward or unconvinced Jews, and Gentiles, of the truth of the Scriptures, Jewish monotheism, and the one, true law.

André Myre has pointed to the heart of Philo's mission: he wanted to reach out to a pagan world he considered sadly misguided and desperately in need of help.[2] It is for this reason that Philo identifies the law of nature with the law of Moses, and for this reason that Philo, though not a traditional Messianist, holds out hope that the entire world will one day follow the law of Moses.[3] Philo's adoption

---

[1] Samuel Sandmel, *Philo of Alexandria: An Introduction* (New York: Oxford University Press, 1979) 135.
[2] Myre, "Les caracteristiques" 66.
[3] Goodenough, *Politics* 105,110,115 sees in this a kind of Messianism. He believes that indeed Philo was awaiting a Messiah-King, a "living law." Richard D. Hecht, "Philo and Messiah" in *Judaisms and their Messiahs Judaisms and Their Messiahs at the*

of Greco-Roman higher law conceptions serves to protect the law of Moses; it serves the aims of Judaism, not Hellenism.[4]

Philo's subtle use of Greek legal terminology bears out his apologetic aims. Every form of Greek higher law which may threaten the law of Moses is considered, including a term, θεσμός, not much in use in Philo's day and Stoic technical terms καθήκοντα *and* κατορθώματα. Philo's discussions are nuanced, yet Philo uses these forms of law to support his own aims, which are the aims of Judaism. Greek concepts of law come to serve the law of Moses. Philo is telling his readers, Jew and Greek, that the law they desire, whether the law of nature, the unwritten law, or the living law, is found in the law of the Jews. Far from removing the law of Moses from its place of significance, discussions of Greco-Roman law serve to buttress its position.[5]

The Apostle Paul, by way of comparison, of course, has the same universalistic tendencies as Philo, with far different implications and results. He too was an apologist, but the message he brought was a radical restatement of Judaism. His abandonment of the law would have struck Philo as great apostasy. The depth of Paul's rejection of the law is not seen in any Jewish source prior to him. Paul, unlike Philo, could not see his way to universalize the law; instead, he claimed it was abolished. This abolition is not Jewish, and it goes further even than Greek discussions of the law of nature and its relationship to the written law. In contrast to Philo, the depth of Paul's rejection is somewhat surprising. Philo shows how far a Jew could go without abandoning the law.[6]

Philo has universalistic tendencies, which were certainly conditioned by claims of Jewish exclusivity. For Philo, the universalism of Hellenism had a profound effect on his thought, though one should not forget

---

Turn of the Christian Era (ed. Ernest Frerichs, William G. Green, and Jacob Neusner; Cambridge: Cambridge University Press, 1987) 139–168 rejects Goodenough's and Wolfson's conclusions regarding traditional Messianic beliefs. He believes that in Philo's work "the first line of meaning for Messiah and Messianic Era was the inner experience in which the soul was transformed" (162).

[4] See Herbert Oppel, "*Kanon*: zur Bedeutungsgeschichte des Wortes und sein Lateinischen Entsprechungen (regula-norma)" in *Philologus* Supplement Band 30/Heft 4 (1937) 57.

[5] J. J. Collins, "Natural Theology and Biblical Tradition: The Case of Hellenistic Judaism" in *CBQ* 60 (1998) 1–15 argues that with respect to "natural revelation" and "particularistic" religious expression you cannot, ultimately, serve two masters: one or the other wins out. He relies, at least partially, on the example of Philo. This study would seem to bear out his contention.

[6] Collins, "Natural Theology and Biblical Tradition," 13.

the impact of the Hebrew account of God's creation of the entire cosmos upon Philo's view of nature.[7] The roots of his universalism are different than those of the early Christians. In Philo, the universalism stems from a Greek reading of the Hebrew account of creation. It was incumbent on the sage to follow the law of Moses, but this was available to all those with wisdom.

While the encounter of the Jews with Hellenism was for some time ignored by Greeks, it became fundamental to the Jews and how they saw themselves.[8] It called for evaluation, whether conscious or not. Such an evaluation took place in Philo's work on the law. He may not have been the first Jewish thinker to treat the law in this manner, but it is difficult to believe that anyone else approached the question with such depth and fervour. Philo is not a servant of Greek thought, however, and he has no difficulty in rejecting that which does not serve his purposes. In the meeting of Hellenism and Judaism, Philo's allegiance is firm.

The truth of the Greeks supports the Bible, it does not undermine it. Philo dons the dress of Hellenism, but does it disturb the core of his thought? At least in the case of the law, the answer is no. Hellenism becomes part of his thought, but it does not undermine the Jewish centre.

According to Arnaldo Momigliano:

> what constitutes the novelty of the Hellenistic age is that it gave international circulation to ideas, while strongly reducing their revolutionary impact. Seen in comparison with the preceding axial age, the Hellenistic age is tame and conservative. Until St. Paul arrives on the scene, the general atmosphere is one of respectability.[9]

Respectability does not seem to have been Paul's strong suit. As far as Hellenism was concerned, though, Philo is less tame and conservative than one expects, though subtly so. In terms of the core of his thought, Philo adapted the thought of Hellenism to his own needs.

---

[7] The impulse to missionize, to tell the world of the one true way—for Philo the law—was certainly due to Jewish claims of exclusivity: we have the one true way. It was, ironically, the universalism of Hellenism which may have given Jews such as Philo and Paul the impetus and confidence to reach out from this small, insignificant people to tell the world of the truth that rested with them.

[8] Arnaldo Momigliano, *Alien Wisdom: The Limits of Hellenization* (Cambridge: Cambridge University Press, 1975) 92.

[9] Momigliano, *Alien Wisdom* 10.

Philo's meeting with Hellenism is conditioned by the fact of his Judaism. The Jews know the one, true God, they are people of the covenant, and they want to tell others of the truth. But as seen in a study of the law, Philo's differences run to the heart of his thought and being: finally, his allegiances are different.

Philo has consciously woven Greco-Roman legal thought into his work because his philosophical reflection has led him to the truth of its concepts, however misunderstood they are by their original creators and proponents. The higher law comes to the fore in Philo's thought because it is not alien to his thought, and it is not serving some higher goal: it is part of the goal. This goal is the supremacy of the Mosaic law and the truth of Judaism.

Philo, whose use of Greek language and concepts has led some to suspect he is something of a disloyal Jew, actually shows how far one could go to ground one's loyalty. Philo could easily have found philosophical justification for the abandonment of the law of Moses; instead, he adapts Greco-Roman legal theory, which could have lead to such abandonment, to protect the law of Moses.[10] The potential destruction of the law of Moses does not take place; Philo protects the law through his use of Hellenistic concepts.[11] Philo, for all of the Hellenism in which he was so deeply steeped, remains a loyal Jew: loyal to the law, to his people, and to the Temple.[12]

The attractions of foreign wisdom were great, but Philo is convinced of the truth of Judaism. The importance of the law, the whole law, for even so Hellenized a Jew as Philo has become obvious in the course of this study. The law separated Jew from Gentile, as it was supposed to. Philo in all earnestness invited the Gentile world to follow the law of Moses—it was necessary because it was the best law. However many accepted the offer, it was a minimal number. Not only did most Gentiles not care, or think, about the law of the Jews, it was not an easy burden to carry.

Philo, whose thought rests upon the truth of his tradition, clearly

---

[10] Barraclough, "Philo's Politics" 444.

[11] The difference in Paul's and Philo's views of freedom points to the radically different place the law occupies in their thought. Freedom is *through* the law for Philo and *from* the law for Paul. See Federico Pastor's excellent discussion in "Libertad helénica" 230,232,235. Both of them, Pastor says, differ from Hellenism, and show their Jewish roots, in stressing God's role in the process of liberation (235). Cf. also Sandmel, *A Jewish Understanding* 50–51.

[12] See Mendelson, *Philo's Jewish Identity*, especially Chapters Two and Three, for a discussion of Philo's allegiance.

had no reason to abandon the Mosaic law, though the temptations of Greco-Roman law led him to defend its importance. He would have found Paul's thought on the law, for instance, treacherous, or worse, anarchic.

Philo's door was opened wider than the Stoics. There was indeed a brotherhood of man in this world, the megalopolis, under the universal law of nature, and it was not only the home of the wise man. Philo offered the ordinary person a way to follow the law of nature: the law of Moses. The Mosaic law had to be followed, though, there was no question of its abandonment; and for those who had the ability to follow nature or right reason there was not a transcendence of the Mosaic law, there was a "transference": transference from a limited understanding to a full understanding of the law.[13]

Those who truly fulfilled the law were those who followed the law, and who in following it without compulsion or thought of reward, through their superior nature and the grace of God, saw its true glory and truth. In this claim, Philo mimics Stoic claims regarding the autonomous virtue of the sage. But unlike the Stoics, those who followed the Mosaic law literally, however, were not hopeless, they too had a place in the megalopolis, because of the status of the Mosaic law. This is a loosening of the entry requirements from a Stoic perspective, but a maintenance of Jewish claims.

Moses and the Patriarchs are described as νόμοι ἔμψυχοι and ἄγραφοι νόμοι; they seem to be Greek sages, not Jewish leaders. From Philo's perspective, the two options were not contradictory. What must not be forgotten is that in Philo's scheme the "unwritten law" is the model in human form for the law of Moses, the "living law" a Jew. The one who follows the law of nature is the one who observes the law of Moses. Hellenism's mark, though everywhere noticeable, is suspiciously faded.

Philo's synthesis may appear unconvincing, forced, or artificial to modern readers, but Philo's writings bear evidence not only of his sincere commitment to the unity of law—Greek (properly understood) and Jewish—but to the effortless manner in which he presents his case. Philo's purposes arise not from apologetic goals, but

---

[13] Klyne Snodgrass, "Spheres of Influence: A Possible Solution to the Problem of Paul and the Law" in *JSNT* 32 (1988) 93–113, argues that this transference takes place in Paul's work; but a true "transference", as Philo shows, does not involve ignoring the commands of the law.

from profound convictions about the nature of reality and the world. The lasting impression is of a man reaching out to a world which has the truth but cannot correctly interpret it. Philo joined the law of Moses together with Greek law, in order to save it and bring it to wavering Jews and the Gentile world.

It is a truism to say that Philo was lost to Judaism and had no effect on Judaism and how it grew; historically, in the narrowest sense, this is true.[14] But there is a sense in which he remains an example, though lost for so long. He met, as a Diaspora Jew, a minority in a vast empire, the thought of his time. He said "yes" to Hellenism, but on his terms. In the face of persecution and misunderstanding he argued and presented his case. Finally, he remained a loyal Jew, true to his people and to the law.

The results of this study may seem rather conservative. Philo remains after all a loyal Jew faithful to the law. The results are not, I hope, the result of a loss of nerve. Rather, they are the result of the nerve of Philo, who stayed the course, who transformed the Philosophy which he loved, all in the service of the living God and the law he gracefully gave.

---

[14] See David Runia, *Philo in Early Christian Literature CRINT*; Section III. Vol. III. (Assen: Van Gorcum 1993), for an assessment and overview of the history of the influence of Philo's thought.

APPENDIX 1

THE DATE OF THE PYTHAGOREAN KINGSHIP TRACTATES

Armand Delatte was the first modern scholar to discuss the date of the Pythagorean texts in depth in his book *Essai sur la Politique Pythagoricienne*.[1] He claimed that all these textual fragments relating to kingship were genuine products of Pythagoras' students. The consensus today has turned to A. Delatte's conclusion regarding Archytas, but away from his conclusions regarding the other three authors. Willy Theiler was the first to take issue with Delatte in *Gnomon* 2 (1926), 147–156. He argued for a Hellenistic date, specifically in the third century B.C.E.

E. R. Goodenough was the next to take up the challenge in his ground-breaking and still significant article "The Political Philosophy of Hellenistic Kingship" in *Yale Classical Studies* 1 (1928), 55–102. He argued for a Hellenistic date for all of the fragments, including Archytas, and rejected their attribution to actual students of Pythagoras. The next major work was that of Lucien Delatte, the son of Armand, who in a display of independence proposed a radical solution in his 1942 work *Les Traités de la Royauté d'Ecphanté, Diotogené et Sthenidas*.[2] He combined a critical text of the fragments, a French translation of the texts, a close study of the language, an overview of kingship in Greek thought, and a commentary on the Pythagorean texts to produce what remains the most important work on the topic. His radical solution? He argued for a second or third century C.E. date, and Philonic influence on the texts, especially those attributed to Ecphantus.

The next major contribution was that of Holger Thesleff, whose *An Introduction to the Pythagorean Writings of the Hellenistic Period* accepted the dating of Goodenough for the kingship fragments, with the exception of Archytas, which he accepted as earlier, though not genuine (fourth century B.C.E.).[3] Thesleff considered not only the kingship fragments,

---

[1] Bibliothèque de la Faculté de Philosophie et Lettres de l'Université de Liége 1922.
[2] Bibliothèque de la Faculté de Philosophie et Lettres de l'Université de Liége 97, 1942.
[3] Åbo: Åbo Akademie, 1961.

but all of the related Pythagorean texts, which gives his work an authority which the other writings lack. He took L. Delatte to task for what he believed was an untenable position in dating the kingship texts. In this regard, he challenged the conclusions of L. Delatte's study of the language, while generally praising the study itself. Thesleff himself published a critical edition of all the Pythagorean texts which he judged to be Hellenistic in *The Pythagorean Texts of the Hellenistic Period.*[4]

Walter Burkert, without reference to Thesleff, published two articles in *Philologus* 105 (1961), 16–43; 226–246 titled "Hellenistische Pythagorica". In these two articles, without much specific reference to the kingship fragments, he too argued for a Hellenistic date for the whole of the Pythagorean pseudepigrapha, giving third century B.C.E. as a *terminus a quo.*

In the meantime, Francis Dvornik, in a large work entitled *Early Christian and Byzantine Political Philosophy: Origins and Background* 2 Vols., agreed with Goodenough and Theiler in opting for Hellenistic dates for all of the kingship tractates, including Archytas.[5] He relies for the most part on Goodenough's work and does not seem to be aware of the work of Thesleff.

The next major work was a re-examination by Holger Thesleff and Walter Burkert of their previous work in *Fondation Hardt: Pour L'étude de L'Antiquité Classique* (1972),[6] a volume dedicated to pseudepigrapha in the ancient world in general. Burkert, in "Zur geistesgeschichtlichen Einordnung einiger Pseudopythagorica," gives a revised position. For the *terminus a quo* he suggests 150 B.C.E. and for the *terminus ad quem* third century C.E. In response, Thesleff, in "On the Problem of the Doric Pseudo-Pythagorica: An Alternative Theory of Date and Purpose," maintains a Hellenistic date for the fragments, but modifies it by giving a lower border of second century B.C.E.

The last major discussion is that of Glenn Chesnut, "The Ruler and the Logos in NeoPythagorean, Middle Platonic, and Late Stoic Political Philosophy" in *ANRW* II.16.2, 1310–1332. He too opts for a Hellenistic date, pre-Ciceronian, though he does not present many new arguments for the date. He does, however, take account of a number of articles published in the late 1920s which argued that

---

[4] Acta Academiae Åboensis. Ser.A: Humaniora, v. 30, no. 1; Åbo: Åbo Akademie, 1965.
[5] Washington, D.C., 1966.
[6] *Fondation Hardt: Pour L'Etude de L'Antiquite Classique Entretiens: Tome XVIII Pseudipigrapha I.* Geneva: Fondation Hardt 1972.

the living law ideal was present in a number of other authors, such as Cicero and Seneca, and so gives more of a sense of the continuity of the idea.[7]

It is clear that there are two trends in the dating of these texts which are still current. These are the various Hellenistic dates (Thesleff, Goodenough) and the second/third century C.E. dates (Burkert, L. Delatte). The two major works are those of Thesleff and L. Delatte, and to them must go pride of place.

Both of them rely on arguments from the nature of the Greek for dating the texts, because the texts are embedded in the anthology of Stobaeus. External criteria for dating are extremely hard to come by. On the basis of the language and syntax, Delatte and Thesleff come to radically different conclusions.[8]

L. Delatte argues that the language of the texts is artificial, namely, it is a mixture of Doric, with elements of Attic, Ionic, and Lyric poetry (85–87). As a result, Delatte concludes that when the texts were written Doric was no longer spoken. Thesleff maintains, however, that the Doric features are essentially consistent and that the archaisms which lend the language its artificiality "are insufficient to prove that the texts belong to an age when Doric was not used in conversation" (*Intro.*, 66). Delatte's study of vocabulary (88–109) and syntax (110–117) convinced him that the texts cannot have been written before first century C.E. Thesleff maintains that Delatte's study "confirms my impression that the texts are Hellenistic", but states "we do not know Hellenistic prose practices sufficiently well to be able to make chronological inferences from matters of style" (*Intro.*, 67).

Thesleff's comments strike me as convincing, but Delatte uses the same syntactical and linguistic arguments to argue for quite another period. As a result, it is difficult on the basis of textual research alone to date the texts.

The other method of dating is a comparison of ideas with those found in other texts. Delatte has, to some degree, depended upon such comparisons, but his conclusions seem weak and he has not

---

[7] William Klassen, "The King as "Living Law" with reference to Musonius Rufus" in *SR* 14/1 (1985) 67 also dates the texts in the Hellenistic period. He is entirely reliant upon E. R. Goodenough's article. Aalders, "νόμος ἔμψυχος", 315–329, also accepts the Hellenistic dating of these tractates, but does not engage the discussion at all.

[8] Thesleff, *An Introduction*, for instance, finds most of Delatte's work on the language of the fragments convincing; he rejects the interpretation on which Delatte bases his findings.

considered all the evidence. His claim that these authors are influenced by the Middle Stoics (cf. 284f.) are not convincing, and Thesleff is correct to point out (*Intro.*, 68–69), as did Goodenough, that none of the Stoic ideas found in these texts is foreign to the early Stoa. I am convinced, however, that a close study of the ideas in the Pythagorean texts makes the Hellenistic period the only possible period in which these texts could have been produced.

The Ptolemaic-Seleucid period was the period from which the worship of Alexander the Great stemmed, the beginning of the Hellenistic cult of the emperors.[9] Though the initial impulses came from Alexander the Great, the actual development of the cult was left to his followers. Not only did a cult of emperors grow, but so too did literature concerning them.[10] This literature had a wide-ranging effect, influencing even a number of Jewish tractates.[11] Most of this literature is lost to us, but such terms as benefactor (εὐεργέτης) and saviour (σώτηρ) began to appear applied to kings in the early Hellenistic period.[12] The Pythagorean kingship fragments, while only a portion of Hellenistic kingship thought, contain many of these terms. In general, then, the Hellenistic period, due to actual monarchical developments and the presence of a flourishing literature of kingship in general, makes the climate ripe for a literature which supports the claims to divinity and perfection and absolutism of the emperors, and gives no external reasons to doubt such a development.

When we consider the ideas in the texts, and compare them to other such texts, the case becomes even stronger. L. Delatte believed that Philo influenced Ecphantus,[13] and so, it would appear, was the originator of the νόμος ἔμψυχος ideal. Others have suggested that

---

[9] W. W. Tarn, *Hellenistic Civilization* (Cleveland and New York Meridian Books 1964) 48–57; W. S. Ferguson in *The Cambridge Ancient History VIII: The Hellenistic Monarchs and the Rise of Rome* (eds. F. E. Adcock; S. A. Cook; M. P. Charlesworth; Cambridge University Press 1954) 17–18; Lily Ross Taylor, *The Divinity of the Roman Emperor* 17–31; Cuthbert Lattey, "The Diadochi and the Rise of King Worship" in *The English Historical Review* 32 (1917) 321f.; Kaerst, *Geschichte des Hellenismus*. 380f., esp. 385; Dvornik, *Early Christian* 210–233.

[10] See Goodenough, "Hellenistic Kingship" 58.

[11] Dvornik, *Early Christian*. Vol. I 261; Günther Zuntz, "Aristeas Studies I: 'The Seven Banquets'" in *JSS* 4 (1959) 21–36; Oswyn Murray, "Aristeas and Ptolemaic Kingship" in *JTS* n.s. 18 (1967) 337–371; James M. Reese, *Hellenistic Influence on the Book of Wisdom and its Consequences* (Rome: Biblical Institute Press 1970) 71.

[12] See Schubart, "Das Hellenistische Königsideal" for the appearance of these and other terms in non-literary settings.

[13] Delatte, *Les Traites* 177–180, 285–288, but cf. 183,200,216,224,235.

Philo uses Ecphantus,[14] or that Ecphantus and Philo have a common source.[15]

Before considering any of these possibilities, we need to establish Philo's connections to this Pythagorean literature. That Philo knows Pythagorean thought in general is not in dispute, as his use of Pythagorean numerology bears witness (e.g. *Opif.* 90–127). Philo also knows, however, specific Pythagorean writings, as his references to writings which he has read by Philolaus (*Opif.* 100) and Okkelos (*Aet.* 12) show. Both of the writings attributed to these authors are dated to the Hellenistic period by Thesleff.[16] Finally, Philo knows of the term νόμος ἔμψυχος (*Mos.* 1.162;2.4; *Abr.* 5) and shares the ideas and the language of the concept (*Mos.* 1.148–162). But could he be responsible for these ideas? The ideal appears in Philo's work, clearly and in full, but is it possible that Philo could have been the source for this ideal?

L. Delatte's suggestion is fraught with problems, even impossibilities. First, one must overlook the clear evidence of the *Rhetorica ad Alexandrum* and the evidence of Cicero that the ideal existed prior to Philo. If we suspend disbelief on this score, we are met by further problems.

L. Delatte believes, for instance, that Ecphantus' view of the king as a special creation in the image of God is actually an adoption of Philo's view that humanity in general was created in God's image, which was then altered by Ecphantus.[17] L. Delatte believes that evidence of this is found in the Eurysos fragment in Clement of Alexandria (*Strom.* 5.5.29), a passage which is in most respects identical to the passage in Ecphantus. In the Eurysos passage, however, the king is not different from the rest of humanity, humanity is different from the rest of creation, that is, from the animals.

L. Delatte's suggestion that Ecphantus is dependent upon Philo meets improbability after improbability. L. Delatte would have us believe that Ecphantus borrowed an idea of the creation of humanity from Philo and altered it to refer to the unique creation of the king. Following this, Ecphantus borrowed the νόμος ἔμψυχος descriptions from Philo, which he used to describe Moses and the Patriarchs, and built a model of ideal kingship based upon these borrowings.

---

[14] Bréhier, *Les Idées* 18–19.
[15] Thesleff, *An Introduction* 50.
[16] Thesleff, *An Introduction* 16–17,114–115; *Texts* 124–138,147–151.
[17] Both Delatte, *Les Traites* 177–180 and Thesleff, *An Introduction* 69, n. 4 seem to overlook that this idea of humanity created in the image of God is not Philo's own idea. Cf. Gen. 1:26.

Ecphantus' modified model of the king was worked into a subsequent political tractate which influenced other Pythagorean pseudepigrapha (the work of Sthenidas and Diotogenes). This was then disseminated to a wider audience and adopted by authors such as Plutarch and Musonius Rufus.

In addition, another Pythagorean author, Eurysos, borrowed a section from Ecphantus and altered it to agree with the accounts of creation in Gen. 1:26. This is the fragment which Clement used.

It does not seem probable that the Jewish writer Philo could have influenced entirely the development of the concept in the Greek world. Philo is, first of all, a borrower and transformer of Greek philosophical concepts, not a creator. More significantly, however, it seems unlikely that Gentile writers would have fastened upon a concept used to describe the Jewish patriarchs in an ideal context, and then developed the concept to support a view of absolute monarchy in the Greco-Roman world. But it is impossible that Philo could have influenced writers who wrote before him.

Let me propose a more probable scenario. Philo had access to these Pythagorean writings, as he did with Philolaus and Okkelos, and used them to present Moses and the patriarchs as types of Greco-Roman wise men, νόμοι ἔμψυχοι. The passage of Eurysos which Clement used was altered by Clement to agree with Gen. 1:26 and to protect the figure of Jesus, elsewhere described as the νόμος ἔμψυχος (*Strom.* 2.4,35–40). The claim that humanity is not like the animals was not the point of the Eurysos passage. We may be certain his point was the one made by Ecphantus: the king is the unique creation of God.[18] Clement's point is related to his polemic against idolatry, specifically worship of animals.[19] The choice is clear: Philo and Clement adapt a pagan concept which was quite widespread by "Judaizing" and "Christianizing" it; or pagan authors borrow a Jewish

---

[18] Thesleff, *An Introduction* 69 n. 4.

[19] He glosses Gen. 1:26 in the context of a polemic against idolatry elsewhere and makes much of the fact that only humans are made in the image and likeness of God (*Exhortation*, 10.79–84; cf. 12.93). Clement also shows anger at Alexander's supposed deification (*Exhortation*, 10.77) and claims that man sui generis was made by the Supreme Artist (ὁ ᾽αριστοτέχνας πατήρ) as a living statue (ἄγαλμα ἔμψυχον) (10.78). For a fuller treatment of all of these questions, refer to John W. Martens, "Nomos Empsychos in Philo and Clement of Alexandria" in *Hellenization Revisited: Shaping a Christian Response in the Greco-Roman World* (ed. Wendy E. Helleman; Lanham, Maryland: University Press of America, 1994) 323–338.

concept, alter and recreate it in political tractates, and disseminate it to a wide audience.

As to Thesleff's contention that Ecphantus and Philo share a source, this seems to multiply probabilities. One could argue that both Philo and Ecphantus were influenced by other, earlier writings which are now lost to us. Ecphantus could then be dated late without it impinging directly upon his relationship with Philo: both would have other, earlier sources. Why is it likelier though that Philo used a source earlier than Ecphantus? The ideas which Philo presents are present in the work of Ecphantus, Diotogenes, and Sthenidas, so why should we propose an earlier source?

I am not certain who Philo is dependent upon as his source, but his use of Okkelos and Philolaus, both of whose writings are considered Hellenistic, leads me to suspect both that Ecphantus, Diotogenes, and Sthenidas are Hellenistic writings and that Philo could have had access to them.

The Pythagorean texts themselves speak for a Hellenistic date and against a late date in two ways: they are not influenced by the syncretistic, philosophical ideas which one expects if they are from the first century C.E./first century B.C.E.; and they give the impression that they are working with a concept in its infancy and developmental stages, not a fully realized concept which was adopted by them.

The writings of Ecphantus, Diotogenes, and Sthenidas do not show any of the syncretism common to the philosophy of the period from the first century B.C.E. and beyond. The ideas and expressions are almost always consistently Pythagorean. The Stoic influence, which L. Delatte sees as an important element in the writings, is not to be seen, except in rare instances, as Goodenough and Thesleff have both noted. If indeed the texts are influenced by Stoic texts, it seems unlikely that the kings in the fragments would not be touted as wise men. It also seems unlikely that a Stoic influenced text would not mention the law of nature in any context; if the kings were Stoic wise men, the law which they represented could only have been the law of nature. All of this is especially unlikely if Philo had any influence on the texts as Delatte claims. For, in Philo's thought, the νόμος ἔμψυχος is related closely to the law of nature.

The texts also seem to be situated in the developmental stage of the concept. All the texts are working with the same ideas, but they express them in unique ways. The ideas, therefore, are not systematized;

they are being created and developed. As a result there is very little similarity in tone among these texts. The ideas do not seem to be in their infancy in the work of Philo or Musonius Rufus, who present finished topics which they have clearly borrowed. One can see fully developed *topoi* in their writings.

Finally, the Hellenistic Pythagorean fragments seem to be aimed at actual kings.[20] This again points to the nascency of the concepts, and also their origin. The texts appear to be written to influence the behaviour of existing kings. There is an urgency and freshness about them, which is not apparent in authors such as Cicero, Philo, or in the *Rhetorica ad Alexandrum*, which in fact purports to be written to an actual king. The Hellenistic period supplies us with the most likely period in which such texts could have been written.

The concept was widespread in the first century B.C.E. and first century C.E. It seems unlikely that an idea which Musonius Rufus calls "ancient" could have stemmed from a first century B.C.E. source, let alone a first century C.E. source, and have been disseminated so quickly and with such success. The influences of the concept are found in Plutarch, Musonius Rufus, Cicero and the pseudo-Aristotelian *Rhetorica ad Alexandrum*. Both Cicero and the *Rhetorica ad Alexandrum* must be dated to the first century B.C.E., but in the case of the *Rhetorica ad Alexandrum* the date usually given is second or third century B.C.E. The fragments should be placed firmly in the Hellenistic period, either at the end of the third century B.C.E. or the beginning of the second century B.C.E.

And yet, these fragments do not seem to have exercised their influence directly upon Musonius Rufus, Plutarch, or the others, except for Philo. It appears that there is a stage missing in the transmission of these ideas. It is probably no accident that the authors who preserve this idea are the heirs or followers of Middle Platonism, such as Plutarch and Cicero. Richard Horsley has argued that Cicero and Philo have a common source for their view of the law of nature, Antiochus of Ascalon, and it could be that Plutarch, Musonius Rufus, and Cicero, among others, also have a common source for their concept of the living law.[21] If this is the case, and it is only a supposition, Middle Platonism could be the missing stage in the transmission of the idea.

---

[20] Thesleff, "On the Problem of the Doric Pseudo-Pythagorica" 85.
[21] Horsley, "The Law of Nature in Philo and Cicero" 35–59.

There is no way to tie the texts to the early stages of Middle Platonism or to a particular author, such as Antiochus of Ascalon or Eudorus of Alexandria, but we can, I think, see evidence of transmission from the Hellenistic authors to another stage of Pythagorean writers. Two fragments of Eurysos exist (in Clement, *Strom.* 5.5.29 and in *Stob.* 1.6.19), but there is no biographical information concerning him. As a result, a couple of possibilities present themselves.

Thesleff believes that Eurysos is simply a citation mistake for Eurytos.[22] We know a fair amount about Eurytos (Diogenes Laertius 8.45; Iamblichus, *vit. Pyth.*, 146,148,267–269), so the suggestion is appealing. There is, however, a problem. If Clement really meant to cite Ecphantus, as Thesleff supposes, then Clement not only made a citation mistake, he also misspelled Eurytos' name. To compound the problem, the same misspelling was made by Stobaeus. Is Eurysos really the creation of two chance misspellings and one citation mistake?

I tend to believe, therefore, that Eurysos was a student of the Hellenistic Pythagorean writings and resonsible to some degree for the transmission of the texts. (To suppose that Eurysos is a citation mistake for Eudorus, a Pythagoreanizing Academic, and someone who might have been responsible for the transmission of the texts, runs into the same problems, more acutely, as with Eurytos.) He is dependent upon Ecphantus in the fragment located in Clement,[23] but what has not been noted is his dependence on Diotogenes (*Stob.* 4.1.133—Περὶ ὁσιότητος) in the fragment preserved by Stobaeus. The Stobaeus fragment of Eurysos has numerous Doric elements, but both in language and ideas he is dependent on the passage attributed to Diotogenes. Both texts are concerned with fate and the things generated by fate, and both claim that fate produces nothing orderly or good. The Eurysos fragment also refers to the nature of the king.

In Eurysos, therefore, we do have a follower of the tractates—his dependence on Ecphantus and Diotogenes points to this[24]—and an indication that these Hellenistic tractates were transmitted, but we are still missing, it seems to me, another stage in the transmission.

---

[22] Thesleff, *An Introduction* 69 n. 4; *Texts* 87–88.

[23] In *Strom.* 5.5,29 (2–3) (also found in Mullach, *FPG* Vol. II, Eurysos, frag. 1, p. 112) Clement quotes a passage which is found in Ecphantus word for word. The only differences that I can see are two case endings.

[24] Cf. Burkert, "Zur geistesgeschictlichen" 52. If Diotogenes and Ecphantus were dependent upon Eurysos one would expect them to have language in common, but this is not the case.

The first stage would be Archytas' development of the Greek concept of ideal kingly rule. The development of this idea, under the influence of actual claims of absolute kingship, would have been undertaken by Pythagorean authors of the Hellenistic period. The development of this ideal might have been a response to absolute rulership not in order to support such absolutism blindly, but to see that the rulers in question became just rulers. The missing step would be the development of the concept among philosophers of the first century B.C.E., the Middle Platonists.[25] Here the concept would have come into contact with Stoicism and the actual *topoi* would have been systematized. This stage is difficult to reconstruct because there is simply no evidence, beyond the possible evidence of Eurysos, but the concept as found in Musonius Rufus and Plutarch does not seem to be dependent upon the actual Hellenistic fragments. The fourth stage would have been the passing down of the concept to the followers of Middle Platonism, men such as Cicero, and Plutarch. From here the idea would have reached out to other authors, such as Philo, Clement of Alexandria and Themistius.

The missing step between the Hellenistic Pythagoreans and men such as Musonius Rufus and Plutarch is difficult to retrace with certainty -it remains possible that the Hellenistic Pythagoreans were themselves read. Whether the transmission of the idea took place in this manner, therefore, is debatable, though there is some evidence, in Eurysos, that the Hellenistic Pythagoreans were being transmitted themselves. More probable, if not certain, is that the texts of the Pythagorean fragments are Hellenistic.

---

[25] On the need for care when speaking of the Middle Platonists, see D. T. Runia's article, "Redrawing the Map of Early Middle Platonism" in *Hellenica et Judaica: Hommage a Valentin Nikiprowetzky* (ed. A. Caquot, M. Hadas-Lebel, and J. Riaud; Leuven-Paris Editions Peeters 1986) 85–104. Cf. also Glucker, *Antiochus and the Late Academy*; and H. Tarrant, *Scepticism or Platonism*.

APPENDIX 2

PHILO AND THE ORAL LAW

For a meaningful dialogue to be held on the subject of Philo and the oral law it is necessary to define "oral law" and then show that Philo knew of it, or its earlier forerunners, and in some way contributed to it or was influenced by it. It was, and is, my contention that such necessary connections have not been demonstrated by Naomi G. Cohen in her study *Philo Judaeus: His Universe of Discourse*, or her earlier study "The Jewish Dimension of Philo's Judaism—An Elucidation of *de Spec. Leg.* IV 132–150" in *JJS* (1987) 165–186 and that Philo's references to the "unwritten law" are better understood in the context of Greek legal and philosophical discussions than the later, Rabbinic compilations of Jewish legal material, *Halakhot*, sometimes known as "oral law" or תורה שבעל פה.[1]

To this, the core of my argument in "Unwritten Law in Philo: Response to Naomi G. Cohen,"[2] Cohen has not responded. It should be clear by this point that my dispute is not that Philo is enamoured of "Greek" or "Roman" laws, that is, that the content of his law is made up of Athenian or Roman laws; indeed, as I have argued throughout this study, I believe Philo is utterly Jewish in his understanding of the content of the true law: it is either the law of Moses or the life of the Sage/Patriarch. Part of the problem may be one of definition, as Cohen herself agrees:

> We suggest that the major reason for the sharp division in the ranks of scholarship over whether Philo was or was not referring to the 'Oral Law' (תורה שבעל פה) when he talked of *traditional customs* is the way this and cognate terms were defined by different scholars.[3]

---

[1] Jacob Neusner, in *Method and Meaning in Ancient Judaism. Brown Judaic Studies 10* (Missoula, Mont.: Scholars Press, 1979) states that "diverse forms of Judaism known to us from late antiquity invariably claim that there is tradition, in addition to the written Torah, possessed uniquely by a particular group" (68), but that "we do not only do not have a reference to oral transmission, we do not even have an unequivocal Pharisaic reference to an oral Torah or to two Torahs... We should not even have called such traditions the Oral Torah (תורה שבעל פה)" (70).

[2] "Unwritten Law in Philo: A Response to Naomi G. Cohen," in *Journal of Jewish Studies* (Spring 1992): 38–45.

[3] Cohen, *Universe of Discourse*, 278.

This is exactly the case. I believe we are operating with different definitions of what constitutes "oral law." Each of our definitions needs to be explicit for the possibility of dialogue to exist.

When I speak of the oral law I am speaking of the *Halakhot*, recorded by the Rabbis long after Philo lived and wrote. Even though, it is true, the term itself is not found in the Mishnah or Tosephta, it seems appropriate to designate these texts as oral law.[4] We are left, though, only with the oral law as it was committed to text, not as it might have existed in Philo's day. This does not imply that customs and traditions of the Rabbis did not exist previous to the codification of the Mishnah, nor does it imply that some of their customs and traditions did not exist at the time of Philo and are not, indeed, located in the Rabbinic documents, but it does suggest that unless some point of contact can be shown between a particular Philonic Biblical interpretation and a particular Rabbinic interpretation, on the one hand, and between the Rabbinic schools in Palestine and Biblical interpreters or schools of interpretation in Alexandria, on the other, such contact cannot be said to exist. It must be shown to exist. It must then be shown that the passage in the particular Rabbinic document which has a parallel in Philo's work can be traced back to Philo's day and that he was aware of such Palestinian traditions. It does not seem appropriate historical practice to assume that the existence of a similar teaching or tradition in a Rabbinic document and in Philo's writings share, a priori, a common provenance, especially when we consider the gap in time between Philo's corpus and the written Rabbinic documents.

Jacob Neusner has written extensively about the assumptions which lie behind the claim that any similarity in an ancient Jewish teaching proves its Rabbinic provenance or origin. He says that "one conclusion, routinely reached, is that congruence or similarity proves in this instance the antiquity of the rabbinic tradition."[5] He adds,

> a second, closely related, and equally ubiquitous assumption is that similarities show parallels, parallels reveal sources, and sources demonstrate dependence. The source of all sources is Pharisaic-rabbinic tradition. Therefore if a saying appears early in Philo, and late in a medieval compilation of midrashim . . . then Philo presumably has borrowed from Pharisaic-rabbinic tradition.[6]

---

[4] Cohen, *Universe of Discourse*, 21–22, 281–283.
[5] Neusner, *Method and Meaning*, 73.
[6] Ibid., 73.

This type of procedure, then, can be used to connect every similarity in ancient Jewish writings to Rabbinic teachings, even if, on the face of it, it is historically more accurate to trace provenance to the source in which it first appeared, in this instance Philo, not to Rabbinic documents appearing hundreds of years later.[7]

This, to my mind, is what Cohen does when she speaks of a "common pool" of traditions which the Rabbis and Philo drew from in composing their documents. Whenever a parallel can be adduced between a Philonic passage and a similarly themed passage in a Rabbinic document, Cohen feels safe in assuming they drew from a common storehouse of oral tradition.[8] This she assumes without arguing for the existence of early traditions in the Rabbinic documents. She states, indeed, that there are early sources in the Rabbinic documents, but does not tell us her methodology for locating them or how she determines early or late provenance. The method seems to boil down to this: if there is a parallel to something Philo wrote, then the Rabbis and Philo drew from an early source. It must be always kept in mind that Philo pre-dates all of the Rabbinic texts and that "influence," a notoriously shady term to pin down, might more easily be said to have moved from an earlier document to a later document and not the other way around. As she states,

> although it is extremely difficult, in fact well nigh impossible, to assign even an approximate date to the vast majority of midrashic traditions contained in the standard midrashic compendia, this does not preclude the possibility, even the likelihood, that some of them are early, even very early.[9]

Again, though, the issue is not *are some traditions early*, but *which ones are early* and *how do we locate them*.

Cohen, to my mind, has started to bridge this gap and has located some points of contact between Philonic interpretation and later Rabbinic interpretation, as has, for instance, Peder Borgen.[10] She

---

[7] Ibid., 73–75.

[8] Cohen, *Universe of Discourse*, 7–10, 31, 37, 56, 65, 143, 284. See, further, Neusner's comments on this procedure by modern scholars in *Method and Meaning*, 73–75 and *The Rabbinic Traditions About the Pharisees Before 70: Part III Conclusions* (Leiden: E. J. Brill 1971) 175–177.

[9] Cohen, *Universe of Discourse*, 77.

[10] Peder Borgen, "Philo of Alexandria" in *Jewish Writings of the Second Temple Period*. (CRINT). Section 2. Vol. 2. (Assen: Van Gorcum 1984) 258–259.

has also, to my mind, shown that we need not assume that Philo's lack of knowledge of Hebrew (if this was the case) and his location in Alexandria pose insuperable difficulties in his awareness of Palestinian Biblical interpretation.[11] Given that Philo made at least one journey to Jerusalem (*Prov.* 2.64), we might be wise to suspect it was not his only trip to Jerusalem.[12] Given, too, his love of Torah and his passion for Biblical interpretation, we might be wise to accept his awareness of Palestinian Biblical interpretation, as well as Biblical interpretation in other cities and regions in the Diaspora.[13]

Cohen, too, is aware of the sources and the problems the Rabbinic sources pose:

> While the 'oral traditions' were clearly very much a part of the fabric of Jewish life in his day—and Philo states in no uncertain terms that he considers behaviour according to these precepts to be incumbent upon committed Jews—*the literature of the Oral Law was of course centuries away from redaction or codification.* Philo could not therefore refer to this *literature,* nor could it have served as a subject for study in his day in the manner that it did in later times . . . so too Philo's 'unwritten laws,' 'traditions of men of old' etc., although they do in fact overwhelmingly reflect either the *halakhah* as we know it or what in Talmudic scholarship are called 'early *halakhot,*' are not to be associated with the literature of the 'oral law.'[14]

She is also aware that the Rabbinic documents pose problems with respect to their historical veracity—"of course not everything in these texts can or should be considered historically accurate"[15]—but rightly rejects the wholesale discrimination of these texts as historically worthless. The problem for me is not her outlook of "goodwill" regarding the Rabbinic texts, but the assumption that whenever Philo's thought is reflected in a Rabbinic text, the Rabbinic parallel is judged thereby as early as Philo and drawing from a "common" source. It is an historical shortcut: I do not a priori reject the historical validity of Rabbinic texts, but if I want to show that texts written centuries apart share the same provenance I must prove this not assume it. This is where the work has not been done. Should we assume that every similar interpretive theme, or even practice, reflects a shared Palestinian—

---

[11] Cohen, *Universe of Discourse,* 16–18, 28–30.
[12] Ibid., 145.
[13] Ibid., 15.
[14] Ibid., 22.
[15] Ibid., 23.

Diaspora tradition? What does it mean to suggest "influence" amongst these communities? Does similar interpretation denote a shared tradition of interpretation? Or should we expect similarity when the text being interpreted, the Torah, is the root of their interpretation?

Jacob Neusner speaks to both of these issues: "the fact of a parallel form or idea, standing by itself, may prove only that two men in the same country and social class reached a similar aesthetic or religious conclusion, at much the same time, about much the same literary or theological problem," which is to be expected when we recognize "the simple fact that all Israel by definition acknowledged the authority of Scripture, its law and theology."[16] It does not imply a Rabbinic origin for any given idea, indeed, it might imply the opposite: borrowing by later Rabbinic documents.

"Oral law" may also refer to the traditions of the Rabbis and the Rabbinical schools before they were committed to writing, that is, in the time of Philo, though I do not believe they were called "oral law" during the period at which Philo lived, which poses a problem when attempting to compare his use of the term ἄγραφος νόμος and cognate terms.[17] The problem inherent in this, however, is that the traditions of the Rabbis which are not committed to writing in the Tannaitic texts are for the most part lost to us, unless we include traditions of the Pharisees preserved in the New Testament and Josephus. Neither Josephus nor the New Testament name these traditions "unwritten law" or "oral law" or any other such equivalent. Rather, these traditions are called just that, παράδοσις, or νόμιμα (customs), as Cohen herself discusses.[18] If we are to use these traditions

---

[16] Neusner, *Rabbinic Traditions III*, 176–77 and *Oral Tradition in Judaism: The Core of the* Mishnah (New York and London: Garland Publishing, 1987) 137.

[17] Cohen, *Universe of Discourse*, 263–64, 267 indicates that many terms were used to refer to the oral traditions, preeminent amongst them the word παράδοσις. Neusner disagrees, pointing out that the "category of 'Oral Torah' makes its appearance, so far as I can discern, only with the Yerushalmi and not in any document closed prior to that time, although a notion of a revelation over and above Scripture— not called 'Oral Torah' to be sure—comes to expression in Avot ... But that tradition is not called 'the oral Torah,' and I was disappointed to find that even in the Yerushalmi the mythic statement of the matter, so far as I can see, is lacking" (*Oral Traditions*, 152–153). Παράδοσις, though it clearly refers to the traditions of the Pharisees, is not an equivalent term to oral Torah.

[18] Cohen, *Universe of Discourse*, 263–64, 267. The major difference in my understanding, and it is major, is that παράδοσις refers to the Pharisaic traditions, not the traditions held by all Jews or "normative" Judaism. See especially, A.I. Baumgarten, "The Pharisaic Paradosis" in *HTR* 80/1 (1987) 63–77 for the argument that παράδοσις refers exclusively to the Pharisees. Cohen also cites Mark 7:3 to support her

to determine influence, we must also show that Philo, in some way, knows of a tradition which is known to us as Pharisaic. Once this is achieved, the problem remains that it is not accepted that the traditions of the Pharisees form the bulk of the Rabbinic material, though some can be located there.[19] Even if this expanded definition is accepted, and even if we accept that the Pharisees were the group from which the Rabbinical schools arose, we must still show, not assert, contact between Philo and the Pharisees. We cannot assume that "the ancient Pharisees, five or ten centuries earlier, had said such a thing, that the writer of the Patriarchal Testament or Philo, heard it from the Pharisees, and in writing it down, exhibited his affinity with, or even dependence upon, rabbinic authority or tradition."[20] Not only must contact be asserted, but it must be shown in concrete ways to exist in Philonic texts.

It is true that if one expands the definition of oral law from that which I offer many other possibilities are open to us. As E. P. Sanders puts it, "every first-century Jew lived by 'oral law,' if oral law means 'the law as interpreted.'"[21] If this is the accepted definition, then any ancient interpretation of a Biblical passage may be considered as oral law. If this is the case, Philo's interpretations of Biblical passages may be considered oral law, but it does nothing to move us closer to whether his "oral law" needs to be understood in the light of Rabbinic interpretation and influence.[22] This definition, I believe, is too wide for Cohen's purposes.

Cohen wants to make a connection between the Rabbinic oral law, or that of the Pharisees, and Philo's use of the Greek term "unwritten law." Such is the connection recently made by Shmuel Safrai in "Oral

---

contention that "all Jews" followed the Pharisaic traditions, but almost all New Testament scholars see the phrase "all the Jews" as an editorial comment. See E. P. Sanders, *Jewish Law From Jesus to the Mishnah: Five Studies* (London: SCM Press; Philadelphia: Trinity Press International, 1990), 108–115; *Judaism: Practice and Belief: 63 B.C.E.–66 C.E.* (London: SCM Press 1992) 448–451.

[19] Shaye J. D. Cohen, "The Significance of Yavneh: Pharisees, Rabbis, and the End of Jewish Sectarianism" in *HUCA* 55 (1984) 41–53.

[20] Neusner, *Rabbinic Traditions III*, 176.

[21] E. P. Sanders, *Jewish Law From Jesus to the Mishnah: Five Studies*, 97.

[22] Indeed, it might be that, as stated earlier, the Rabbis learned such and such a teaching or saying from Philo: for who knows which way influence flows? "It may be more reasonable to suggest that some time after the first writing down of a tradition in, e.g., Qumranian writings or Apocrypha and Pseudipigrapha or Philo or Josephus, a rabbi heard the tradition from someone familiar with such literature (excluding the Qumranian instance) or learned it himself in its original location" (Neusner, *Method and Meaning*, 75).

Tora" in *The Literature of the Sages*.²³ Cohen herself says that she wants to tie Philo's references not to the *Halakhot*, but to "forerunner(s) of what later became formalized as oral law."²⁴ But how does one show a connection between the forerunners of the oral law and Philo? One must rely on the written compilations of Jewish legal material which post-date Philo by over 100 years and in some of the examples brought by Cohen by over 600 years. What is the option? Unless one claims that the existence of Biblical interpretation in Alexandria itself shows connection to Rabbinic Biblical interpretation, one must claim that Philo had some dependence upon the actual forerunners of the *Halakhot*, namely, Pharisaic or Rabbinic traditions. This has not been shown, either specifically or generally. Again, some traditions in the Rabbinic texts may be "early, even very early," but how are these decisions made?²⁵

Recently, E. P. Sanders has tried to show that many of Philo's Jewish traditions or customs, that is, customs which are extrabiblical, have no parallel in Rabbinic, or Pharisaic, tradition.²⁶ He has shown, successfully, that many of Philo's customs reflect Diaspora rather than Palestinian practice. We do know, of course, that Philo went at least once to Jerusalem and so was presumably aware of Pharisaic practice,²⁷ but this does not mean he followed it. This must be shown. Obviously, there would be overlap amongst the customs of Jews in Palestine and the Diaspora since they were deriving custom in order to adhere to the demands of the Torah. They were all, whether in Palestine or beyond, Jews and observant Jews everywhere adhered, as best they understood, to the dictates of the Torah. I do not believe, however, that in Philo's day Pharisaic traditions were dominant for all Jews everywhere.

What then did Philo intend when he wrote of the unwritten law (ἄγραφος νόμος or cognates)? Since the term "oral law" or, more correctly, "oral Torah" did not come into usage, if the literary evidence

---

²³ Shmuel Safrai, "Oral Tora" in *The Literature of the Sages*, Part I (CRINT II.3.1), ed. S. Safrai, (Assen and Philadelphia 1987) 40f.
²⁴ Cohen, "Jewish Dimension," 177; "A Response to John W. Martens" in *JJS* 44/1 (1993) 114.
²⁵ Cohen, *Universe of Discourse*, 77; also, cf. 19, 52.
²⁶ E. P. Sanders, *Jewish Law From Jesus to the Mishnah: Five Studies*, 255–308.
²⁷ Though it is important to keep in mind the relative influence of the Pharisees at the time Philo lived; it is not as great as commonly assumed. See Neusner, *From Politics to Piety: The Emergence of Pharisaic Judaism* (Englewood Cliffs, N.J.: Prentice-Hall, Inc., 1973), esp. 10–11, for an assessment of all the evidence.

can be trusted, until hundreds of years after Philo's death, it is not possible that Philo is writing with the Hebrew term in mind. The term probably existed before it was committed to the written page, but the fact that it appears in neither the Mishnah nor the Tosephta indicates that it originated sometime between 200–450 C.E. The burden of proof rests with whoever brings the argument, and the proof is not adequate to support Cohen's contention that when Philo speaks of the unwritten law we ought not look to the Greek source material which he mimics and quotes, but to Rabbinic traditions which we are not certain Philo knew and to a term which was not written down until hundreds of years after his death.

As I argued in "Unwritten Law in Philo," Philo is not referring to concepts of "higher" law each time he uses the phrase ἄγραφος νόμος.[28] Indeed, Cohen adopts my correction that unwritten law is not, necessarily, the equivalent of "eternal" law or the "law of nature" in *Philo Judaeus: His Universe of Discourse*, but attributes to me the belief that I consider it to represent the law of nature in *Spec. Leg.* 4.149–150.[29] I do not. I believe that the Greek context for Philo's claims indicate that he is speaking about customs which are observed as ἄγραφος νόμος.[30]

If he is not referring to ἄγραφος νόμος as "eternal" law, does this clear the way for us to see his references to *Halakhot*? In Cohen's words, does he "in *Spec. Leg.* IV. 149–150 . . . use the words ἄγραφος νόμος to refer to what eventually became codified as the Oral Law in Rabbinic sources?"[31] My claim is simple: he does not. Philo speaks here of customs which are observed by peoples everywhere, including the Jews, but it does not refer to the "παράδοσις" which Cohen claims is "'the ancestral customs' which were considered 'normative' in his day,"[32] because there is no indication that the Pharisaic παράδοσις was normative in Philo's day. Nor is there any sense that Philo is referring in this passage to any particular Pharisaic or early Rabbinic tradition. The connections Cohen draws are amongst Philo and late Midrashic texts, but even here the issues shared do not represent a common *Halakhic* tradition but a common heritage: the Torah.

---

[28] Martens, "Unwritten Law in Philo," 40–44.
[29] Cohen, *Universe of Discourse*, 258, n. 37.
[30] For a fuller discussion of the relevant texts, please refer to chapters one and five.
[31] Cohen, *Universe of Discourse*, 261.
[32] Ibid., 267.

APPENDIX 2: PHILO AND THE ORAL LAW

Philo is also not referring in *Spec.* 4.149–150 to anything which has the weight of later Tannaitic *Halakhah*. In *Spec.* 4.150, Philo states that praise is not due to one who obeys the unwritten laws, but that commendation is due to one who observes written laws. Cohen remarks that this does not indicate that the unwritten laws are optional, only that "no sanction is specified for their transgression."[33] But why would this distinction even be drawn? Does not the *Halakhah* have the same weight as Torah? As Cohen herself states, "the law to observe unwritten laws is itself a written law."[34] Where then, and why then, the distinction if Philo considers these laws to be the equivalent of Torah? Should one not do the written and unwritten laws with the same mind, neither deserving commendation?

The best way to see the unwritten laws in this passage, as I argue elsewhere in chapter five and in "Unwritten Law in Philo," is as customs which are incumbent upon people to follow, but are not the equivalent of written laws, and are certainly not "a body of traditional practices which were considered obligatory by the rank and file of committed Jews (including of course the Pharisees, but not them exclusively) and which eventually served as the cornerstone of the *halakhic* literary compositions."[35] If the issue is not one of terminology, that is, "unwritten laws" are equal to "oral laws" because of the similarity in the phrases, but content, that content is not yet clear to me: I do not see the connections in Philo's work to either Midrashic or Tannaitic *Halakhah*.[36]

Cohen ultimately explains her dismissal of the Greek sense of "unwritten law" which I prefer as being based upon a "frame of reference ... very different from his {Martens}." Therefore, "not surprisingly my conclusions from these very same classical sources are quite different."[37] Cohen returns to this issue of personal biography in her book, stating that "the difference between the two views apparently stems from a different conceptual and semantic frame of reference."[38] I am not certain how my frame of reference is different than hers, or how this directs me to falsehood and her to truth, since I take my framework to be the work of Philo, but I have my suspicions.

---

[33] Ibid., 268.
[34] Ibid., 251.
[35] Ibid., 268.
[36] Ibid., 283.
[37] Cohen, "A Response to John W. Martens" in *JJS* 44/1 (1993) 114.
[38] Cohen, *Universe of Discourse*, 285–286.

A frame of reference, as I suspect she is using the phrase, may be construed in two ways: one religious and theological; the other having to do with issues of personhood, i.e., I am a man and a Canadian. Both of these have to do, I think, with a suspicion of prejudices which manifest themselves in an interpretation of a text. The fact that we are subjects coming from different backgrounds, and have personal perspectives, demands two comments. First, it is impossible to keep one's personal perspectives from one's writing and it is not desirable to attempt to do so, though it is necessary to screen for bias and to check always for oversights and blind spots which may serve not the interpretation of a text, but the advancement of ideology. I am not certain how, though, she knows my personal "frame of reference" on the basis of my conclusions about a certain text, though she might have her suspicions. Because we reach different positions does not imply that my "frame of reference" is different from hers. Second, if frame of reference refers to aspects of my person it is of no consequence, unless it can be shown that these are controlling my reading of the data to the detriment of what would be considered reasonable. My subjectivity, finally, should not be the deciding factor in how others judge my conclusions; the significant issue is how my conclusions accord with the reality of the data, in this case Philo's writings.

While we may disagree on the importance of the Greek sources, I would not like to chalk this up to different frames of reference, but to a different reading of the evidence, which may be influenced by factors of subjectivity but is not controlled by them. If a frame of reference determines different conclusions in advance then not only is dialogue fruitless it is meaningless. Is it fair, for instance, for me to dismiss her arguments not on the basis of scholarship, but on the basis of her "different frame of reference"? This is a path which we should not take. Though it is not now in vogue, I am still naive enough to believe that an author, including Philo, writes with an intended sense, and that readers of goodwill may ideally achieve an understanding of this intention, regardless of different frames of reference. The text is the key, and I hope it is the text, in conjunction with my different frame of reference, whatever it might be, which leads me to a different reading of these passages than Cohen.

My framework is the work of Philo. I consider Philo to be a deeply committed Jew, who often expressed his beliefs in the rhetoric and language of Greek philosophy. These twin concerns of Philo, his Judaism and his devotion to Greek philosophical thought, are not dichotomous. They are especially apparent when he refers to the unwritten law, a term which he borrowed from the Greeks and which in some cases refers to customs of the Jews but not to the *Halakhah* or its forerunners.

BIBLIOGRAPHY

Modern Authors

Aalders, G. J. D. "νόμος ἔμψυχος" in *Politeia und Res Publica. Palingenesia IV*. ed. Peter Steinmetz. Wiesbaden: Franz Steiner, 1969, 315–329.
Adams, James Luther. "The Law of Nature: Some General Considerations" in *Journal of Religion* 25 (1945) 88–96.
———. "The Law of Nature in Greco-Roman Thought" in *Journal of Religion* 25 (1945) 97–118.
Alon, Gedalia. *Jews, Judaism, and the Classical World*. Trans. Israel Abrahams. Jerusalem: Magnes Press 1977.
Altman, Marian. "Ruler Cult in Seneca" in *Classical Philology* 33 (1938) 198–204.
Amir, Yehoshua. "Mose als Verfasser der Tora bei Philon" in *Die Hellenistische Gestalt des Judentums bei Philon von Alexandrien*. Neukirchen-Vluyn: Neukirchner 1983.
Andrews, M. E. "Paul, Philo and the Intellectuals" in *Journal of Biblical Literature* 53 (1934) 150–166.
Aune, David. *Greco-Roman Literature and the New Testament*. SBL Sources for Biblical Study. Atlanta, Georgia: Scholars Press 1988.
Baldry, H. C. *The Unity of Mankind In Greek Thought*. Cambridge: The University Press 1965.
———. "Zeno's Ideal State" in *JHS* 79 (1959) 3–15.
Barclay, William. "Hellenistic Thought in New Testament Times" in *Expository Times* 72 (1960–61).
Barker, Ernest. *Greek Political Theory*. London: Methuen, 1951.
Barraclough, Robert. "Philo's Politics. Roman Rule and Hellenistic Judaism" in *ANRW* II 21.1 417–553.
Baumgarten, A. I. "The Pharisaic Paradosis" in *HTR* 80/1 (1987) 63–77.
Belkin, Samuel. *Philo and the Oral Law: The Philonic Interpretation of Biblical Law in Relation to the Palestinian Halakhah*. Cambridge, Mass.: Harvard University Press 1940.
Bentzen, Aage. *King and Messiah*. London: Lutterworth 1955.
Berchman, Robert M. "The Categories of Being in Middle Platonism" in *The School of Moses: Studies in Philo and Hellenistic Religion: In Memory of Horst R. Moehring*. Brown Judaic Studies 304. Studia Philonica Monographs 1. Ed. John Peter Kenney (Atlanta: Scholars Press, 1995).
———. *From Philo to Origen: Middle Platonism in Transition*. Chico, California: Scholars Press 1984.
Bickerman, Elias. *From Ezra to the Last of the Maccabees: Foundations of Postbiblical Judaism*. trans. Moses Hadas. New York: Schocken Books 1962.
Bigg, Charles. *The Christian Platonists of Alexandria*. Oxford: Clarendon Press 1913.
Bloch, Ernst. *Natural Law and Human Dignity*. Cambridge, Mass.: MIT Press 1986.
Böhlig, H. *Die Geisteskultur von Tarsos im augusteischen Zeitalter mit Berucksichtigung der Paulinischen Schriften*. FRLANT, NF 2. Göttingen 1913.
Borgen, P. "Observations on the Theme 'Paul and Philo'" in *Die Paulinische Literatur and Theologie*. Skandinavische Beitrage: Aarhus-Gottingen 1980, 85–102.
———. "Philo of Alexandria" in *Jewish Writings of the Second Temple Period. Compendia Rerum Iudaicarum ad Novum Testamentum*. Section 2. Vol. 2. Assen: Van Gorcum 1984, 233–282.
———. "Emperor Worship and Persecution in Philo's In Flaccum and De Legatione ad Gaium and the Revelation of John" in *Geschichte—Tradition—Reflexion*. Tübingen: J. C. B. Mohr Press 1996, 493–509.

———. "Moses, Jesus and the Roman Emperor: Observations in Philo's Writings and the Revelation of John" in *Novum Testamentum* 38 (April 1996) 145–159.

———. *Early Christianity and Hellenistic Judaism*. Edinburgh: T&T Clark 1996.

———. and Søren Giversen eds. *The New Testament and Hellenistic Judaism*. Peabody, Mass.: Hendrickson Publishers 1997.

Born, Lester. "Animated Law in the Republic and Laws of Cicero" in *TAPA* 64 (1933) 128–137.

Bornkamm, Gunther. "Gesetz und Natur (Rom. 2.14–16)" in *Studien zu Antike und Urchristentum*. BevTH Band 28. Munich: Chr. Kaiser 1959 93–118.

———. "Die Offenbarung des Zornes Gottes (Rom. 1–3)" in *Das Ende des Gesetzes: Paulusstudien: Gesammelte Aufsätze*. BevTh Band 16. Munich: Chr. Kaiser 1958 9–33.

Bossier, F. et al. eds. *Images of Man in Ancient and Medieval Thought: Studia Gerardo Verbeke*. Leuven: Leuven University Press 1976.

Bousset, Wilhelm. *Kyrios Christos*. Nashville/New York; Abingdon Press 1970.

Bréhier, Emile. *Les Idées philosophiques et religieuses de Philon d'Alexandrie*. Paris: Librairie Philosophique J. Vrin 1950.

Broneer, Oscar. "Paul and the Pagan Cults at Isthmia" in *HThR* 64 (1971) 169–187.

Buckland, W. W. *A Textbook of Roman Law from Augustus to Justinian*. Cambridge: The University Press 1963.

Bultmann, Rudolf. "The Stoic Idea of the Wise Man" in *Primitive Christianity*. Cleveland and New York: Meridian Books 1956, 135–145.

Burkert, Walter. "Hellenistische Pythagorica" in *Philologus* 105 (1961) 16–43; 226–246.

——— "Zur geistesgeschichtlichen Einordnung einiger Pseudo-pythagorica" in *Fondation Hardt: Pour L'Étude de L'Antiquité Classique Entretiens: Tome XVIII Pseudipigrapha I*. Geneve: Fondation Hardt 1972 27–55.

Burnet, John. "Law and Nature in Greek Ethics" in *Essays and Addresses*. London: Chatto & Windus 1930, 23–28.

Calabi, Francesca. *The Language and the Law of God: Interpretation and Politics in Philo of Alexandria*. South Florida Studies in the History of Judaism 188. Atlanta: Scholars Press 1998.

Cerfaux, Lucien. *Christ in the Theology of St. Paul*. Freiburg: Herder 1962.

———. "Le Titre Kyrios et la Dignité Royale de Jésus" in *Revue des Sciences Philosophiques et Théologique* 11 (1922) 40–71.

Chadwick, Henry. "St. Paul and Philo of Alexandria" in Bulletin of the John Rylands Library 48 (1965–66) 286–307.

Chesnut, Glenn. "The Ruler and the Logos in Neopythagorean, Middle Platonic, and Late Stoic Political Philosophy" in *ANRW* II. 16.2 (Berlin: New York: W. de Gruyter, 1972–) 1310–1332

Christenson, Johnny. *An Essay on the Unity of Stoic Philosophy*. Copenhagen: Munksgaard 1962.

Chroust, Anton-Hermann. "On the Nature of Natural Law" in *Interpretations of Modern Legal Philosophies*. New York: Oxford University Press 1947, 70–84.

Cohen, Naomi G. "The Jewish Dimension of Philo's Judaism—An Elucidation of" *de Spec. Leg*. IV 132–150 in *JJS* (1987) 165–186.

———. "A Response to John W. Martens" in *JJS* 44/1 (1993) 114–115.

———. "Philo and Midrash" in *Judaism* 44 (Spring 1995) 196–207.

———. *Philo Judaeus: His Universe of Discourse*. Frankfurt: Peter Lang 1995.

Cohen, Shaye J. D. "The Significance of Yavneh: Pharisees, Rabbis, and the End of Jewish Sectarianism" in *HUCA* 55 (1984) 27–53.

———. *From the Maccabees to the Mishnah*. Philadelphia: The Westminster Press 1987.

Colish, Marcia L. *The Stoic Tradition from Antiquity to the Early Middle Ages*. Vol. 1. Leiden: E. J. Brill 1985.

Collins, J. J. *Between Athens and Jerusalem: Jewish Identity in the Hellenistic Diaspora*. New York: Crossroad Publishing Co. 1986.

———. "Messianism in the Maccabean Period" in *Judaisms and their Messiahs at the Turn of the Christian Era*. eds. Ernest Frerichs, William S. Green, Jacob Neusner. Cambridge: Cambridge University Press 1987, 97–110.

———. "Natural Theology and Biblical Tradition: The Case of Hellenistic Judaism" in *CBQ* 60 (1998) 1–15.

Cope, E. M. *An Introduction to Aristotle's Rhetoric*. London: Macmillan 1867.

Crowe, Michael Bertram. *The Changing Profile of the Natural Law*. The Hague: Martinus Nijhoff 1977.

Deissmann, Adolf. *Light from the Ancient East*. London: Hodder and Stoughton 1927.

Deissner, Kurt. "Das Idealbild des Stoischen Weisen" in *Greifswalder Universitätsreden 24*. Greifswald: Ratsbuchhandlung L. Bamberg 1930, 1–15.

Delatte, A. *Essai sur la politique pythagoricienne*. Bibliothèque de la Faculté de Philosophie et Lettres de l'Université de Liége 1922.

Delatte, Lucien. *Les Traités de la Royauté d'Ecphanté, Diotogené et Sthenidas*. Bibliothèque de la Faculté de Philosophie et Lettres de l'Université de Liége 97, 1942.

Delling, Gerhard. "Wunder-Allegorie-Mythus bei Philon von Alexandrie" in *Studien zum Neuen Testament und zum hellenistischen Judentum*. Göttingen: Vandenhoeck & Ruprecht 1970, 72–129.

Dey, Lala Kalyan Kumar. *The Intermediary World and Patterns of Perfection in Philo and Hebrews*. SBL Dissertation Series. Missoula, Mont.: Scholars Press 1975.

Dillon, John M. *The Middle Platonists*. London: Duckworth 1977.

———. "'Orthodoxy' and 'Eclecticism': Middle Platonists and Neo-Pythagoreans" in *The Question of "Eclecticism."* John Dillon and A. A. Long eds. Berkeley-Los Angeles: University of California Press 1988, 103–125.

Dix, Dom Gregory. *Jew and Greek*. Westminster: Dacre Press 1953.

Dodd, C. H. *The Bible and the Greeks*. London: Hodder and Stoughton 1954.

Donini, Pierluigi. "The History of the Concept of Eclecticism" in *The Question of "Eclecticism": Studies in Later Greek Philosophy*. John Dillon and A. A. Long eds. Berkeley-Los Angeles: University of California Press 1988, 15–33.

Dover, K. J. *Greek Popular Morality in the Time of Plato and Aristotle*. Oxford: Basil Blackwell 1974.

Drummond, James. *Philo Judaeus or the Jewish-Alexandrian Philosophy*. Amsterdam: Philo Press 1969; repr. of London 1888 ed.

Dvornik, Francis. *Early Christian and Byzantine Political Philosophy: Origins and Background*. Vol. I. Washington, D.C.: Dumbarton Oaks Center for Byzantine Studies 1966.

Dyck, Andrew R. *A Commentary on Cicero, De Officiis*. Ann Arbor: the U. of Michigan Press, 1996.

Eckstein, H. E. *Der Begriff Syneidesis bei Paulus*. Tübingen: J .C. B. Mohr 1983.

Edelstein, Ludwig. *The Meaning of Stoicism*. Martin Classical Lectures XXI; London: Oxford University Press 1966.

Ehrenberg, Victor. "Anfänge des griechischen Naturrechts" in *Archiv für Geschichte der Philosophie* xxxv Band, Neue Folge xxviii (1923) 119–143.

———. *Die Rechtsidee im frühen Griechentum*. Leipzig: S. Hirzel 1921.

———. *Sophocles and Pericles*. Oxford: Basil Blackwell 1954.

Ehrhardt, Arnold. "Ein antikes Herrscherideal: Phil. 2,5–11" in *Evangelische Theologie* 1948–49 101–110.

———. "Jesus Christ and Alexander the Great" in *The Framework of the New Testament Stories*. Manchester: University Press 1964, 37–43.

Farnados, Giorgios D. *Cosmos und Logos nach Philon von Alexandria*. Amsterdam: Rodopi 1976.

Ferguson, W. S. in *The Cambridge Ancient History VIII: The Hellenistic Monarchs and the Rise of Rome*. eds. F. E. Adcock; S. A. Cook; M. P. Charlesworth; Cambridge: University Press 1954.

Finnis, John. *Natural Law and Natural Rights*. Oxford: Clarendon Press 1980.

Fortenbaugh, William W. *On Stoic and Peripatetic Ethics: The Work of Arius Didymus.* Vol. I. New Brunswick, N.J. 1983.
Frede, Michael. "The Stoic Doctrine of the Affections of the Soul" in *The Norms of Nature: Studies in Hellenistic Ethics.* ed. Malcom Schofield and Gisela Striker. Cambridge: Cambridge University Press, 1986.
Gagarin, Michael. *Early Greek Law.* Berkeley: University of California Press 1986.
———. *Drakon and Early Athenian Homicide Law.* New Haven: Yale University Press 1981.
Gärtner, Bertil. *The Areopagus Speech and Natural Revelation.* Uppsala: C. W. K. Gleerup 1955.
Geytenbeek, A. C. *Musonius Rufus and Greek Diatribe.* Assen: Van Gorcum 1963.
Gigon, Olaf. "Cicero und die griechische Philosophie" in *ANRW* I.4 226–261.
Gilat, Yitchak D. "The Sabbath Laws in the Writing of Philo" in *Torah and Wisdom: Studies in Jewish Philosophy, Kabbalah, and Halakhah*: Essays in Honor of Arthur Hyman. Ed. Ruth Link-Salinger. New York: Shengold Publishers 1992, 61–73.
Glucker, John. *Antiochus and the Late Academy.* Hypomnemata 56. Göttingen: Vandenhoeck and Ruprecht 1978.
Goodenough, E.R. *An Introduction to Philo Judaeus.* Oxford: Basil Blackwell 1962.
———. *The Jurisprudence of the Jewish Courts in Egypt.* New Haven: Yale University Press 1929.
———. "Kingship in Early Israel" in *JBL* 48 (1929) 169–205.
———. *By Light, Light: The Mystic Gospel of Hellenistic Judaism.* New Haven: Yale University Press 1935.
———. with A. Thomas Kraabel. "Paul and the Hellenization of Christianity" in *Religions in Antiquity: Essays in Memory of E. R. Goodenough.* Leiden: Brill 1968, 23–68.
———. "The Political Philosophy of Hellenistic Kingship" in *Yale Classical Studies* 1 (1928) 55–102.
———. *The Politics of Philo Judaeus: Practice and Theory.* New Haven: Yale University Press 1938.
Goodwin, W. W. *Demosthenes: On the Crown.* New York: Hildesheim 1973.
Grant, Frederick C. *Roman Hellenism and the New Testament.* New York: Charles Scribner's Sons 1962.
Grant, Michael. *Myths of the Greeks and Romans.* New York: A Mentor Book 1962.
Grant, Robert M. "Hellenistic Elements in 1 Corinthians" in *Early Christian Origins.* ed. A. Wikgren. Chicago: Quadrangle Books 1961, 60–66.
———. *Miracle and Natural Law in Graeco-Roman and early Christian Thought.* Amsterdam: North-Holland Publishing Co. 1952.
Greene, W. C. *Moira: Fate, Good, and Evil in Greek Thought.* Gloucester, Mass.: Peter Smith 1944.
Greenwood, David. "Saint Paul and Natural Law" in *Biblical Theology Bulletin* 1 (1971) 262–279.
von Gierke, Otto Friedrich. *Natural Law and the Theory of Society.* Cambridge: The University Press 1934.
Guthrie, W. K. C. *History of Greek Philosophy.* Vol. 3. Cambridge: The University Press 1962–1981.
——— *The Sophists.* Cambridge: The University Press 1971.
Hall, Jerome. "Plato's Legal Philosophy" in *Indiana Law Journal* 31 (1956) 171–206.
Harrison, Jane Ellen. *Themis: A study of the Social Origins of Greek Religion.* Gloucester, Mass.: Peter Smith, 1974.
Hecht, Richard D. "Philo and Messiah" in *Judaisms and their Messiahs at the Turn of the Christian Era.* eds. Ernest Frerichs, William S. Green, Jacob Neusner. Cambridge: Cambridge University Press 1987 139–168.
Heinemann, Isaac. "Hellenistica" in *MGWJ* 74 (1929) 425–443.
———. "Jüdisch-hellenistische Gerichtshöfe in Alexandrien?" in *MGWJ* 74 (1930) 363–369.

———. "Die lehre vom ungeschriebenen Gesetz" in *HUCA* 4 (1928) 149–171.
———. *Philons griechische und judische Bildung*. Hildesheim: Georg Olms Velrag 1973.
Heinimann, Fritz. *Nomos und Physis*. Darmstadt: 1965. Wissenschaftliche Buchgesellschaft.
Hengel, Martin. *Between Jesus and Paul*. trans. John Bowden. Philadelphia: Fortress Press 1983.
———. *Judaism and Hellenism*. 2 Vols. trans. John Bowden. Philadelphia: Fortress Press 1974.
Herzog-Hauser, Gertrud. "Kaiserkult" in *Pauly-Wissowa Real Encyclopädie. Supplement IV* 806–853.
Hicks, R. D. *Stoic and Epicurean*. New York: Russell and Russell 1910.
Hirzel, Rudolf. *Agraphos Nomos*. Abh. d. Sachs. Gesellsch. d. Wissenschaft 20.1. Leipzig: B. G. Teubner 1900.
———. *Themis, Dike, und Verwandtes: Ein Beitrag zur Geschichte der Rechtsidee bei den Griechen*. Hildesheim: Olms 1966; repro. of, Leipzig: S. Hirzel, 1907.
Höistad, Ragnar. *Cynic Hero and Cynic King: Studies in the Cynic Conception of Man*. Uppsala: Lund 1948.
Hommel, Hildebrecht. "Denen, die Gott lieben... Erwagungen zu Romer 8,28" in *ZNW* (1989) 126–129.
Horowitz, Maryanne Cline. "The Stoic Synthesis of the Idea of Natural Law in Man: Four Themes" in *JHI* 35 (1974) 3–16.
Horsley, Richard. "The Law of Nature in Philo and Cicero" in *Harvard Theological Review* 71 (1978) 35–59.
Hurtado, Larry W. *One God, One Lord: Early Christian Devotion and Ancient Jewish Monotheism*. Philadelphia: Fortress Press 1988.
Inwood, Brad. "Commentary on Striker" in *Proceedings of the Boston Area Colloquium in Ancient Philosophy* Vol. II. Boston: University Press of America 1987, 95–101.
———. *Ethics and Human Action in Early Stoicism*. Oxford: Clarendon Press 1985.
———. "Rules and Reasoning in Stoic Ethics" in *Topics in Stoic Philosophy*. ed. Katerina Ierodiakonou; Oxford: Clarendon Press 1999, 95–127.
Jaeger, Werner. *Paideia*. Vol. III. New York: Oxford University Press 1944.
———. "Praise of Law: The Origin of Legal Philosophy and the Greeks" in *Interpretation of Modern Legal Philosophies*. New York: Oxford University Press 1947 352–375.
Kaerst, Julius. *Geschichte des Hellenismus*. Band II. Leipzig and Berlin: B. G. Teubner 1926.
Kerferd, G. B. "The Image of the Wise Man in Greece before Plato" in *Images of Man in Ancient and Medieval Thought: Studia Gerardo Verbeke*. Leuven: University Press 1976, 17–28.
———. "The Search for Personal Identity in Stoic Thought" in *Bulletin of the John Rylands Library* 55 (1972–73) 177–196.
———. "What Does the Wise Man Know?" in *The Stoics*, Berkeley and Los Angeles: University of California 1978, 125–136.
Kidd, I. G."Moral Actions and Rules in Stoic Ethics" in *The Stoics*. Berkeley and Los Angeles: University of California Press 1978, 247–258.
———. *Posidonius. Commentary*. Vol. II. Cambridge: Cambridge University Press 1972.
———. "The Relation of Stoic Intermediaries to the *Summum Bonum*, with Reference to Change in the Stoa" in *CQ* n.s. 5 (1955) 181–194.
———. "Stoic Intermediaries and the End for Man" in *Problems in Stoicism*. London: The Athlone Press 1971, 150–172.
Kirk, G. S. *Heraclitus: The Cosmic Fragments*. Cambridge: University Press 1954.
Klassen, William. "The King as 'Living Law' with reference to Musonius Rufus" in *SR* 14/1 (1985) 63–72.
Klausner, Joseph. *The Messianic Idea in Israel from its Beginning to the Completion of the Mishnah*. New York: The Macmillan Co. 1955.

Klebs, E. "Ampius" in *Pauly-Wissowa Real-Encyclopädie* I.2 1978–1979.
Knox, W. L. *Some Hellenistic Elements in Primitive Christianity*. London: Oxford University Press 1944.
Koester, Helmut. "νόμος φύσεως: The Concept of Natural Law in Greek Thought" in *Religions in Antiquity: Essays in Memory of E. R. Goodenough*. Leiden: Brill 1968 521–541.
Kugel, James L. "Two Introductions to Midrash" in *Midrash and Literature*. eds. Geoffrey H. Hartman and Sanford Budick. New Haven: Yale University Press 1986.
Lapidge, Michael. "*Archai* and *Stoicheia*: A Problem in Stoic Cosmology" in *Phronesis* 18 (1973) 240–278.
Laserson, Max M. "Positive and 'Natural Law' and their Correlation" in *Interpretations of Modern Legal Philosophies*. New York: Oxford University Press 1947, 443–449.
Latte, Kurt. θεσμός. In *Pauly-Wissowa Real-encyclopädie der classischen Altertumswissenschaft*. Ed. August Friedrich Pauly, Georg Wissowa, Wilhelm Kroll, and Kurt Witte, Stuttgart: J. B. Metzler, 1894–1982.
Lattey, Cuthbert. "The Diadochi and the Rise of King Worship" in *The English Historical Review* 32 (1917) 321–334.
Leisegang, Hans. "Physis" in *Pauly-Wissowa Real Encyclopädie* 20.1 1129–1164.
Levin, Flora R. *The Harmonics of Nicomachus and the Pythagorean Tradition*. Amer. Class. Stud. 1. University Park, Pa. American Philological Association 1975.
Lewy, Heinrich. "Philologische Streifzuge in den Talmud. 4. Ein greichisches Sprichwort" in *Philologus* 52 (1893) 567–572.
Lieberman, Saul. *Greek in Jewish Palestine*. New York: P. Feldheim 1965.
———. *Texts and Studies*. New York: Ktav Publishing House 1974.
Lohse, Bernhard. *Askese und Mönchtum in der Antike und in der alten Kirche*. Munich: Oldenbourg 1969.
Long, A. A. "Carneades and the Stoic Telos" in *Phronesis* 12 (1967) 59–90.
———. "The Early Stoic Concept of Moral Choice" in *Images of Man in Ancient and Medieval Thought*. Leuven: Leueven University Press 1976, 77–92.
———. and D. N. Sedley. *The Hellenistic Philosophers*. Cambridge: University Press 1987.
———. ed. *Problems in Stoicism*. London: The Athlone Press 1971.
———. "Soul and Body in Stoicism" in *Phronesis* 27 (1982) 34–57.
Lovejoy, A. D. "Meaning of *Physis* in the Greek Physiologres" in *Phil Rev* 18 (1909) 369–383.
Lutz, Cora. "Musonius Rufus: The Roman Socrates" in *Yale Classical Studies* 10 (1947) 3–147.
Lyall, Francis. "Legal Metaphors in the Epistles" in *Tyndale Bulletin* 32 (1981) 81–95.
———. "Roman Law in the Writings of Paul—Aliens and Citizens" in *EQ* 49 (1976) 3–14.
McClure, M. T. "The Greek Conception of Nature" in *The Philosophical Review* 2/63 (1934) 109–124.
McKenzie, John L. "Aspects of Old Testament Thought" in *Jerome Biblical Commentary*. eds. Raymond E. Brown, Joseph A. Fitzmyer, Roland E. Murphy. Englewood Cliffs, New Jersey: Prentice-Hall, Inc. 1968, 736–767.
MacDowell, Douglas Maurice. *Andocides*. Oxford: Clarendon Press 1962.
Maguire, Joseph P. "Plato's Theory of Natural Law" in *Yale Classical Studies* 10 (1947) 151–178.
Malherbe, Abraham. *The Cynic Epistles*. SBLSBS. Missoula, Mont.: Scholar's Press 1977.
Marchant, E. C. *Andocides: De Mysteriis and De Reditu*. London Longmans: 1906.
Martens, John W. "νόμος ἔμψυχος in Philo and Clement of Alexandria," in *Hellenization Revisited: Shaping a Christian Response within the Greco-Roman World*. ed. Wendy Helleman. Lanham, Maryland: University Press of Americas 1994, 323–338.

———. "Unwritten Law in Philo: A Response to Naomi G. Cohen," in *Journal of Jewish Studies*. Spring 1992, 38–45.
———. "Philo and the 'Higher Law'" in *SBL Seminar Papers 1991*. Atlanta: Scholars Press, 1991, 309–322.
Mayer, J. P. *Political Thought: The European Tradition*. London: J. M. Dent & Sons, Ltd. 1939.
Mayer, Reinhold. "Geschichtsfahrung und Schriftauslegung—zur Hermeneutik des frühen Judentums" in *Die hermeneutische Frage in der Theologie*. eds. Oswald Loretz and Walter Strolz. Wien-Freiburg: Herder 1968, 290–355.
Meeks, Wayne. *The Prophet-King*. Leiden: E. J. Brill 1967.
Mendelson, Alan. *Philo's Jewish Identity*. BJS 161; Atlanta, GA.: Scholars Press 1988.
———. *Secular Education in Philo of Alexandria*. Cincinnati: Hebrew Union College Press 1982.
Meyer, B. F. *Critical Realism and the New Testament*. Allison Park, Penn.: Pickwick Publications 1989.
———. *The Early Christians: Their World Mission and Self-Discovery*. GNS 16; Wilmington, Delaware: Michael Glazier Inc. 1986.
Momigliano, Arnaldo. *Alien Wisdom: The Limits of Hellenization* Cambridge: Cambridge University Press 1975.
Montefiore, C. G. *Judaism and St. Paul*. London: Max Goschen Ltd. 1914.
Moehring, Horst. "Arithmology as an Exegetical Tool in the Writings of Philo of Alexandria" in *The School of Moses: Studies in Philo and Hellenistic Religion: In Memory of Horst R. Moehring*. Brown Judaic Studies 304. Studia Philonica Monographs 1. Ed. John Peter Kenney (Atlanta: Scholars Press, 1995).
Morrison, J. S. "Pythagoras of Samos" in *CQ* 6 (1956) 135–156.
Morrow, Glenn. *Plato's Cretan City: A Historical Interpretation of the Laws*. Princeton, N.J.: Princeton University Press 1960.
Murray, Oswyn. "Aristeas and Ptolemaic Kingship" in *JTS* n.s. 18 (1967) 337–371.
Myre, André. "Les characteristiques de la loi mosaïque selon Philon d'Alexandrie" in *Science et Esprit* 25 (1973) 35–69.
———. "La loi dans l'ordre cosmique et politique selon Philon d'Alexandrie" in *Science et Esprit* 24 (1972) 217–247.
———. "La loi dans l'ordre moral selon Philon d'Alexandrie" in *Science et Esprit* 24 (1972) 93–113.
———. "La loi de la nature et la loi mosaïque selon Philon d'Alexandrie" in *Science et Esprit* 28/2 (1976) 163–181.
———. "La loi et la Pentateuque selon Philon d'Alexandrie" in *Science et Esprit* 25 (1973) 209–225.
Neusner, Jacob. *The Rabbinic Traditions About the Pharisees Before 70: Part III Conclusions* (Leiden: E. J. Brill, 1971).
———. *From Politics to Piety: The Emergence of Pharisaic Judaism* (Englewood Cliffs, N.J.: Prentice-Hall, Inc., 1973).
———. *Method and Meaning in Ancient Judaism. Brown Judaic Studies 10* (Missoula, Mont.: Scholars Press, 1979).
———. *Oral Tradition in Judaism: The Core of the* Mishnah (New York and London: Garland Publishing, 1987).
Nikiprowetzky, Valentin. *Le Commentaire de l'écriture chez Philon d'Alexandrie*. Leiden: E. J. Brill 1977.
Nock, A. D. *Essays on Religion and the Ancient World*. Vols. 1–2. ed. Zeph Stewart. Cambridge, Mass.: Harvard University Press 1972.
Norden, Eduard. *Die Antike Kunstprosa*. II. Stuttgart: B. G. Teubner 1958.
Nussbaum, Martha. "The Extirpation of the Passions in Stoicism" in *Apeiron* 20/2 (1987) 129–177.
Oppel, Herbert. "*Kanon*: zur bedeutungsgeschichte des Wortes und sein Lateinischen

Entsprechungen (regula-norma)" in *Philologus*. Supplement Band 30\Heft 4 (1937) 1–108.
Ostwald, Martin. *Nomos and the Beginnings of Athenian Democracy*. Oxford: Clarendon, 1969.
———. *From Popular Sovereignty to the Sovereignty of Law: Law, Society, and Politics in Fifth Century Athens*. Berkeley: University of California Press 1986.
Pastor, Federico. "Libertad helénica y libertad paulina" in *Miscelanea Comillas* 37 (1979) 219–237.
Pfitzner, Victor C. *Paul and the Agon Motif: Traditional Athletic Imagery in the Pauline Literature*. Leiden: E. J. Brill 1967.
Pohlenz, Max. "*Nomos*" in *Philologus* 97 (1948) 135–142.
———. "*Nomos und Physis*" in *Hermes* 81 (1953) 418–438.
———. "Paulus und die Stoa" in *ZNW* 42 (1949) 69–104.
Pollock, Sir Frederick. *Essays in the Law*. London: Macmillan and Co. 1922.
von Premerstein, Anton. *Vom Werden und Wesen des Principats*. Abhandlungen der Bayerischen Akademie der Wissenschaften. Philosophisch-historische Abteilung. Neue Folge. Heft 15. Munich Verlag der Bayerischen Akademie der Wissenschaften 1937.
Rawson, Elizabeth. "The Interpretation of Cicero's 'De Legibus'" in *ANRW* I.4 (Berlin; New York: de Gruyter, 1972–) 243–334.
Reese, James M. *Hellenistic Influence on the Book of Wisdom and Its Consequences*. Rome: Biblical Institute Press, 1970.
Reinhartz, Adele. "The Meaning of *nomos* in Philo's *Exposition of the Law*" in *SR* 15/3 (1986) 341–342.
Remus, Harold. "Authority, Consent, Law: Nomos, Physis, and the striving for a given" in *SR* 13 (1984) 5–18
Richardson, W. "A Motif of Greek Philosophy in Luke-Acts" in *Studia Evangelica*. Vol. II (vol. 87). ed. F. L. Cross. Texte und Untersuchungen zur Geschichte der Altchristlichen Literatur. Berlin: Akademie 1964, 628–634.
———. "νόμος ἔμψυχος: Marcion, Clement of Alexandria and St. Luke's Gospel" in *Studia Patristica*. Vol. VI (vol. 81). ed. F. L. Cross. Texte und Untersuchungen zur Geschichte der Altchristlichen Literatur. Berlin: Akademie 1964 188–196.
———. "The Philonic Patriarchs as νόμος ἔμψυχος" in *Studia Patristica*. Vol. I. Berlin: Akademie-Verlag 1957, 515–525.
Rist, J. M. ed. *The Stoics*. Berkeley and Los Angeles: University of California Press 1978.
———. *Stoic Philosophy*. Cambridge: Cambridge University Press 1969.
Robson, E. Iliff. "Composition and Dictation in New Testament Books" in *JThS* 18 (1917) 288–301.
Runia, D. T. "Redrawing the Map of Early Middle Platonism" in *Hellenica et Judaica: Hommage a Valentin Nikiprowetzky*. eds. A. Caquot, M. Hadas-Lebel, and J. Riaud. Leuven-Paris: Editions Peeters 1986, 85–104.
———. "How to Search Philo" in *The Studia Philonica Annual* 2 (1990) 106–139.
———. "Witness or Participant? Philo and the Neoplatonic Tradition" in *The Neoplatonic Tradition: Jewish, Christian, and Islamic Themes*. eds. D. Pätzold and A. Vanderjagt. Köln: Dinter 1991.
———. *Philo in Early Christian Literature. Compendia Rerum Iudaicarum ad Novum Testamentum*. Section III. Vol. III. Assen: Van Gorcum 1993.
Safrai, Shmuel. "Oral Tora" in *The Literature of the Sages*. Part I (CRINT II.3.1). ed. S. Safrai. Assen and Philadelphia 1987.
Sanders, E. P. *Paul, the Law, and the Jewish People*. Philadelphia: Fortress Press 1983.
———. *Jewish Law From Jesus to the Mishnah: Five Studies*. London: SCM Press; Philadelphia: Trinity Press International 1990.
———. *Judaism: Practice and Belief: 63 B.C.E.–66 C.E.* London: SCM Press 1992.
Sandmel, Samuel. *A Jewish Understanding of the New Testament*. New York: Ktav Publishing House 1974.

———. "Parallelomania" in *JBL* 81 (1962) 1–13.
———. *Philo of Alexandria: An Introduction.* New York: Oxford University Press 1979.
———. "Philo's Place in Judaism" in *HUCA* 25 (1954) 225–228.
Schiffman, Lawrence. *From Text to Tradition.* New York: KTAV 1991.
Schmid, Wilhelm. "Die Rede des Apostels Paulus vor den Philosophen und Areopagiten in Athen" in *Philologus* 95 (1943) 79–120.
Schofield, Malcolm; Burnyeat, Myles; and Barnes, Jonathan edd. *Doubt and Dogmatism: Studies in Hellenistic Epistemology.* Oxford: Clarendon Press 1980.
Schubart, Wilhelm. "Das Hellenistische Konigsideal nach Inschriften und Papyri" in *Archiv für Papyrusforschung und verwandte Gebiete.* Band 12. Leipzig and Berlin: B. G. Teubner 1937 1–26.
Scott, Kenneth. "Plutarch and the Ruler Cult" in *TAPA* 60 (1929) 117–135.
Sherwin-White, A. N. *The Roman Citizenship.* Oxford: Clarendon Press 1973.
———. *Roman Society and Roman Law in the New Testament.* Oxford: Clarendon Press 1963.
Shroyer, Montgomery J. "Alexandrian Jewish Literalists" in *JBL* 55 (1936) 261–284.
Sinclair, T. A. A. *A History of Greek Political Thought.* Routledge and Kegan Paul Ltd.: London 1951.
Singh, Raghuveer. "Heraklitos and the Law of Nature" in *JHI* 24 (1963) 457–472.
Skemp, J. B. *The Theory of Motion in Plato's Later Dialogues.* Cambridge: The University Press 1942.
Smallwood, E. Mary. *Philonis Alexandrini: Legatio ad Gaium* Leiden: E. J. Brill 1961.
Snodgrass, Klyne. "Spheres of Influence: A Possible Solution to the Problem of Paul and the Law" in *JSNT* 32 (1988) 93–113.
Solmsen, Friedrich. *Plato's Theology.* Ithaca, New York: Cornell University Press 1942.
Sowers, Sidney. *The Hermeneutics of Philo and Hebrews.* Richmond, Virginia: John Knox Press 1965.
Stalley, R. F. *An Introduction to Plato's Laws.* Indianapolis: Hackett Publishing Co. 1983.
Sterling, Gregory. "'Wisdom Among the Perfect': Creation Tradition in Alexandrian Judaism and Corinthian Christianity" in *Novum Testamentum* 37 (October 1995) 355–384.
Stowers, Stanley K. *The Diatribe and Paul's Letter to the Romans.* SBLDS 57. Chico, Calif.: Scholar's Press 1981.
Strack, Herman L. and Stemberger, G. *Introduction to the Talmud and Midrash.* trans. Marcus Bockmuehl. Minneapolis: Fortress Press 1992.
Strauss, Leo. *Natural Right and History.* Chicago: The University of Chicago Press 1953.
Striker, Gisela. "Origins of the Concept of Natural Law" in *Proceedings of the Boston Area Colloquium in Ancient Philosophy.* Vol. II. Boston: University Press of America 1987, 79–94.
Talmon, Shemaryahu. "Waiting for the Messiah: The Spiritual Universe of the Qumran Covenanters" in *Judaisms and their Messiahs at the Turn of the Christian Era.* eds. Ernest Frerichs, William S. Green, Jacob Neusner. Cambridge: Cambridge University Press 1987 111–138.
Tarn, W. W. *Hellenistic Civilization.* Cleveland and New York: Meridian Books 1964.
Taylor, Lily Ross. *The Divinity of the Roman Emperor.* Chico, Calif.: Scholars Press 1981; a reprint of the 1931 Ed., Middletown, Conn.: American Philological Association.
Tcherikover, V. *Hellenistic Civilization and the Jews.* New York: Atheneum 1975.
Theiler, Willy. "Review of A. Delatte" in *Gnomon* 2 (1926) 147–156.
Thesleff, Holger. *An Introduction to the Pythagorean Writings of the Hellenistic Period.* Åbo: Åbo Akademie 1961.
———. "On the Problem of the Doric Pseudo-Pythagorica: An Alternative Theory of Date and Purpose" *Fondation Hardt: Pour L'Étude de L'Antiquite Classique Entretiens: Tome XVIII Pseudipigrapha I.* Geneve: Fondation Hardt 1972, 59–87.
———. *The Pythagorean Texts of the Hellenistic Period.* Acta Akademiae Aboensis. Ser. A: Humaniora, v. 30, no. 1; Åbo: Åbo Akademie 1965.

Thiede, D. L. *The Charismatic Figure as Miracle Worker.* SBLDS 1; Missoula, Mont.: Scholar's Press 1973.
Urbach, E. *The Sages.* Jerusalem: Magnes Press 1979.
van Unnik, W. *Sparsa Collecta I.* NTS 29. Leiden: E. J. Brill 1973.
Vander Waerdt, Paul. *The Stoic Theory of Natural Law.* Diss. Princeton 1989.
Verbeke, Gérard. "Aux Origines de la Notion de 'loi naturelle'" in *Atti del 3 Congresso internazionale di filosofia medioevale.* Posso della Mendola (Trento), 31 agosto–5 settembre 1964. Milano Società Editrice Vita e Pensiero 1966, 164–173.
von Gierke, Otto Friedrich, *Natural Law and the Theory of Society, 1500 to 1800.* Cambridge: The University Press, 1934.
Watson, Gerard. "The Natural Law and Stoicism" in *Problems in Stoicism.* A. A. Long ed. London: The Athlone Press 1971, 216–238.
Weinreb, Lloyd L. *Natural Law and Justice.* Cambridge, Mass.: Harvard University Press 1987.
Wendland, Paul "Die Schriftstellerei des Anaximanes von Lampsakos" in *Hermes* 39 (1904) 419–443; 499–542.
———. "*Soter*" in *ZNW* 5 (1904) 335–353.
Westerholm, Stephen. *Israel's Law and the Church's Faith.* Grand Rapids, Michigan: Eerdman's Publishing Co. 1988.
———. "The Law and the 'Just Man' (1 Tim. 1:3–11)" in *Studia Theologica* 36 (1982) 79–95.
———. "Letter and Spirit: The Foundation of Pauline Ethics" in *NTS* 30, 229–248.
———. "On Fulfilling the Whole Law (Gal. 5:14)" in *Svensk Exegetisk Årsbok* 51–52 (1986–87) 229–237.
White, Nicholas P. "Stoic Values" in *Monist* 73/1 (Jan. 1990) 42–58.
———. "Two Notes on Stoic Terminology" in *AJP* 99 (1978) 111–119.
Wiens, D. H. "Mystery Concepts in Primitive Christianity and in its Environment" in *ANRW* II.23.2 1248–1288.
Wild, John. *Plato's Modern Enemies and the Theory of Natural Law.* Chicago: The University of Chicago Press 1954.
Wilson, T. *St. Paul and Paganism.* Edinburgh: T&T Clark 1927.
Winston, David. *Wisdom of Solomon: A New Translation with Introduction and Commentary.* Garden City, N.Y.: Doubleday 1979.
———. *Logos and Mystical Theology in Philo of Alexandria.* Cincinnati: Hebrew Union College Press 1985.
———. "Philo's Conception of the Divine Nature" in *Neoplatonism and Jewish Thought.* ed. Lenn E. Goodman. Albany: State University Press 1992, 21–42.
Winter, Bruce W. *Philo and Paul Among the Sophists.* Cambridge: Cambridge University Press 1989.
Wolf, Eric. *Griechishes Rechtsdenken* Band IV\Teil 2. Frankfurt am Main: V. Klostermann 1950–70.
Wolfson, H. A. *Philo: Foundations of Religious Philosophy in Judaism, Christianity, and Islam.* 2 Vols. Cambridge, Mass.: Harvard University Press 1947.
Woodbridge, F. J. E. "The Dominant Conception of the Earliest Greek Philosophy" in *Phil. Rev.* 10 (1901) 359–374.
Zeller, Eduard. *The Stoics, Epicureans, and Sceptics*, London. Longmans, Green, 1870.
Zuntz, Gunther. "Aristeas Studies I: 'The Seven Banquets'" in *JSS* 4 (1959) 21–36

Ancient Authors and Texts

Aristotle. *Metaphysics.* 2 vols. trans. H. Tredennick. Cambridge, Mass.: Harvard University Press 1966. The Loeb Classical Library.

———. *Eudemian Ethics*. trans. H. Rackham. Cambridge, Mass.: Harvard University Press 1935. The Loeb Classical Library.
———. *Nichomachean Ethics*. trans. H. Rackham. Cambridge, Mass.: Harvard University Press 1962. The Loeb Classical Library.
———. *Politics*. trans. H. Rackham. Cambridge, Mass.: Harvard University Press 1967. The Loeb Classical Library.
———. *The Works of Aristotle Translated into English: Vol. 11*. ed. W. D. Ross; trans. E. S. Forster. Oxford: Clarendon Press 1908–1952.
Bible. *Novum Testamentum Graece*. Edited by E. Nestle and K. Aland. 25th Edition. London: United Bible Societies 1973.
———. The New Oxford Annotated Bible with the Apocrypha. RSV Translation. Edited by Herbert G. May and Bruce M. Metzger. New York: Oxford University Press Inc. 1965, 1977.
———. *Septuaginta*. Edited by Alfred Rahlfs. Stuttgart: Deutsch Bibelgesellschaft 1935, 1979.
Cicero. *De Officiis*. trans. Walter Miller. Cambridge, Mass.: Harvard University Press 1913. The Loeb Classical Library.
———. *De Finibus bonorum et malorum*. trans. H. Rackham. Cambridge, Mass.: Harvard University Press 1961. The Loeb Classical Library.
———. *De Natura Deorum and Academica*. trans. H. Rackham. Cambridge, Mass.: Harvard University Press 1961. The Loeb Classical Library.
———. *De Republica and De Legibus*. trans. Clinton W. Keyes. Cambridge, Mass.: Harvard University Press 1966. The Loeb Classical Library.
Clement of Alexandria. *Clemens Alexandrinus. Stromata Buch I–VI*. O. Stählin ed. Berlin: Akademie 1960.
Corpus Inscriptionum Latinarum. Inscriptiones vrbis Romae Latinae. Vol. 6. eds. E. Bormann et G. Henzen. Berlin: G. Reimer 1863–1975.
Demosthenes. *De Corona and De Falsa Legatione*. trans. C. A. Vince and J. H. Vince. Cambridge, Mass.: Harvard University Press 1963. The Loeb Classical Library.
———. *Meidias, Androtion, Aristocrates, Timocrates, Aristogeiton*. trans. J. H. Vince. Cambridge, Mass.: Harvard University Press 1964. The Loeb Classical Library.
Dio Cassius. *Roman History*. 9 Vols. trans. E. Cary. Cambridge, Mass.: Harvard University Press 1961. The Loeb Classical Library.
Dio Chrysostom. Vol. 5. trans. H. Lamar Crosby. Cambridge, Mass.: Harvard University Press 1951. The Loeb Classical Library.
Diogenes Laertius. *Lives of Eminent Philosophers*. 2 vols. trans. R. D. Hicks. Cambridge, Mass.: Harvard University Press 1966. The Loeb Classical Library.
Epictetus. 2 Vols. trans. W. A. Oldfather. Cambridge, Mass.: Harvard University Press 1926. The Loeb Classical Library.
Euripides. 4 Vols. trans. A. S. Way. Cambridge, Mass.: Harvard University Press 1962. The Loeb Classical Library.
Fragmenta Philosophorum Graecorum. 3 Vols. ed. Friedrich Wilhelm August Mullach. Paris: Firmin-Didot & Sociis 1928–1935.
Horace. *Satires, Epistles, Ars Poetica*. trans. H. R. Fairclough. Cambridge, Mass.: Harvard University Press 1961. The Loeb Classical Library.
Isocrates. 3 Vols. trans. George Norlin and LaRue Van Hook. Cambridge, Mass.: Harvard University Press 1962. The Loeb Classical Library.
Justinian. *Corpus Iurus Civilis*. Vol. 1, *Institutiones* ed. P. Krueger; *Digesta* ed. T. Mommsen; Vol. 2, *Codex Iustinianus* ed. P. Krueger; *Novellae* ed. R. Schöll. Berlin: Weidmann 1963–66.
Marcus Aurelius. trans. C. R. Haines. Cambridge, Mass.: Harvard University Press 1930. The Loeb Classical Library.
Migne, Jacques Paul. *Patrologiae Cursus Completus. Series Completus*. Lutetiae Parisorum: Migne, 1857–66.

Panaetius. ed. M. van Straaten in *Panaetii Rhodii Fragmenta*. Leiden: Brill 1962.
Philo. 11 vols. Vols. I–V trans. F. H. Colson and Rev. G. H. Whitaker; Vols. VI–XI trans. F. H. Colson. Cambridge, Mass.: Harvard University Press 1981. The Loeb Classical Library.
———. *Philonis Alexandrini opera quae supersunt*. I–VI. L. Cohn and P. Wendland eds. *Indices*. VII. H. Leisegang ed. Berlin 1896–1930.
Philostratus. *The Life of Apollonius of Tyana*. 2 Vols. trans. F. C. Conybeare. Cambridge, Mass.: Harvard University Press 1960. The Loeb Classical Library.
Plato. *The Collected Dialogues*. eds. Edith Hamilton and Huntington Cairns. Bollingen Series LXXI; Princeton, N.J.: Princeton University Press 1982.
———. *The Laws*. trans. Rev. R. G. Bary. Cambridge, Mass.: Harvard University Press 1961. The Loeb Classical Library.
———. *The Laws*. trans. Thomas L. Pangle. New York: Basic Books, Inc. 1980.
Pliny. *Letters*. 2 Vols. trans. Betty Radice. Cambridge, Mass.: Harvard University Press 1963. The Loeb Classical Library.
Plutarch. *Moralia*. 16 vols. I–V trans. F. C. Babbitt; VI trans W. C. Helmbold; VII trans. P. H. De Lacy and B. Einarson; VIII trans. P. A. Clement and H. B. Hoffleit; IX trans. E. L. Minar, Jr., F. H. Sandbach, and W. C. Helmbold; X trans. H. N. Fowler; XI trans. L. Pearson and F. H. Sandbach; XII–XIII trans. H. Cherniss and W. C. Helmbold; XIV trans. P. H. De Lacy and B. Einarson; XV trans F. H. Sandbach. Cambridge, Mass.: Harvard University Press 1962. The Loeb Classical Library.
Pomponi Porfyrionis: Commentum in Horatium Flaccum. ed. Alfred Holder. Innsbruck 1894. New York: Arno Press, 1979.
Posidonius. edd. L. Edelstein and I. G. Kidd in *Posidonius. The Fragments*. Vol. I. Cambridge: Cambridge University Press 1972.
Proclus. ed. W. Kroll. *In Rem Publican*. II. Amsterdam: Hakkers 1965 repr.
Seneca. *Epistulae Morales*. 3 vols. trans. R. M. Gammere. Cambridge, Mass.: Harvard University Press 1967. The Loeb Classical Library.
Sextus Empiricus. 4 Vols. trans. Rev. R. G. Bury. Cambridge, Mass.: Harvard University Press 1933–49. The Loeb Classical Library.
Sophocles. *Oedipus the King. Oedipus at Colonus. Antigone*. trans. F. Storr. Cambridge, Mass.: Harvard University Press 1981. The Loeb Classical Library.
Stobaeus. *Anthologium*. Vols. 1–2 ed. C. Wachsmuth; Vols. 3–5 ed. O. Hense. Berlin: Weidmann 1884.
Stoicorum Veterum Fragmenta. 3 vols. ed. H. von Arnim. Leipzig: Teubner 1903–5. Vol. 4 Indices. ed. M. Adler, 1924. Repr. 4 vols., Stuttgart: Teubner 1979.
Strabo. *Geography*. 4 Vols. trans. Horace L. Jones. Cambridge, Mass.: Harvard University Press 1961. The Loeb Classical Library.
Suetonius. 2 Vols. trans. J. C. Rolfe. Cambridge, Mass.: Harvard University Press 1970. The Loeb Classical Library.
Themistius. ed. Wilhelm Dindorf. *Themistius*. Leipzig: C. Cnobloch 1832.
Xenophon. *Cyropaedia*. 2 Vols. trans. Walter Miller; *Memorabilia and Oeconomicus*. trans. E. C. Marchant. Cambridge, Mass.: Harvard University Press 1960. The Loeb Classical Library.

Translation and Research Aids

Ast, Friedrich. *Lexicon Platonicum*. Bonn: R. Habelt 1956.
Bauer, Walter. *A Greek-English Lexicon of the New Testament and other Early Christian Literature*. trans. William F. Arndt and F. Wilbur Gingrich. Chicago and London: The University of Chicago Press 1979.
Blass, F. and Debrunner, A. *A Greek Grammar of the New Testament and Other Early Christian Literature*. Chicago: University of Chicago Press 1961.

Bonitz, H. *Index Aristotelicus*. Berlin 1870. Repr. Darmstadt: Wissenschaftliche Buchgesellschaft 1960.
Kleinknecht, H. and Gutbrod, W. νόμος in *TDNT*, IV, eds. Gerhard Kittel, Geoffrey William Bromiley, and Gerhard Friedrich; Grand Rapids, Mich: Eerdmans, 1964–1976.
Lampe, G. W. H. *A Patristic Greek Lexicon*. Oxford: Clarendon Press 1961.
Liddell, Henry George and Scott, Robert A. *A Greek-English Lexicon*. Oxford: Clarendon Press 1968.
Mayer, Günter. *Index Philoneus*. Berlin and New York: Walter De Gruyter 1974.
Moulton, James. *A Grammar of New Testament Greek. Vol. III. Syntax*. Edinburgh: T&T Clark 1963.
Runia, D. T. and Radice, Robert eds. *Philo of Alexandria: An Annotated Bibliography. 1937–1986*. Leiden: Brill 1988.
Saunders, Trevor J. *Bibliography on Plato's Laws 1920–1970*. New York: Arno Press 1976.

INDEX OF MODERN AUTHORS

Aalders, G. J. D. 33, 35, 37, 61
Adams, J. L. 1
Aland, K. 86
Altman, M. 24
Amir, Y. 127
Arndt, W. F. 107

Baldry, H. L. 25
Barker, E. 13, 31, 33
Barraclough, R. 85, 93, 100, 112, 117, 128, 162
Bauer, W. 107
Baumgarten, A. I. 179
Berchman, R. 75, 76, 78, 109
Bigg, C. 96, 103
Bloch, E. 13
Borgen, P. 177
Born, L. 46, 63
Bréhier, E. 86, 91, 95, 98, 120
Buckland, W. W. 49
Bultmann, R. 18
Burkert, W. 35, 166
Burnet, J. 16

Calabi, F. 93, 100
Chesnut, G. 46, 47, 166
Christenson, J. 26
Chroust, A.-H. 13, 14
Cohen, N. G. 15, 87, 175–185
Cohen, S. J. D. 180
Colish, M. 125, 153
Collins, J. J. 160
Colson, F. H. 84, 134, 141
Cope, E. M. 6, 7, 8, 10, 42
Crowe, M. 13

Deissner, K. 26
Delatte, A. 9, 10, 35, 54, 55, 59, 165–174
Delatte, L. 9, 33, 35, 40, 53, 57, 58, 62, 165–174
Delling, G. 68
Dillon, J. 83, 85, 125, 130, 154
Dindorf, W. 45
Donini, P. 125
Dover, K. J. 8
Drummond, J. 68
Dvornik, F. 46, 47, 166

Edelstein, L. 2, 21, 23, 25, 152
Ehrenberg, V. 1, 3, 7, 8, 15, 89, 134

Ferguson, W. S. 168
Finnis, J. 13
Forster, E. S. 42, 43
Frede, M. 76

Gagarin, M. 140
Geytenbeek, A. C. 45
Gigon, O. 20
Gingrich, F. W. 107
Glucker, J. 174
Goodenough, E. R. 9, 35, 37, 39, 41–43, 46, 47, 49, 54–60, 62–65, 68, 73, 76, 80, 91–94, 96, 100, 103, 107, 111, 112, 117–119, 128, 159
Goodman, L. E. 75
Goodwin, W. W. 68
Grant, M. 133
Greene, W. C. 1, 14, 16, 67
Gutbrod, W. 96, 103, 128
Guthrie, W. K. C. 1, 2, 16, 19, 74, 133

Hall, J. 14, 26, 53
Heinimann, F. 1, 16, 19, 67, 74, 132, 133
Heinimann, I. 87, 93, 112, 117
Hense, O. 36
Herzog-Hauser, G. 48
Hirzel, R. 1, 4–9, 11, 12, 19, 89, 133
Hoistad, R. 92
Holder, A. 4
Horowitz, M. C. 16, 20, 22
Horsley, R. 15, 85, 89, 119

Inwood, B. 16, 20, 22, 26, 28, 76, 137, 151, 152

Jaeger, W. 1, 15, 31, 133
Jones, H. S. 60

Kaerst, J. 62, 168
Kenney, J. P. 109
Kerferd, G. 23, 27, 158
Kidd, I. G. 22, 28, 29, 151, 152
Kirk, G. S. 1
Kittel, G. 96

Klassen, W. 167
Klebs, E. 49
Kleinknecht, H. 96, 103, 128
Knox, W. L. 76
Koester, H. 14, 18, 76, 85, 106, 113, 126, 129

Lapidge, M. 27, 158
Laserson, M. 13
Latte, K. 145
Lattey, C. 168
Leisegang, H. 67, 68
Lewy, H. 4
Liddell, H. G. 60
Lieberman, S. 4
Lohse, B. 97
Long, A. A. 26, 27, 73, 155, 157
Lovejoy, A. O. 16, 68
Lutz, C. 44, 55, 56, 59, 63

MacDowell, D. 3, 7
Maguire, J. P. 14
Marchant, E. C. 4
Martens, J. W. 175–185
Mayer, J. P. 13
Mayer, R. 129
McLure, M. T. 1
Meeks, W. 49, 91, 92, 111, 112
Mendelson, A. 70, 72, 73, 79, 92, 94, 97, 100, 115, 120, 126–129, 162
Migne, J. P. 143
Moehring, H. 109, 110
Momigliano, A. 161
Morrison, J. S. 9
Morrow, G. 14
Murray, O. 168
Myre, A. 80, 84, 85, 95–99, 103, 121, 128, 130, 159

Neusner, J. 14, 160, 175–185
Nikiprowetzky, V. 120, 127, 128
Nock, A. D. 62, 63
Nussbaum, M. 76

Oppel, H. 160
Ostwald, M. 134, 145,

Pastor, F. 97, 162
Pohlenz, M. 19
Pollock, F. 14

Rawson, E. 20
Reese, J. 168
Reinhartz, A. 68, 126
Richardson, W. 46, 86, 93
Rist, J. 23, 26, 27, 151, 157, 158
Ross, W. D. 42
Runia, D. T. 164

Safrai, S. 181
Sanders, E. P. 175–185
Sandmel, S. 87, 96, 103, 104, 159, 164
Schubart, W. 62, 63, 168
Scott, K. 47
Scott, R. 60
Sedley, D. 27, 73, 155, 157
Shroyer, M. J. 105, 127
Singh, R. 14
Smallwood, E. M. 87
Snodgrass, K. 163
Solmsen, F. 14
Sowers, S. 103
Stalley, R. E. 14
Strauss, L. 13
Striker, G. 14, 15, 76

Tarn, W. W. 168
Tarrant, H. 174
Taylor, L. R. 48, 168
Theiler, W. 35, 165
Thesleff, H. 9, 35, 54, 175–185
Thiede, D. L. 94, 99

vander Waerdt, P. 14, 15, 17, 18, 21, 28, 29, 105, 120, 125, 152, 153, 154, 157
Verbeke, G. 14
Vince, J. H. 9
von Gierke, O. F. 13
von Premerstein, A. 48

Wachsmuth, C. 36
Watson, G. 14, 18, 29
Weinreb, L. 13
Wendland, P. 42, 62
Westerholm, S. 125
Wild, J. 14
Winston, D. 75, 148
Wolfson, H. 70, 72, 73, 87, 129
Woodbridge, F. J. E. 16, 68

Zeller, E. 23
Zuntz, G. 168

INDEX OF ANCIENT SOURCES

Andocides
  De Mysteriis
    85f   3

Appolonius
  Harpocration Grammaticon   139
  Lexicon Homericum
    87:22   139

Archytas of Tarentum
  Peri Nomou Kai Dikaiosynes   9, 35
  Stobaeus
    4.1,61   54
    4.1.132   9, 36, 54, 55, 91
    4.1.135   9, 31, 36, 54, 57, 58, 60, 64, 122
    4.1.135,7–13   36
    4.1.135,15   31, 36
    4.1.135,20–21   36
    4.1.135–138   54, 64
    4.1.136   54, 59
    4.1.137   54
    4.1.138   54, 62
    4.5.61   36, 54
    4.5.61,13   37
    4.5.61,19   37
    4.6,22   54
    4.7,61   54
    4.7,61:263f   55
    4.7,62   54
    4.7,64   54
    4.7,64–66   54
    4.7,67   54, 55
    4.1,135–82,15–17   57
    4.1,135–82,19   60
    4.1,136–83,19   59

Aristotle
  Athen. Const.
    7.1   95
    7.2   95
  Eth. Eud
    4.2,34   23
  Eth. Nic.
    4.8,10   23, 34
    5.4,7   34
    8.10,4   35
    8.10–11   31, 34
    8.11,1–2   35
    10.9,4   6
  Pol.
    1.1,9   23, 34
    3.6,5   6
    3.8,1–2   23, 34, 88
    3.11,6   6
    3.11,1–9   34
    3.11,11–13   34
    3.11,13   53
  Rhetorica
    1.10,8   87
    1.13,1–7   87
    1.13,18   87
    1.14,7   87
    1.1368bf   10
    1.1368bff   6
    1.1374a, 18f   6

Pseudo-Aristotle
  Rhetorica ad Alexandrum
    1420a,22–25   43
    1420a,20–23   43
    1420a,21–23   54
    1420a,23–25   43
    1420b,12–14   43
    1420b,13–19   60
    1420b,15–19   43, 57
    1421b,35f   10
    1422a   10

Bible
  Apocrypha
    2 Maccabees
      6:20   148
      12:14   148
    3 Maccabees
      6:36   148
    4 Maccabees
      1:8–9   125
      1:15–18   125
      1:28–30   125
      1:34–35   125
      2:6   125
      2:23   125
      3:17–18   125

5:17–26	125	2.39	71
6:31–35	125	82	18
7:7–9	125	86	18
8:7	149	*De Officiis*	
13:1–6	125	1.98–100	18
13:16–18	125	1.100	29
16:1–3	125	1.106–113	71, 73
18:1–3	125	1.148	22, 26
Deuteronomy		2.41	44, 57
17:15f	112	2.42–42	64
33:3f	108	3.15	24
Exodus		3.16	23
22:18	117	3.63	28
Genesis		3.69	21, 25, 28, 29, 96, 97, 119, 153, 154, 157
26:5	107, 108		
Numbers			
28	115		
28:3	116	41–42	44
29	115	*De Republica*	
Wisdom of Solomon		1.54	44, 57
14:23	148	1.62	44
		2.43	44
Chrysippus		3.7	23, 26
Fragmenta Moralia		3.18	22, 25, 28
314 (SVF 3)	19	3.33	18, 20, 71
337.7 (SVF 3)	137	52	44
Cicero		52–56	44
De Finibus		*Parad. Stoic*	
2.104	24	14	18
3.71	24	*Pro Milone*	
3.75	24, 26	10	11
20–26	17		
De Legibus		Cleanthes	
1.17	21, 28, 157	*Hymn to Zeus*	
1.18–19	21	SVF 1.537	19, 25, 31
1.34	18	Clement of Alexandria	
1.42	21, 25, 28, 29, 120, 154, 156, 157	*Stromata*	
		5.5,29.2–3	45
		Corpus Inscriptionum Latinarum	
1.44	28, 29, 105, 120, 154, 156	6.930	48
		Demosthenes	
2.8–11	28, 154	*In Aristocratem*	
2.10	95	61	7
2.11	28, 120, 153, 154, 156	70	5
		De Corona	
2.13	18, 21, 25, 157	274–275	8
		In Stephanum	
2.26	125	1.53	8
3.2–3	18, 43	Dio Cassius	
18–19	18	52.1,3	50
20	17	52.15,2	50
De Natura Deorum		52.15,3	50
1.23	23, 26	52.34,1	50
2.34	18, 71		

INDEX OF ANCIENT SOURCES

52.34,6–8	50	4.7,61,266,19–23	41
52.39,3	50	4.7,61,267,1–268,12	41
52.40,1–2	50	4.7,61,268,12–14	42
53.9,5	50	4.7,61,268,14–269,17	42
53.11,4–12,1	51	4.7,61,270,1–11	42
53.18,1–2	51	4.7,61–62	64
59	112	4.7,62	64
59.10,2	51	4.7,62,265f	57
59.14,3	51	4.7,62,268,12	58
59.15,1	51	4.7,62,269,2	58
		4.7,62,269,3	58

Dio Chrysostom
75.1	31
76.1	7
76.4	22, 26, 89

Ecphantus
Stobaeus
4.7,61	58
4.7,62	58, 61
4.7,64	56, 58, 59, 60, 61, 62, 64

Diogenes Laertius
7.43	73
7.87	17
7.87–89	19
7.88	17
7.116	23
7.117–118	23
7.119	24
7.121	24
7.122	24, 122
7.123	26
7.125	22, 24, 26, 29, 88, 152
7.127	24
7.128	19

4.7,64–66	64
4.7,65	57, 59
4.7,66	61
4.7,66,272, 14f	38
4.7,66,274, 1f	38
4.7,66,274,4–9	38
4.7,66,274,20–275,5	38
4.7,66,276,2–9	39
4.7,66,276,4–9	39

Epictetus
1.11,15	29
1.26,1–2	28
1.29,19	20, 25
3.3,11–12	27
3.24,107	25, 29
4.3,11–12	20, 21, 25, 157
4.7,34	28, 29

Dionysus of Halicarnassus
Antiquitates Romanae
7.41	11
7.52	11

Rhet.
5.118	138

Euripides
Suppliants   35

Gaius
Institutes
1.4–5	52

Diotogenes
Stobaeus
4.7,61	55, 62, 64
4.7,61,263,15–16	40
4.7,61,263,15–19	92
4.7,61,263,16–20	40
4.7,61,264,1	92
4.7,61,264,9	40
4.7,61,264,11	58
4.7,61,264,12–265,1	41
4.7,61,264,15	58
4.7,61,264,18	58
4.7,61,265,1–10	41
4.7,61,265,1–12	92
4.7,61,265,10	58
4.7,61,265,10–12	41
4.7,61,265f	41

Heraclitus
frag. B91   132

Herodotus
1.65	95
1.66	95
4.106	132
7.104	31

Hesiod
  Works and Days
    276f   132
    388f   132
Horace
  Epist.
    1,106–108   23
Isocrates
  Ad Demonicum
    36   35
Josephus
  Antiquities
    16   107
    27   107
  Contra Apion
    1.223–320   98
    1.309   98
    2.1–296   98
    2.148   98
  The Jewish Wars
    4.386.2   138
Lysias
  Epitaph
    18–19   31
Marcian
  1 (SVF 3.314)   31
Marcus Aurelius
  1.17,6   20
  4.4,1–4   20
  7.9   20
  7.67   25, 27
Methodius
  Symp.
    3.2   143
Musonius Rufus
  Stobaeus
    4.7,67   44, 56, 60
Palestinian Talmud
  Rosh Hashanah
    I, 3, 57a   4
Philo
  Abr.
    1–5   89
    3   89, 96, 119
    3–6   114
    4   107
    4–6   103
    5   75, 91, 107
    5–6   88, 89
    6   75, 143
    16   90, 99
    21   74
    52–55   74
    123   128
    193–195   69
    202   78
    248–249   68
    275–276   107
    276   88, 89, 108
  Aet.
    12   169
    35–37   69, 72, 74
    57–59   77
    59   144
  Agr.
    1   74
    7–8   68
    30–31   68
    31   84
    56   70
    157   104
  Cher.
    14–15   121, 155, 156
    39   75
    86   78
    90–92   74
  Conf.
    46   71
    49   74
    52   74
    59   84
    68   77
    87   71
    174   142
    180–181   78
  Congr.
    4   68
    61   78
    71   74
    120   89, 98, 141
    122   72
  Contempl.
    24   98
    28   73
    70   77
  Decal.
    1   89, 103, 108
    15   98

INDEX OF ANCIENT SOURCES

16	142	71	75
32	141	84	79
41–43	68, 69, 142	95	75
64	74	121	68
132	77, 84	142	74
136	88	167	141
142	71	168	89, 141
150	77	168–172	141
Det.		295	87
52	75	*Hypoth.*	
66–68	103	7.6	87, 88
68	95	*Ios.*	
83–84	70	25	72
89	78	28–31	75, 77
122	120, 156	29	84
141	111	29–31	99, 115
142	142	30	89, 143
161–162	92	81–83	74
274	71	118	79
Deus		129	75
37–38	68	142	74
55	78	*Leg.*	
61–63	70	1.18	70
151	79	1.52	73
Ebr.		1.56	120, 155, 156
18	88		
34	75	1.92–94	72
36–37	100	1.94	103
55	74	1.107	69
80	84	2.1–3	78
80–81	100	2.10	78
141	84	2.17	120, 156
142	84	2.94	89
164–167	72	2.105	70
169	74	3.3	98
193	99	3.7	70
211–212	74	3.24	73
Fug.		3.25	73
14	74	3.27	73
34	74	3.28	73
112	77	3.29	73
120	74	3.64	69
146	128	3.71	74
163	79	3.75	70
171–172	75	3.77	71
172	74	3.77–78	70
Gig.		3.79	93
25	73	3.79–81	73
30	70, 71	3.83–84	73
60–63	72	3.85–87	73
Her.		3.88–89	71
8	108	3.104	72
45–46	72	3.126	121, 156, 158
49	74		

208 INDEX OF ANCIENT SOURCES

3.130	74	1.158	79, 92
3.144	103	1.159	92
3.145–147	69	1.160	92
3.1577	3	1.162	92
3.165	120, 156	2.4	92, 94
3.204	142	2.5–7	76
3.206–207	78	2.11	96, 103, 119
3.210	73, 120, 156	2.12	98, 103
		2.12–13	115
3.245	84, 89	2.13	88, 89, 96, 98, 105
3.252	78		
Legat.		2.14	103, 119
7	104	2.17	98, 115
56–57	68	2.20	98
68	89, 144	2.21	144
75	72	2.26–27	115
115	87, 88	2.34	98, 115, 142
115–117	98	2.43	98
118	71, 78	2.43–44	115
119	48, 111	2.48	95, 96, 103, 119
126	68		
190	68	2.51	89, 98, 105, 115, 119
210	98		
277	98	2.51–52	103
353	98	2.52	119
Migr.		2.58	70
26	74	2.100	74
46–52	94	2.133–134	74
68	70	2.142	74
78	70	2.211	103
89–93	129	2.281	69
92–93	105, 114	2.288–292	92
94	103	*Mut.*	
130	108	7	78
171	128	14	70, 78
174–175	103	35–37	114
206–207	73	46	72
Mos.		71	73
1.1	98	84–86	70
1.2–7	79	108	74
1.21–22	70	117	70
1.26–28	69	140	78
1.39	75	162	68
1.59–60	70	167	74
1.87	98	184	78
1.97	74	197–199	71
1.117	77	219	79
1.148	91	225	72
1.148–162	92	266	74
1.149	91	*Opif.*	
1.151	91	2–3	103
1.154	92	3	73, 84, 97, 116
1.155	92		
1.156	92	13	84

INDEX OF ANCIENT SOURCES

14	142	75–87	99
16	73	79	144
19–22	73	81	120, 156
44	73	*QE*	
46	73	1	68
54	84	1.16	74
61	83	1.42	95
69	96	2.1	77
70	84	2.6	111
71	96	2.19	103
73	73	2.42	98, 103
74	120, 156	2.106	71
82–85	69	*QG*	
90–127	169	1.62	79
95–97	69	2.6	100
100	169	3.3	104
130	73, 103	4.42	77, 84
133–135	79	4.62	73
141	147	4.90	77, 84
143	137, 143	4.152	100
145	73	4.184	74, 77, 103, 108
148	93		
159	74	4.243	72
172	143	*Sacr.*	
Plant.		4	70
91	78	8–9	92, 93
100	120, 155, 156	19–20	120, 156
		43	155
132	103	68–69	70
Post.		98–102	68
4–5	73, 77	99	120, 156
13	78	111	115
20	78	131	95, 146
26–28	79	*Sobr.*	
31–32	74	33	84
103–104	68	46–48	75
109	74	53	73
115	79	*Somn.*	
160	70	1.6	73
182	74	1.11	75
185	84	1.20	73
Praem.		1.27	68, 73
29	103	1.44	128
82	104	1.106	5
Prob.		1.109–111	70
3	89, 142, 147	1.114	74
37	84	1.135–137	79
46	75	1.143	79
57	100, 117	1.150	74
60	120, 156	1.167–169	74
61	120, 156	1.171–172	70
62	88, 112, 114	1.176	70
72	114	1.188–189	79
72–75	112, 115	1.191	103

INDEX OF ANCIENT SOURCES

1.232	78
1.236	70
2.6	68
2.79	74
2.90	75
2.136	74
2.174	143
2.262	68

Spec.

1.36–40	128
1.116	79
1.202	76, 89, 143
1.325	77
2.6	68
2.13	84, 144
2.37	84
2.39	115
2.42	115
2.42–48	103, 115
2.44	115
2.45	116
2.46	116
2.47	116
2.48	69, 75, 116
2.50–52	73
2.58	77
2.73	116
2.100	75
2.104	98
2.122–124	74
2.129	95
2.158–159	68
2.163	103
2.170	144
2.170–173	77
2.233	89, 144
2.239–241	75
3.30	142
3.32	84
3.45–48	77
3.61	142
3.63	142
3.93–98	117
3.121	77
4.61	100
4.149f	87
4.150	87
4.164	103
4.179	98, 103
4.215	144

Virt.

70	111, 112
73–75	92
94	103
104	142
112	142
132	144
182	98, 115
194	89
211–219	94
212–218	93
217	94
218	94

Pindar
   Frag. 169   25, 133

Plato
  Crito

46b	22
50b	22
51b	22
52a	22

  Epist.

355b	136
355c	136

  Gorgias

484b	31

  Leg.

644b	34
679e–680a	23
773e	5
793a–d	5
822d	5
835e	5
838b	5
839a	5
841b	5
875a–d	23
875c–d	34

  Phaedrus

248c	136

  Politicus

293b–d	33
295a–296c	5
295a–e	5
298d	5
300c	53
301d	33
302e	33

  Respublica

425a–c	53
425a–e	5
425b	5
473c–e	33

Pliny
  Epist.

3.20	49
10.56	49

Plutarch
Ad Principem Ineruditem
  779d–782f   45
  780b   45, 57, 59
  780c   45, 54
  780e   45, 64, 92
  781b   45, 56
Adversus Stoicus
  1062a   27
Apoph. Lacon.
  221b   7
De Alexandri Magni
Fortuna aut Virtute
  329a–b (SVF 1.262)   18
De Fato
  568.c.7   138
  570.a.8   138
  570.b.5   138
Lycurgus
  4.1   95
Sept. Sap. Conviv.
  163a   7
Solon
  15.2   95
  19.5.1   138
  19.5.8   138
  25.1   95
Stoic. Repug.
  1038   24
  1038a   29
  1048e   27, 157
  1057e   24
  1061e   24
Virt. Sent. Prof.
  75d   24
  76a   27, 157

Pomponius Porphyry
Satires
  2.3,188   4, 51

Proclus
In Rem Publican
  11.15f   119

Procopius of Gaza
Comm. In Proverbs
  6:20   143

Pseudo-Dionysius
Areopagita
  d.n. 2.9   143

Seneca
Ad Poly.
  7,2   51
De Clem.
  1.8,5   51
Epistulae Morales
  9.45   24
  14   26, 29
  17.115   24
  30   20, 28, 29
  35   27
  35.245   24
  45   20
  48   20
  59.513   24
  66   20
  66.18   24, 28
  71.27   24
  73.14   24
  75   27
  81.2   24
  85.41   24
  87.19   24
  90.5   137
  90.27–28   157
  90.34–36   157
  94.21   157
  94.29   157
  94.37–40   157
  95.36–37   157
  95.40   28, 157
  99.36   24

Septuagint
Proverbs
  1:8   147
  6:20   147, 148

Sextus Empiricus
Adv. Dogm.
  1.432   23, 26
  3.133   23, 26
  5.181   23
Adv. Rhet.
  2.33   33
Pyrrhoniae Hypotyposes
  2.38–42   23, 26

Sophocles
Ajax
  1104   135
Antigone
  450f   7

Sthenidas of Lokri
Stobaeus
  4.7,63   56, 57, 60, 64
  4.7,64, 270,13–14   40

4.7,64,270,14–16	40	Thucydides	
4.7,64,271,1–2	40	2.37,2	6
4.7,64,271,6–7	40	5.105,1–2	9

Suetonius
  1.77   49
  4   112
  4.14   50
  4.29   50
  4.34   50
  4.52   50

Ulpian
  Justinian's Digest
    1.3,31   52
    1.4,1   52

The Sybylline Oracles
  5.166   138
  5.430   138
  8.9   138
  13.31   138

Xenophon
  Cyropaedia
    8.1,21   32
    8.1,22   33
    8.1,24   33
  Memorabilia
    4.4,19f   8

Themistius
  212d   45
  228a   45

INDEX OF SUBJECTS

Abraham, 84, 88–91, 107–108
ἀδιάφορα, 156
ἄγραφος νόμος, 3–12, 87, 133, 134, 163
Alexander the Great, 32, 48
Animate law, *see* living law ideal
Antinomianism, 3, 29
Antiochus of Ascalon, 17, 29, 105, 125, 154–155
Anti-Semitism, 98
Archytas
  Dating of texts, 9, 35, 165–174
  On kingship and living law ideal, 35–37, 54–64
  Περί νόμον καὶ δικαιοσύνης, 35
Aristotle, 10, 11, 14, 34–35
Athens, 5–6
Augustus, 50–51

Barbarians, 115

Chrysippus, 19, 137
Cicero
  On kingship and living law ideal, 43, 44, 64
  And law of nature, 14, 18, 20–23, 24–29, 125–126, 151–158
  And transcendent God, 85–86
  On wise man, 22–23
City law, unwritten law as a component of, 4–6, 10–11
Common law, 10, 17–19
Community standards, *see* customs
Convention, 74
Creation, 74–77
Customs, 4–6, 86–88
Cyrus, 32–33

De Abrahamo, 88–89
Democracy, 54
Dio Cassius
  On living law ideal in Roman imperialism, 50–51
Diogenes Laertius, 21–22
Diotogenes
  On communion, 61
  On kingship and living law ideal, 40–42, 54–64

Divine order of the world, 1, 7
Draco, 95

Eclecticism, 83
Ecphantus
  On communion, 61
  On kingship and living law ideal, 38–40, 54–64
Embodiment of law, *see* living law ideal
Epictetus, 29
Equity, 6
Euripides, 35
Evil, 70–71

Fear, as a restraint on lawlessness, 6
Feast of "every day," 115–116
Fools, mankind as, 27, 157
Free will, 70, 72, 73

Gaius (emperor), 48, 49, 50, 51, 112
Gaius (lawyer), 52
Gentiles, and law of nature, 115–118, 159
God, in Philo, 77–80, 85, 86, 97–98
Greek literature, 132–136
Greek society, Sophists' view of law, 1–2

Habit, 74
Halakhah, 87, 175–185
Harmony, 57–59
Hellenism, universalism of, 159–164
Heraclitus, 14, 132
Hesiod, 132
Higher law
  Material law falls short of ideal, 2
  Translation problem of concepts, 8–9
  See also law of nature; living law ideal; unwritten law
Hippias, 8
Human nature, 69–73, 77, 78–81

Infants, 5
Intentionality, 9
Isaac, 94
Isocrates, 35

INDEX OF SUBJECTS

Jewish oral law, 87, 175–185
Joseph, 93
Judaism, 109–113, 159–163
    See also Jewish oral law; Mosaic law
Julius Caesar, 49–50

καθήκοντα, 120, 125, 151–158
κατορθώματα, 120, 125, 151–158
king/kingship
    as benefactor, 61–62
    in Bible, 92
    Cicero on, 43, 44, 64
    and closeness to god, 40–42, 55–56
    communion and, 60, 61
    deified, 50, 55–56
    and harmony of people, 57–59
    Homer's conception of, 31–32
    as imitator of God, 38–42, 59–60
    justness of, 63–65
    and Moses, 91–94
    in relation to subjects, 34, 35, 36–42, 56–61, 64
    as saviour, 61–62
    virtue of, 38
    and virtue of the people, 39–42, 44–46, 56–57

law of nature
    and common law, 17–19
    connection to reason and God, 17–22, 84
    contents identified by Philo, 84
    and Gentiles, 115–118
    its relation to human law, 99–100
    "jarring" nature of phrase, 19
    and Mosaic law, 99–101, 118–121, 124–130
    and natural justice, 15
    officia of, 28, 125, 154–155
    origins, 13–16
    and the Patriarchs, 88–89, 107–110, 113–114
    in Philo, 67, 74–78, 102–121, 151–158
    and Sophists, 1, 16
    and Stoicism, 15–18, 75, 80, 151–158
    transcended written law, 19–21, 25–27, 118–120
    and unwritten law, 2, 12
    and wise man, 22–27, 157–158
living law ideal
    and absolute rulership, 32–35
    Cicero on, 43–44, 64
    communion of king and subjects, 60–61

deified king, 50, 55–56
    Diotogenes on, 40–42, 54–64
    Ecphantus on, 38–40, 54–64
    as godgiven, 31–32
    and harmony of people, 57–59
    just king, 63–65
    king as benefactor, 61–62
    king as imitator of God, 38–42, 59–60
    king as living law, 32
    king as saviour, 61–62
    king is law, 55
    king's closeness to god, 40–42, 56–57
    king's relation to subjects, 34, 35, 36–42, 56–61, 64
    and Mosaic law, 111–113
    and Moses, 91–94
    in Musonius Rufus, 44–45, 59, 63
    origins, 31–37
    in Philo, 90–95, 111–113, 121–123
    Plutarch on, 59, 122
    and Roman imperialism, 46–51
    transcending written law, 32–35, 43
    virtue of king, 36–37
    virtue of subjects and, 39–42, 44–46, 56–57
Lycurgus, 95

magistrates, 43
Middle Platonists, 85, 122
monarchy, 31
morality, 12, 25
Mosaic law
    and Gentiles, 115–118
    and law of nature, 99–101, 118–121, 124–130, 162–163
    and living law ideal, 111–113
    for ordinary people, 7–99, 108–110, 162–163
    Philo's view of, as divine, 95–99
Moses, 78, 79, 92–95, 162–164
Musonius Rufus, 44–45, 59, 63

nature
    Philo's and Stoics' views of, 67, 75–76, 77–80, 151–158
    and virtue, 17–18, 84
    see also law of nature
νόμος
    origins, 132–133
    in Philo, 139–141
    and θεσμός, 84, 89, 131–135, 143–144, 147–149
νόμος ἔμψυχος. *see* living law ideal
νόμος φύσεως, 151

INDEX OF SUBJECTS

Panaetius, 154
Patriarchs, 88–89, 107–110, 113–114
Paul (apostle), 88, 160–161
penalties, 104
φυλάσσω, 108
physis
  explained, 67
  and nature of God, 77–80
  as nature of things and persons, 69–74
  as ordering nature, 74–77
  as power of growth and life, 68–69
Plato, 14, 23, 33
Pliny, 49
Plutarch
  on kingship and living law ideal, 59, 122
  use of θεσμός, 138
  on wise man, 24
Pomponius Porphyry, 51
Posidonius, 154
Proclus, 119

reason
  in kingly rule, 54
  and law of nature, 17–22
  in Philo's view of nature, 74–77, 80
religious law, unwritten law concerned with, 7
Rhetorica ad Alexandrum, 10, 43, 54
Roman imperialism, and living law ideal, 46–51
Roman law, and law of nature, 125, 153

sages. *see* wise man
Seneca
  on living law ideal in Roman imperialism, 51
  on wise man, 24
sin, law leads to, 88
Solon, 95
Sophists/Sophism, relativism of, towards law, 1–2, 8
Sthenidas of Lokri, 40, 54–64
Stoics/Stoicism
  and common law, 17–19
  on καθήκοντα and κατορθώματα, 164–174
  and law of nature, 15–18, 19–27
  and Philo's view of nature and natural law, 67, 75–76, 77–80, 151–158

  and the Sage, 22–27, 118, 157–158
  theory of indifferents, 156
Suetonius, 49–50

theodicy, in Philo, 76
θεσμός
  in literature, 135–139
  and νόμος, 84, 89, 107–110, 113–114
  origins of, 133–135
  in Philo, 137–138, 141–143
θεσμὸς ἄγραφος, 89, 144, 147–149
θεσμὸς φύσεως, 143–144, 147–149
Tiberius, 49
tyranny, 31, 37

Ulpian, 52
unity of law, in Philo, 100–101, 103–130
universalism, of Hellenism, 159–164
unwritten law
  alluded to, 8–9
  as custom, 4–6, 86–87
  as eternal or divine, 7–11, 88–90
  and law of nature, 7, 12
  perfect men as, 89, 123–124
  in Philo, 86–90, 123–124
  problems in defining, 3, 12
  vis a vis written law, 3–4, 7–11
"unwritten nature", 89

Vespasian, 48
virtue
  and free will, 73
  and kingship, 38
  as law itself, 89
  and nature, 17–18, 84
  and subjects of king, 39–42, 44–46, 56–57
wise man
  κατορθώματα of, 151–158
  and law of nature, 22–27
  in Philo, 85
  and Stoics, 23–27, 118
written law
  as god-given, 36
  and higher laws, 105–110
  vis a vis law of nature, 25–27, 118–121

Zeno, 17, 18
Zeus, 31